Security in a Post-Cold War World

Edited by

Robert G. Patman
Senior Lecturer in International Relations
University of Otago
Dunedin
New Zealand

First published in Great Britain 1999 by
MACMILLAN PRESS LTD
Houndmills, Basingstoke, Hampshire RG21 6XS and London
Companies and representatives throughout the world

A catalogue record for this book is available from the British Library.

ISBN 0–333–73226–X

 First published in the United States of America 1999 by
ST. MARTIN'S PRESS, INC.,
Scholarly and Reference Division,
175 Fifth Avenue, New York, N.Y. 10010

ISBN 0–312–22062–6

Library of Congress Cataloging-in-Publication Data
Security in a post-Cold War world / edited by Robert G. Patman.
    p.   cm.
Essays evolved from papers delivered at the 32nd Otago Foreign
Policy School, University of Otago, 1997.
Includes bibliographical references (p.   ) and index.
ISBN 0–312–22062–6 (cloth)
1. National security—Congresses.   2. Military policy—Congresses.
3. World politics—1989– —Congresses.   4. National security—Asia–
–Congresses.   5. National security—Pacific Area—Congresses.
I. Patman, Robert G.   II. Otago Foreign Policy School (32nd : 1997 :
University of Otago)
UA10.S385   1999
355'.03—dc21   98–42207
                                                            CIP

This book is printed on paper suitable for recycling and made from fully managed and
sustained forest sources.

10   9   8   7   6   5   4   3   2   1
08   07   06   05   04   03   02   01   00   99

Printed and bound in Great Britain by
Antony Rowe Ltd, Chippenham, Wiltshire

SECURITY IN A POST-COLD WAR WORLD

Also by Robert G. Patman

NEW ZEALAND AND BRITAIN: A Special Relationship in Transition

THE SOVIET UNION IN THE HORN OF AFRICA: The Diplomacy of Intervention and Disengagement

Contents

Tables and Figures

Acknowledgments

I am indebted to a number of people and institutions for assistance in the preparation of this book. The essays in this volume evolved from papers delivered at the 32nd Otago Foreign Policy School. As Director of that School and Editor of the resulting book, I wish to acknowledge the considerable help which made both projects possible.

My first debt of gratitude is to my colleagues on the Academic Committee of the 32nd School: Dr William Harris, Dr Ralph Hayburn, Dr Louis Leland, Dr Elena Poletti, Dr Rob Rabel, Associate Professor Martin Richardson, Associate Professor Antony Wood, Mr John Terry, Professor Ann Trotter and Mrs Pam Quin. Their support has been substantial. Members of the committee not only provided encouragement and practical advice in the planning of the School, but also agreed to chair various sessions and thus played a significant part in making a success of the occasion. Four individuals deserve a special mention. Antony Wood, a former colleague in the Department of Political Studies, put the book into camera-ready form and gave unstinting technical aid at many stages of the project. I owe him much. Pam Quin, the organiser for the 32nd School, provided efficient and energetic administrative support that extended into the preparations for publication. Elena Poletti helped to ensure that the School operated within budget and Louis Leland rendered significant assistance on the publication side, including the co-ordination of manuscripts.

Second, I would like to thank all the contributors to this book. They cheerfully accepted editorial guidelines and took the time to revise the papers that they delivered at the 32nd School into thoughtful and very solid chapters.

Third, I wish to thank all those organisations whose support and sponsorship made it possible to bring together such a distinguished cast of contributors. Without this support, there would have been no conference and no book. I am grateful to: The British Council, the United States Information Service, Peace and Disarmament Education Trust, Public Advisory Committee on Disarmament and Arms Control, the Division of Humanities at the University of Otago, the Federation of University Women, the New Zealand Ministry of Foreign Affairs and Trade, the Centre for Strategic Studies (Wellington), the New Zealand Institute of International Affairs, the New Zealand Ministry of Defence, the Army General Staff of the New Zealand Defence Force, the Australian High Commission, Westpac Banking Corporation, Otago Chamber of Commerce and Industry, Tourism Dunedin, Statistics New Zealand and Cook Allan Gibson.

Fourth, I was fortunate to have the able assistance of the staff at Macmillan, notably Tim Farmiloe, the Publishing Director, Annabelle Buckley, the Commissioning Editor, and Karen Brazier, the Copy-Editor. And I would like to express my appreciation to Dr Douglas Little for his proof-reading of the manuscript.

Finally, and most importantly, I was fortunate to have the loving support of my wife, Martha. Our baby daughter, Jennifer, also provided her own brand of vocal encouragement from her cot.

Robert Patman
University of Otago
New Zealand

List of Abbreviations

ANZAC	Australia New Zealand Army Corp
ANZUS	Australia New Zealand United States Defence Arrangement
APEC	Asia Pacific Economic Cooperation
ARF	ASEAN Regional Forum
ASEAN	Association of South-east Asian Nations
ASEM	Asia Europe Meeting
BW	biological weapons
BWC	Biological Weapons Convention
CD	Conference on Disarmament
CNN	Cable Network News
COCOM	Coordinating Committee for Multilateral Export Controls
CPRF	Communist Party of the Russian Federation
CSCAP	Council for Security Cooperation in Asia-Pacific
CSIS	Centre for Strategic and International Studies
CTBT	Comprehensive Test Ban Agreement
CW	chemical weapons
CWC	Chemical Weapons Convention
DFAT	Department of Foreign Affairs and Trade
DMZ	De-militarised Zone
DPRK	Democratic Peoples Republic of Korea (North Korea)
EU	European Union
ENZL	Zapatista National Liberation Army
FAR	Forces Armes Rwandaises
FMCT	fissile material cut-off treaty
FPDA	Five Power Defence Arrangement
FSU	Former Soviet Union
GATT	General Agreement on Tariffs and Trade
IAEA	International Atomic Energy Agency
IBRD	International Bank for Reconstruction and Development
ICRC	International Committee of the Red Cross
IFOR	Peace Implementation Force

IMF	International Monetary Fund
INF	intermediate-range nuclear forces
IWC	Inhumane Weapons Convention
KEDO	Korea Energy Development Organisation
MFN	Most Favoured Nation
MTCR	Missile Technology Control Regime
NAFTA	North American Free Trade Agreement
NAM	non-aligned movement
NATO	North Atlantic Treaty Organisation
NCCPD	National Consultative Committee on Peace and Disarmament
NGO	non-governmental organisation
NPT	Non-Proliferation Treaty
NSG	Nuclear Suppliers Group
NWC	Nuclear Weapons Convention
NWFZ	Nuclear-Weapon Free Zones
NWS	nuclear weapon states
NZDF	New Zealand Defence Force
ONUC	UN Operation in the Congo
OPEC	Organization of Petroleum-Exporting Countries
PRI	Partido Revolucionario Institucional
PTBT	1963 Partial Test Ban Treaty
QDR	(US) Quadriennial Defence Review
RMA	Revolution in Military Affairs
ROK	Republic of Korea (South Korea)
SDF	Japanese Self-Defence Force
SEATO	South East Asia Treaty Organisation
SFOR	International Stabilisation Force
SPNFZ	South Pacific Nuclear Free Zone
START	Strategic Arms Reduction Talks
START I	Strategic Arms Reduction Treaty 1991
SWP	Stiftung Wissenschaft und Politik
UN	United Nations
UNEP	UN Environment Programme
UNFICYP	UN Peacekeeping Force in Cyprus
UNIFIL	UN Interim Force in Lebanon
UNGA	United Nations General Assembly
UNPROFOR	UN Protection Force (Former Yugoslavia)
UNSCOM	UN Special Commission

UNSSOD IV	Fourth Special Session of the UN General Assembly on Disarmament
UNTAC	UN Transitional Authority in Cambodia
WEOG	Western Europe and Others caucus group
WMD	weapons of mass destruction
WTO	World Trade Organistion

About the Contributors

Byung-joon Ahn is Professor of Political Science at Yonsei University, South Korea. He is the author of many academic articles and books on Korean foreign policy and diplomacy in the Asia-Pacific. Recent books include *Political Economy of Chinese Modernisation* (1992) and *Post-Cold War International Politics and Korean Clarification* (1993).

Mats Berdal is Research Fellow and Research Co-ordinator at the Centre for International Studies, Oxford University, United Kingdom. He has specialised in the study of United Nations peacekeeping as well as the problems of ethnic conflict after the Cold War. His publications include *Norway, the US and the Cold War 1954-60* (1996), *Whither UN Peacekeeping?*, Adelphi Paper 281 (1993) and *Disarmament and Demobilisation after Civil Wars*, Adelphi Paper 303 (1996).

Bryce Harland is Director of the New Zealand Institute of International Affairs. Formerly a career diplomat, he was New Zealand's First Ambassador to China (1973-75), New Zealand's Permanent Representative to the UN (1982-85) and New Zealand's High Commissioner in London (1985-91). He is the author of *Collision Course: America and East Asia, in the Past and in the Future* (1996).

Rt. Hon. Don McKinnon is Minister for Foreign Affairs and Trade of New Zealand. Having entered parliament in 1978, he has risen to a number of high-level posts. These include the position of Deputy Prime Minister, Minister for Pacific Island Affairs and Leader of the House. He became Foreign Minister in 1990.

Walter Russell Mead is a political economist and a Senior Contributing Editor at *Worth* magazine, a contributing editor at the *Los Angeles Times* and serves on the editorial board of the *World Policy Journal*. His internationally syndicated articles on economic policy and foreign affairs have appeared in major newspapers around the world. He is a member of the US Council of Foreign Relations and wrote *Mortal Splendor: The American Empire in Transition* (1987).

Dianne Otto is a Senior Lecturer in Law at the University of Melbourne, Australia. Her research interests lie primarily in the areas of international and human rights law. She has published widely on issues concerning global democracy and the possibilities for women, indigenous sovereignty in Australia and the emerging role of international civil society in journals such as *Human Rights Quarterly, Syracuse Journal of International Law and Commerce* and *Transnational Law and Contemporary Problems.*

Sir Michael Quinlan is Director of the Ditchley Foundation, Chipping Norton, United Kingdom, which mounts international conferences on public policy themes. Before taking up his current position in 1992, he was a United Kingdom civil servant whose posts included Permanent Secretary at the Department of Employment and Permanent Secretary at the Ministry of Defence. He has written numerous articles on defence and public service issues. His study 'Thinking About Nuclear Weapons' (1997) was published by the Royal United Services Institute for Defence Studies.

Terence O'Brien is Director of the Centre for Strategic Studies (CSS) in Wellington, New Zealand. Prior to this he was a diplomat with the New Ministry of Foreign Affairs and Trade. His service included spells as New Zealand's Permanent Representative to the United Nations (1990-93), New Zealand's Ambassador to the EC (1983-86) and New Zealand's Permanent Representative to the UN in Geneva (1980-83). He has written extensively on international and strategic issues. A recent publication was a CSS working paper entitled 'The United Nations: Legacy and Reform' (1996)

Robert G. Patman is Senior Lecturer in the Department of Political Studies at the University of Otago, New Zealand. His research interests centre on Russian foreign policy and international relations. He is the author of *The Soviet Union in the Horn of Africa: the Diplomacy of Intervention and Disengagement* (1990) and editor of *New Zealand and Britain: A Special Relationship in Transition* (1997).

Michael Renner is Senior Researcher at the Worldwatch Institute, Washington D.C., United States. His research and writing deals with disarmament, arms conversion, peacekeeping, the military-environment relationship and new conceptions of security. He is the author of *Economic Adjustments after the Cold War: Strategies for Conversion* (1992) and *Fighting for Survival: Environmental Decline, Social Conflict and the New Age of Insecurity* (1996).

Peter Shearman is Senior Lecturer in the Department of Political Science at Melbourne University, Australia. He specialises in Russian politics and international relations. His publications include *The Soviet Union and Cuba* (1987), *The Superpowers, Central America and the Middle East* (co-edited with Phil Williams,1988) and has edited *Russian Foreign Policy Since 1990* (1995).

John Simpson is Professor of International Relations at the University of Southampton, United Kingdom, and the founding Director of its Mountbatten Centre for International Studies. He has published widely on the military use of nuclear energy and nuclear non-proliferation. Recent publications include *The Future of the Non-Proliferation Treaty* (co-edited with D.Howlett,1995) and *The Preparatory Committees for the 2000 NPT Review Conference: Issues Regarding Substance* (1997).

Ramesh Thakur is Professor of International Relations and Vice Rector at the United Nations University in Tokyo, Japan. Formerly the Director of the Peace Research Centre at the Australian National University, he has a major research interest in UN Peacekeeping and the diplomacy of the Asia-Pacific region. Among other works, he is the author or editor of *Peacekeeping in Vietnam: Canada, India, Poland and the International Commission* (1984), *International Peacekeeping in Lebanon: United Nations Authority and Multinational Force* (1987) and *A Crisis of Expectations: UN Peacekeeping in the 1990s* (1995).

Martin van Creveld is Professor of History at the Hebrew University, Jerusalem, Israel. His principal research interests are military history and strategy. He is the author of *Supplying War* (1977), *Fighting Power* (1982), *Command In War* (1985),

Technology and War (1998), *The Transformation of War* (1991) and *The Rise and Fall of the State* (forthcoming).

Jiemian Yang is Director and Senior Fellow of the Department of American Studies at the Shanghai Institute for International Studies, China. He has written numerous articles and books on international relations and American foreign policy. His most recent book is *Sino-US Relations in the Post-Cold War Era: Elaboration and Exploration* (1997).

Introduction

Security in a Post-Cold War Context

Robert G. Patman

For much of the post-war era, the nature and scope of international security was defined by the parameters of the Cold War. This term was used to describe a climate of hostility and rivalry that developed between the Western (non-communist) and Eastern (communist) blocs shortly after the Second World War. A pervasive sense of threat meant that the hegemonic bloc leaders, the US and the USSR, engaged in a political competition, not only with each other, but also for the allegiance of the world at large.[1] No continent was spared from the effects of the Cold War. This global struggle was waged through ideological means, economic rivalry, arms races, propaganda, diplomatic outbursts, threats of force and the use of client states to promote each side's course. While the Cold War contained many of the features of traditional great power rivalries, it fell short of direct armed conflict between the two main antagonists. It was a condition of 'neither peace nor war'. Such an uneasy mix was upheld by nuclear weapons and the superpower fear of mutual assured destruction.[2]

Yet the Cold War did not culminate in a nuclear Armageddon. To the surprise of most observers, the Cold War era passed away peacefully in the late 1980s. A series of momentous changes in the international landscape saw to that. The Soviet military withdrawal from Afghanistan, the collapse of the Soviet Empire in East Europe, the unification of Germany, the demise of the Warsaw Pact and the

1   John Groom, 'The End of the Cold War: Conceptual and Theoretical Implications for the Study of International Relations', Paper delivered at the University of Otago, 4 July 1995, p. 1.
2   Gustav Däniker, 'The Need for a Strategy of Stabilization' in Klaus Schwab, ed., *Overcoming Indifference: Ten Key Challenges in Today's Changing World* (New York: New York University Press, 1995), p. 51; Graham Evans and Jeffrey Newnham, *The Dictionary of World Politics* (Hemel Hempstead: Harvester Wheatsheaf, 1992), pp. 42-43.

disintegration of the Soviet Union signalled the end of the bi-polar world. But what has replaced it? Is the post-Cold War world a wholly new order or is it merely a new form of an earlier system?[3] While there is little agreement over the shape of the emerging international order, a general recognition exists that a different global context requires a reappraisal and reformulation of the concept of security.

The Problem of Interpretation

This, however, is no easy task. In W. B. Gallie's terms, security is an 'essentially contested concept'.[4] Such a concept involves fierce disputes about the proper application on the part of its users. A classic attempt to define the term provides some insight into its controversial nature. Arnold Wolfers argued that 'security, in any objective sense, measures the absence of threats to acquired values and in a subjective sense, the absence of fear that such values will be attacked'.[5] This definition alerts to the perceptual aspect of the concept. What matters ultimately for the security of an individual or a nation-state is not an absolute level of capabilities, but capabilities which are relative and clearly apparent to those possessed by a perceived or potential adversary.[6] That judgement will, in turn, partially depend on an assessment of the environment in which these actors are located.

In the international arena, there has been a high degree of agreement that security implies freedom from threats to 'acquired values', but whether such threats exist at the national or international level remains a far more contentious point. For much of the twentieth century, the discipline of international relations has witnessed a lively debate between Idealists and Realists over the appropriate focus of

3   Ian Clark, *Globalization and Fragmentation: International Relations in the Twentieth Century* (Oxford: Oxford University Press, 1997), p. 173.

4   W.B. Gallie 'Essentially Contested Concepts' in Max Black, ed., *The Importance of Language* (Englewood Cliffs, New Jersey: Prentice Hall, 1962), p. 121.

5   Arnold Wolfers, *Discord and Collaboration* (Baltimore: Johns Hopkins University Press, 1962), p. 150.

6   Robert G. Patman, *The Soviet Union in the Horn of Africa: the Diplomacy of Intervention and Disengagement* (Cambridge: Cambridge University Press, 1990), p. 9; Trevor C. Salmon, 'The Nature of International Security' in Roger Carey and Trevor C. Salmon, eds., *International Security in the Modern World* (Basingstoke: Macmillan Press, 1992), pp. 13-14.

enquiry in security studies.[7] These two schools of thought were respectively optimistic and pessimistic on the prospects for greater international order.

During the inter-war years between 1919 and 1939, Idealism was the favoured perspective. A defining characteristic of Idealism was that it viewed international politics from the perspective of moral values and legal norms. Convinced that the major lesson of the First World War was an inability of military force to achieve its objectives, Idealism contended that internationalism was the key to a more fundamentally peaceful world order. This reflected the assumption that human affairs, at both the domestic and international levels, were characterised by the potential for harmony and co-operation. Such an approach promoted the importance of the principles of collective security via institutions like the League of Nations, established in 1919, and international law through treaties such as the Kellogg-Briand Pact of 1928 which denounced war as an instrument of national policy. But the events of the 1930s, epitomised by Hitler's assault on the international order, challenged the basic tenets of Idealism. By 1939, E.H. Carr had launched a sustained attack on the 'utopianism' of the idealists and advocated a paradigm shift to what he called Realism.[8]

The impact of the Second World War and its successor, the Cold War, helped to consolidate Realism's status as the dominant intellectual framework in world politics. Known sometimes as the power-politics model, Realism was sceptical that a permanent international peace was possible. Because human nature was deemed to be driven by a lust for power, war and violent conflict were seen as perennial features of an anarchic international system. Moreover, in the absence of any higher authority, sovereign states had no alternative but to assume responsibility for determining security. During the Cold War period, security thinking centred on the idea of national security, which was largely defined in military terms. However, realists insist that the militarisation of the state system is not necessarily a recipe for unending war. Instead, the pursuit of national security compels states to form alliances which, when weighed against one another in a balance of power configuration, may ensure prolonged periods of

7　Martin Hollis and Steve Smith, *Explaining and Understanding International Relations* (Oxford: Clarendon Press, 1991), pp. 17-28.
8　A. Reynolds, *An Introduction to International Relations,* 3rd Edition (London: Longman, 1994), p. 5.

international stability. Thus, according to the realists, the creation of a bi-polar world order based on a balance of comparable US and Soviet power blocs led to an effective system of deterrence and helped to maintain a general peace during the Cold War.

The Post-Cold War Debate

With the end of the Cold War, the debate between the Idealists and Realists has renewed and intensified albeit in new guises. For the neo-idealists (a perspective on international politics that emphasises morality is a practical as well as a desirable aspiration), the collapse of the East-West ideological confrontation was a momentous turning point ushering in a 'new world order' in which common international norms and values would gradually subdue conflict between states and groups. Several factors have been shaping this view. First, the advent of the US as the sole superpower has coincided with the global expansion of democracy. A new wave of democratization erupted in Eastern Europe in 1989, spread to the former Soviet Union and extended to parts of Africa, Asia and the Middle-East in the 1990s.[9] The spread of democratization enhanced the prospect of 'one world' speaking with 'one voice'. Second, the process of globalization had accelerated to the point where the clear outlines of a global society were now evident. The emergence of a global economic system, global communications and the elements of a popular global culture has created a vast network of linkages which encompass people and states all over the world.[10] Third, the realities of an interdependent world mean that the security agenda is shifting from one centred on the military capability of a state towards that of common or co-operative security. This change acknowledges that many contemporary security threats, whether the breakdown of the global financial system, global warming, human rights protection, the proliferation of weapons of mass destruction, forced migration and so forth, are largely beyond the control of individual states and therefore require international, not national, responses. According to the neo-idealists, this process began with Mikhail Gorbachev's emphasis on 'mutual security' in the late

9   Samuel P. Huntington, 'Democracy's Challenge' in Klaus Schwab, ed., *Overcoming Indifference*, p. 81.

10   John Baylis, 'International Security in the Post-Cold War Era' in John Baylis and Steve Smith, eds., *The Globalization of World Politics* (Oxford: Oxford University Press, 1997), p. 207; Ian Clark, *Globalization and Fragmentation*, p. 174.

1980s and gathered impetus in the 1990s with tentative steps by the international community in the direction of humanitarian intervention in Iraq, Somalia and Bosnia. Such intervention was evidence of a shift away from the sanctity of the state as the central focus in security concerns.[11]

However, for neo-realists (a perspective on international politics that modifies the power-politics model by highlighting the structural constraints of the international system) very little had fundamentally changed as a result of the events of 1989. While it was conceded that the threat of global nuclear war had receded, the highly durable structure of anarchy in the international arena determined that one conflictual relationship, the Cold War, was being replaced by another, intra-state strife, characterised by the fragmentation of racial, ethnic and regional identities. Because the Cold War stimulated a sense of external threat (be it international communism or capitalist encirclement), it is argued that it promoted internal cohesion in most states by constraining pre-existing ethnic and sub-national aspirations.[12] The collapse of the external threat, however, has helped to unleash centrifugal pressures in places such as Chechnya, Bosnia, Somalia and Rwanda. According to the neo-realists, the very fact that the UN became involved in a wide range of peacekeeping activities, including humanitarian interventions around the globe, lent little credence to the idea that peace was breaking out. Far from establishing a new world order based on respect for justice and human rights, the end of the Cold War was said to mark a return to the kind of genocidal and nationalist violence that had so plagued international politics since the seventeenth century. On this view, the period 1947-89 is seen as an oasis of stability sandwiched between the instabilities of the periods which preceded and succeeded it.[13]

Clearly, each of these perspectives has some validity. But neither is wholly convincing. The neo-idealist view tends to assume that the post-Cold War World will see uniform progress towards global and common security. By stressing the growing importance of the non-

11 Ian Clark, *Globalization and Fragmentation*, p. 181; Robert G. Patman, 'Russia's New Agenda in Sub-Saharan Africa' in Peter Shearman ed., *Russian Foreign Policy Since 1990* (Boulder, Colorado: Westview Press,1995), p. 286.
12 Terence Taylor, 'Security Policy in a World of Complexity' in Klaus Schwab, ed., *Overcoming Indifference*, pp. 66-67.
13 John Mearsheimer, 'Back to the Future: Instability in Europe after the Cold War', *International Security*, Vol. 15, no.1 (Summer 1990).

military aspects of security, there is too often a concomitant readiness to devalue the military dimension. But has military power become progressively redundant after the Cold War? A cursory glance at the world during the 1990s underlines the continuing importance of military force, especially in internal conflicts. At the same time, there is little evidence yet that the tension between national and international security interests will be easily resolved. The issue of nuclear deterrence is instructive in this respect. While developments in nuclear arms control such as the START I and II treaties, the extension of the Non-Proliferation Treaty and the Comprehensive Test Ban Agreement reflect a willingness by national governments to enhance international security, there is little sign that the major nuclear weapon states such as the US and Russia are prepared to completely relinquish possession of these weapons. Such reluctance not only poses an implicit threat to existing or potential adversaries, but also betrays a lack of confidence that a common security regime will really replace one based on national security.[14]

On the other hand, the neo-realist approach exaggerates the peace and stability of the Cold War era and, in doing so, obscures the depth and range of the changes which became evident in world politics in the 1990s. It should not be forgotten that turbulence, whether in the Taiwan Straits (1954), Cuba (1962) or the Middle-East (1973), led to nuclear sabre-rattling by one or both superpowers. Moreover, the trend towards instability and fragmentation had already deepened from the late 1960s. Internal conflicts such as Biafra (1970), Lebanon (1972-74), Angola (1975-76), Zaire (1979), Eritrea (1961-91) and Poland (1980-81) occurred long before the Cold War ended. But if the instabilities of the 1990s did not come out of a clear blue sky, the same was true for the globalising forces of this period. By the mid-1980s, the capitalist-oriented world had experienced a revolution in information and communications technology, a massive expansion of the role of foreign direct investment in the market economies[15] and a growing consciousness that the risks posed by environmental destruction did not respect state frontiers. Not surprisingly, the impact

---

14   John Baylis, 'International Security in the Post-Cold War Era', p. 210.
15   Andrew Fraser, 'Increasing Economic and Trade Cooperation Gateways: to Respective Regions; Expanding Trade Liberalisation', paper presented at a conference on *Britain and New Zealand: Refocusing the Link*, Wilton Park, Steyning, UK, 31 August - 1 September 1998; Ian Clark, *Globalization and Fragmentation*, pp. 183-184.

of these inter-connected changes was magnified with the collapse of Soviet style communism. In the 1990s, it was possible to speak of a genuinely global economic system with a 'global information infrastructure' which included around 50 million Internet users from more than 100 countries.[16] It was also a time when, at least one state Russia, cited environmental concerns in opposing UN sanctioned military action against another, Iraq.[17] These profound changes have eroded the traditional distinction between a state's internal and external policy and advance a conception of security which is much broader than that envisaged by the 'Back to the Future' neo-realists.

What can we deduce from this discussion of the competing claims about international security in the late 1990s? Despite the different perspectives outlined above, there remains a wide measure of agreement that the post-Cold War World is being shaped by the contradictory, but interrelated forces of globalization and fragmentation. This new global context has direct implications for the role of the nation-state in the realm of security. While it would be premature to anticipate the sudden collapse of the function of the state in this area, a combination of transnational pressures from without and separatist pressures from within have seriously called into question the state's capacity to serve as the only focus of security considerations.

Mapping the New Security Agenda

But if we do concede there is now a new security agenda, the key task facing the scholar and the statesperson is to distinguish what is unique and what is perennial in the current international circumstances.[18] The structure of the book reflects this central concern. It attempts to map out the nature of post-Cold War security by focussing on four broad, but interlocking themes. The first examines the battle of ideas surrounding patterns of international conflict; the second looks at non-state challenges to security; the third considers international co-operation in security matters; and the fourth assesses security dynamics in the Asia-Pacific region.

---

16   Gebhard Geiger, 'International Security in the Information Age: New Structures and Challenges', *Aussenpolitik*, Vol. 48, No. 4, 1997, p. 402.

17   Gennedy Tarasov, Russian Foreign Ministry spokesman, cited in *Reuters*, 10 February 1998; see also *Izvestiya*, 12 February 1998.

18   Jack Spence, 'Entering the future backwards: some reflections on the current international scene' *Review of International Studies*, Vol. 20, No.1 (January 1994), p. 4.

The first three essays in this volume analyze the military implications of a new international order. Don McKinnon, the New Zealand Foreign Minister, notes that the higher degree of uncertainty and fluidity in the 1990s has had mixed results in security terms. While multilateral diplomacy in Asia and global disarmament mechanisms had made welcome strides, growing competition for resources and markets, regional tensions and 'increasingly complex challenges' in UN peacekeeping made it imperative for New Zealand 'not to lose sight of the continuing importance of traditional sources of security'. This meant, amongst other things, that New Zealand had to bolster defence spending after cutting its defence budget in real terms since 1991.

According to Martin van Creveld, if the last fifty years or so provide any guide, future wars would be within states, not between or among them. The advent of nuclear weapons has made large scale warfare between sovereign states 'almost as rare as the dodo'. This trend is marginalising conventional military establishments and will almost certainly lead, in van Creveld's view, to radical changes in military doctrine as well as the jettisoning of large amounts of redundant but expensive heavy military equipment.

While Sir Michael Quinlan agrees that 'the likelihood of old-style interstate conflict has indeed greatly declined' he does not rule it out altogether. The volatile nature of the world, the political diversity of states and the tendency of armed conflicts to escalate are factors which weigh heavily here. For the foreseeable future, the US will remain the key provider of heavyweight force to the international community. That applies equally to inter- and intra-state conflicts. In the present conditions, the call to abolish nuclear weapons 'is neither feasible nor necessarily desirable unless and until we first manage to change the whole global political environment'.

The next four essays deal with various aspects of insecurity that transcend state boundaries. Mats Berdal observes that UN peacekeeping has been transformed in terms of scale, scope and context since the passing of the Cold War. But the UN's use of force during this period indicates 'much more careful consideration must be given to the choice of instrumentality'. The experience of UN operations in Bosnia and Somalia underlines the need 'to reassert the distinction' between consent-based peacekeeping and peace enforcement. This distinction makes it more difficult for political decision-making to 'fudge' hard decisions in situations where peacekeeping is inappropriate and helps to ensure that the use of peace enforcement reflects 'a deliberate choice' rather than organisational drift.

Writing from a feminist perspective, Dianne Otto argues that the dramatic expansion of UN peacekeeping after 1989 had both negative and positive effects on international security. Developments such as the increased power assumed by the Security Council, the extension of militarism to ever more local forms and the neo-colonial overtones of many peacekeeping efforts have reinforced an oppressive status quo 'that is hardly distinguishable from the gender blind security system of the Cold War years'. At the same time, the growth of peacekeeping had the potential to enhance liberating outcomes by promoting de-militarization, eroding militarized gender identities and facilitating a concern with the causes of global insecurity.

In the view of Michael Renner, the media and other observers in the 1990s habitually ascribe the outbreak of civil war and the collapse of states to just one factor: the resurfacing of 'ancient ethnic hatreds' revolving around seemingly irreconcilable religious and cultural differences. But such disputes were often triggered by 'the effects of environmental decline, the repercussions of social divisions and stress, and . . . an unchecked arms proliferation that is a direct legacy of the Cold War period'. Citing conflicts in Bougainville, Nigeria, India, the Sudan and Mexico, Renner argues there is an 'urgent need' for a new global human security approach, which addresses the neglected issues of demilitarisation, environmental sustainability and social well-being.

The economic dimension of international security is highlighted by Walter Russell Mead's account of America's changing foreign policy. With the end of the Cold War, geoeconomics has displaced military strategy as Washington's main focus. This change 'for as important a power as the United States' will have implications for other countries. The emerging economic diplomacy reflects very specific interests: the US is a global nation, a 'middle' nation and a service nation. While Mead believes that these geo-political interests will remain fairly constant, he anticipates that this stance could generate problems. These include a rise in tension between the West and Asia as Asia's export-orientated development model encounters serious limitations and the possible destabilisation of the international system through a vibrant, liberal capitalism and the rising power of civil society.

Three subsequent chapters focus on elements of security that have endured as sources of international concern into the late 1990s. With respect to the issue of nuclear weapon non-proliferation, John Simpson says the global risk of a surprise nuclear attack has substantially diminished since the disintegration of the USSR in 1991. But there remains an 'inherent contradiction between the norm of non-possession which is at the basis of the NPT and the probability that nuclear weapon possession by the nuclear weapon states will continue into the indefinite future'. While de facto nuclear states like India, Israel and Pakistan are unlikely to join the NPT regime until regional political solutions are found, the five permanent members of the UN Security Council are unlikely to eliminate their nuclear stockpiles until the de facto nuclear states sign the NPT. Moreover, even if these obstacles are overcome, Simpson observes it is 'an open question' whether a world without nuclear weapons would be more stable than a low salience nuclear one.

Noting that military alliances 'in classical and common practice, have been generated by a common threat', Peter Shearman maintains the rationale and logic of NATO expansion after the implosion of the Soviet Union 'is fatally flawed'. By backing the inclusion of Poland, Hungary and the Czech Republic in NATO, realists rely 'on selective and distorted accounts of history' in which Russia is seen as an inherently imperialist power. But this view seriously underestimates the scale of change in Russia. At a time of economic crisis, Moscow is simultaneously engaged in transitions to political democracy and the capitalist market. Given this, Shearman argues NATO expansion could prompt anti-Western Russian nationalism, a countervailing strategic partnership between Moscow and China and possibly reverse the democratisation process in Russia. What is needed is not a military bloc from Vancouver to Warsaw 'but a proper inclusive security community from Vancouver to Vladivostok'.

The role of Australia, 'a self-conscious middle power', in international arms control and disarmament is analyzed by Ramesh Thakur. Despite anomalies and inconsistencies in areas such as the export of uranium and conventional arms, Australia has in the past decade made a notable contribution 'to the global delegitimisation of WMD'. Guided by an emphasis on co-operative security, the Labour administrations of Bob Hawke and Paul Keating actively promoted the NPT, the Comprehensive Test Ban Treaty (CTBT), the work of the Canberra Commission on the Elimination of Nuclear Weapons and

Australia was one of the 22 countries which made a submission to the World Court on the legality of nuclear weapons. According to Thakur, Australia's effectiveness in this area is due to decades of faithful membership of the Western alliance, the decision not to develop nuclear weapons despite an undoubted capacity to do so and a pool of relevant scientific expertise to underpin credible initiatives for moving 'to a nuclear-weapon-free world.'

The final three essays provide a distinctly regional perspective on security. Jiemian Yang observes that China is 'an important component' of the Asia-Pacific region. Convinced that the world was moving from a bi-polar to a multi-polar system, China has 'started to conceptualise security in a broader way'. In contrast to the Cold War period, Beijing was now responding positively to multilateral and collective security initiatives in forums such as the ARF, CSCAP and ASEAN. But factors such as the explosive situation in the Korean Peninsula, territorial disputes, a spiralling arms race and a conspicuous lack of trust among states in the region cast a shadow over the Asia-Pacific. If a new security order was to emerge in the Asia-Pacific, key players like the US would have to reconsider its military presence there - 'a legacy of the Cold War' - and embrace a security framework that was consistent with the globalising forces of 'the scientific and technological revolution' impacting on the region.

Byung-joon Ahn agrees that the security situation in East Asia is complex, but offers a different perspective on the role of the US. In the near term, a lot, in Ahn's view, will depend on the process of Korean unification. If present trends continue, North Korea will slowly collapse and unification will occur largely on South Korea's terms. Whatever the scenario, the Sino-American relationship remains the key to maintaining regional stability. In order to prevent a power vacuum from developing in East Asia, the US must mitigate the revival of Sino-Japanese rivalry over Korea. There is 'a critical need for a token American military presence in a unified Korea as an insurance policy against hegemonism either by China or Japan' and to deter the development of nuclear weapons on the Peninsular. Thus, the US must perform a stabilising role in the region until either collective security or a 'concert of power' takes root.

In a broadly-based assessment, Terence O'Brien notes that 'speculation abounds' as to whether the rate of East Asian economic advance is sustainable. Certainly, the consequences of this remarkable transformation - for instance, environmental degradation, resource depletion and population growth - 'could provide seeds for conflict' particularly in a region with longstanding disputes over land and sea boundaries. That is why regional co-operation should be directed to a management order 'that sustains a balance of interest as much as a balance of power between states'. According to O'Brien, the stability of the Asia-Pacific depends essentially on the triangle of relationships encompassing the US, China and Japan. If one of these relationships 'goes sour, they all go sour'. Given that the three states either have nuclear weapons or are capable of developing them (Japan), it follows genuine nuclear disarmament could make a 'real contribution' to regional and global security.

By way of conclusion to this book, Bryce Harland argues that security essentially means what President Roosevelt called freedom from fear. In that sense, the post-Cold War World has not reduced the quantum of human suffering, but has actually increased it in many parts of the world. An old problem, the threat of nuclear war, has diminished without disappearing entirely. But a relatively new problem - the trend of intra-state conflict - has mushroomed in often what are the most brutal circumstances. This presents Preventive Diplomacy with a fundamental challenge: how to discourage divergent groups within a single society from pursuing the right of self-determination to the point of conflict. If there is an answer to this or any other problem of contemporary security, Harland observes, it probably lies in 'that old-fashioned virtue' called tolerance.

Chapter 2

Security in the 1990s: New Zealand's Approach

Don McKinnon

In this chapter I want to talk about security in the 1990s and beyond: the post-Cold War period. First in terms of the ways the world is changing, and second in terms of how New Zealand is reacting to those changes.

The World in the 1990s

It seems clear that global strategic order is still, in 1997, in transition from the Cold War framework. Having said that, some broad patterns are beginning to emerge.

The first is that we are all getting used to a more fluid pattern of inter-relationships, and a higher degree of uncertainty in security relations. This may not be a temporary phenomenon. It now seems clear that no one structure is going to emerge neatly to replace the adversarial lines of the Cold War. People now speak of a multi-polar world, in which economic and political power is increasingly diffuse. There is plenty of evidence, for example,

- China is emerging as a major political player;
- in Europe, efforts to develop a common foreign policy edge cautiously forward;
- ASEAN is wielding a regional influence few would have predicted a decade ago.

Japan, Russia and India could be added to the list of 'poles'.

At the same time let's not forget that in 1997 one country - the United States - remains pre-eminent, particularly in military power.

Early indications from the US Quadrennial Defence Review suggest confidence in Washington that the US will remain the only military superpower, with the capability to defeat any foreseeable regional power or coalition through to 2015. Perhaps a surprising realisation. New Zealand's own Defence White Paper, produced in 1991 just as the Soviet Union was collapsing, spoke of a declining US security role in the region and predicted that the US would reduce its military presence in the Asia-Pacific. We were wrong. In the face of scepticism about their relevance, the US has moved to reinforce its major alliances - NATO in the Atlantic and the US/Japan alliance in the Pacific. This has been a welcome development. We continue to see a solid US forward presence in Asia as an important underpinning of regional stability.

Nonetheless, it is clear that fundamental shifts in economic - and to a lesser extent military - power are changing the balance of interests between the major powers. In this part of the world the main factors have been the extraordinary economic growth of East Asia, and the burgeoning economic advances of China. These developments are unsettling for some because they threaten the status quo. There is no doubt that the structure of regional relations is going to have to change to accommodate that new balance - and that much of that change still lies ahead.

The New Zealand government sees these developments not as a threat, but as a major opportunity for New Zealand, and for the wider region. Our task is to reinforce and sustain the economic dynamism, and to work with all the key players in the region. The development of multilateral regional structures is making a major contribution to that process. The birth of APEC in 1989 was followed by the arrival of its younger brother, the ASEAN Regional Forum, in 1994. Both processes have quickly cemented roles for themselves in a part of the world with little tradition of multilateral diplomacy.

We have also seen progress on the disarmament front. Global mechanisms in place now include a Comprehensive Test Ban Treaty, an indefinitely extended Non-Proliferation Treaty, strengthened IAEA safeguards, and a Chemical Weapons Convention. We now have a network of nuclear-weapon free zones around the Southern Hemisphere. Efforts are underway to strengthen restrictions on biological weapons and ban landmines - the latter not moving fast in Geneva but there's promise in the Ottawa process. But I confess to being disappointed, in particular at the failure of the Nuclear-Weapon

States to produce a greater 'disarmament dividend' from the end of the Cold War. We have not seen as much progress on the disarmament front as was thought possible, given the end of the Cold War confrontation. New Zealand is not alone in believing the world would be much safer without nuclear weapons, as the reports of the Canberra Commission and the judgment of the International Court of Justice indicated.

Despite these positive developments, plenty of security challenges remain. We need to understand that economic growth is not a one-way street to peace. Competition for resources and markets can get out of control. Closer trade and other economic ties do not guarantee stability - they simply increases the cost to everyone when a conflict does break out. A further consequence of the end of the Cold War has been to bring security concerns closer to home. In many places long-standing local and regional tensions - historical, ethnic, nationalist - have re-emerged. States are for the most part more concerned with these than with avoiding global superpower conflict. Our region contains some of the world's most volatile pressure points, including the Korean peninsula, the Taiwan Straits and Myanmar. We cannot dismiss the prospect of serious conflict breaking out within the region even in the short-term. As a signatory to the Armistice in Korea, New Zealand is 'involved' - if conflict were to erupt, we could well be called on to play a role.

Closer to home, tragic conflict continues on Bougainville. We were relieved that the prospect of foreign mercenaries operating in the region was headed off earlier this year - but there is still no resolution to what is a lengthy and damaging dispute. It remains to be seen whether the current elections will open the way to progress in settling the underlying problem of the status of Bougainville. New Zealand has always said that as a neutral neighbour, we would be happy to assist the parties of the Bouganville dispute to resolve their differences. We are going to work harder and where we can be of some help through the process then we will.

At the end of the Cold War it was widely hoped that the UN system, freed from the straitjacket of competitive superpower vetoes, might work as it had been designed to do to deal with some of these smaller conflicts. Although there have been some reasonable successes - such as Cambodia - by and large the picture has instead been one of increasingly complex challenges in peacekeeping. Peace operations are becoming more multi-faceted, sometimes in the form of a 'coalition of the willing' rather than UN leadership; sometimes involving a higher intensity of combat operations, often requiring new kinds of skill.

All things considered, I think this all adds up to a positive security picture for New Zealand. In Asia-Pacific we have a dynamic and prosperous region, which is now working together as a region in many areas for the first time. The other side of the coin is greater uncertainty and a continuing high pace of change and fluidity, and as a result some risk of maintaining forward movement. But, New Zealand needs to stay on guard, to watch developments around us closely, and to do our part in working with others to ensure potential threats are not realised.

New Zealand's Approach to Security

How do New Zealanders feel about this? Is there a distinctively New Zealand approach to security? As in many other relatively young societies, I see a streak of optimism and idealism in New Zealanders' attitudes towards the world. It is sometimes suggested that older-established societies in Europe and Asia, particularly those with a recent experience of major wars on their territory, tend to take a fairly pessimistic view of international relations, and to see competition and conflict between states as the norm rather than cooperation and peace. An internationalist and collective outlook has been a key part of New Zealand's foreign policy from its beginnings. As a nation with little clout, but with interests and trading lines circling the globe, New Zealand has always sought to speak up for the rights of the weak against the powerful, and for a fair and democratic international order.

The search for collective security has been a constant of our diplomacy. The global media age has if anything made those feelings stronger. New Zealanders find it hard to sit and watch images on CNN from Bosnia or Rwanda without wanting to do something to help - we believe our actions can make a difference. Recently that sense of idealism has been overlaid with two considerably more pragmatic realisations:

- that the countries of our region are increasingly interdependent, both for their prosperity and their security; and
- that New Zealand's interests are increasingly engaged in Asia.

In 1970 just over 20% of New Zealand exports went to East Asia and Australia. Now the proportion is nearly 60%. This region has become our strategic community. It matters to us. New Zealand has made tremendous economic gains from the explosion of economic growth in East Asia over the past twenty years. That growth would not have been possible without a stable and peaceful environment. The pace of future growth depends on continued stability.

Interdependence means that what happens in one part of the Asia-Pacific - famine and instability in Korea, some confusion in Cambodia, uncertainty about Myanmar or the future of Aung Sung Siu Kyi, the leader of the pro-democracy movement, affects all other members. This is because we are so tightly tied together by a multitude of political, business, investment, educational, tourism and people-to-people links. As in any community, our partners in that community expect us to take an interest in their welfare, in their security. Standing aside from that responsibility, opting out, is seen as irresponsible and unfriendly. In this sense, New Zealand supports the concept of a comprehensive approach to defence and security policy. Thanks to the world's largest moat, this country has the luxury of facing no obvious direct threat. But given the diversity and importance of our global linkages, we are obliged to look at our security interests as broadly as possible. As a result, our security policy concentrates not just on our immediate needs - on protecting the nation in event of war. It considers the whole range of our security interests.

We have identified security as one of four interlocking goals of our external policy: the others are economic prosperity, human values, and environmental values. This reflects our view that our security as a nation, and the stability of our neighbours and partners, is the essential foundation for New Zealand to pursue all its external interests and values. Security is closely interconnected, for example, to the economic environment we face. Our ability to trade - our livelihood - depends on an open and fair trading system. Hence we see organisations such as the WTO and APEC as playing an important role in New Zealand's security. So too, we are working to build a robust international legal framework to deal with areas such as environmental problems and human rights. Development assistance is another important tool, in contributing to the sustainable development and prosperity of our neighbours.

I have already mentioned the role of disarmament, which we see as very much the other side of the coin of security. But we need to keep a good dose of realism about the world around us. While welcoming the role of new multilateral organisations such as the ARF in contributing to regional stability, we should not lose sight of the continuing importance of traditional sources of security:

- strong and well-disposed friends and allies who can help us when necessary; and
- an appropriately-sized and well-equipped defence force.

New Zealand's Commitment to Defence

This is one area of our security policy where things have slipped. When we returned to Government in 1990, we were faced with a major fiscal crisis requiring some tough and unpalatable cuts across the government sector. Defence was hard hit by these cuts. Coupled with subsequent reductions and adjustments the defence budget has lost around 30% of its funding in real terms since 1990/91. Given the circumstances, our international friends understood our decisions. In making savings, Defence achieved some significant productivity gains, which have attracted interest from partners overseas. There is no doubt New Zealanders are now getting more bang for every buck spent on defence.

But those bucks now look pretty small by regional standards. And now that we are enjoying fiscal surpluses and a strong economy, it is hard to justify continued rock-bottom spending to our friends around the region. Figures produced by Australia show that New Zealand spent 1.0% of its GDP on defence in 1994 - the lowest equal among Australia's partners. We keep company with Japan, which has a constitutional limitation on what it can spend. On the same figures, Australia spent around 2.0% of GDP. Or put another way, per capita, Australia spent $384; USA $1011 and New Zealand $211. Other figures vary according to who produced them, but consistently show New Zealand second to bottom in the region behind Japan, and occasionally Indonesia. Canada, Fiji, the Philippines spend proportionally more than we. So do comparable sized European countries like Denmark and Ireland. And as said before Australians spend more than twice as much as New Zealanders - despite their much higher population. Singaporeans, with a similar population, spend nearly five times as much.

Statistics of course are slippery beasts, and perhaps best left as food for statisticians who like that sort of thing. I am not suggesting that New Zealand should increase defence expenditure to a level near that of Australia, or Singapore. Those countries are both wealthier than we are. More importantly, they have different strategic situations and policies. But these sorts of figures are widely published around the region, and seen as one measure of a country's commitment to defence. And the message in the numbers is repeated on the ground. It has become clear we are struggling to maintain our capability at present levels. It is no secret that putting Kiwi company into Bosnia put a major strain on our Defence Force.

To maintain a similar peacekeeping unit now would be all but impossible. This is not the fault of the personnel in the Defence Force, who do a terrfic job in the circumstances. But we must avoid a situation where first-rate people are being let down by second-rate equipment. The Chief of Defence Force's 1996 report to Parliament reported that resource constraints prevented the Force from meeting its required level of capability in numerous areas, including the naval frigates, Orion and Skyhawk aircraft, and the landforce. This has real implications not just for how we're perceived but for what we can do. It means that even activities like search and rescue, or fisheries surveillance become real strains in the system.

Some reinvestment is taking place. Over the last year we have seen the launch of a second ANZAC frigate, and some major equipment purchases including naval helicopters. But we can no longer ignore that there is a stark gap between what we say we need - as laid out in our 1991 White Paper - and what we actually have and are able to do. That Paper described our policy as Self-Reliance in Partnership - and the concept of a credible minimum level of capability. Not surprisingly, our partners are letting us know our credibility is in question. New Zealand's security policy has always been based on working in pursuit of collective security in partnership with others. We are not neutral, and I don't think New Zealanders want to be neutral.

Working in partnership with others is a fundamental element of our policy. To make partnership work, we have taken on certain responsibilities, whether in alliance with Australia, the Five Power

Defence Arrangements, or the United Nations Charter. Membership of the ARF too carries some sense of responsibility to the other members of our security community. In return, we can expect that others will take some interest in our welfare when the time comes. Those partnerships are now under pressure because - bluntly - we are perceived to be not paying our way. As I have indicated, I am arguing that our environment has become much more dangerous since 1990. It is uncertain and fluid. I have mentioned the sort of risks that we should take seriously. But fundamentally the requirement for New Zealand to defend itself and contribute to the protection of others remains essentially the same as when the 1991 White Paper was written.

The problem is we have failed to maintain our capability at the levels we promised. We do not need a 'stronger New Zealand defence force'. What we do need is to get the NZDF back on the track that it is supposed to be on. That means:

- stopping the long-term decline in our capability; and
- starting to build back towards currently mandated levels.

Staying where we are is not an option. We cannot anchor the partnerships which are the basis of our defence on current spending levels. The choice is between

- *either* a reasonable increase in spending and capability
- *or* a fundamental rethink of our defence policy.

In effect the latter would mean walking away from our decades-long commitment to collective security. I do not believe that is what New Zealanders want.

If you ask New Zealanders if they want:

- international and regional respect;
- to be listened to by others;
- to play a positive role in helping regional neighbours defuse potential problems;
- to play a part in drafting the new security architecture in the Western Pacific;

- to play an active role in peace building and peace keeping;
- to be able to provide logistical aid to our neighbours in times of distress;
- to be able to patrol our own waters for search and rescue or for resource protection or to keep an eye on craft transiting near our area;
- to be regarded as a country which pulls its oar with partners in the same boat -

then a commitment to defence is important.

Invariably the answer would be yes to all and that in itself underpins the direction we are heading.

I expect this message to come through clearly in the Defence Assessment which the Government will be considering shortly. We will be faced with some hard choices, given all the other priorities within Government spending. As the Prime Minister said recently, in a political contest, hospitals and schools win over guns every time. But, after years of economic rigour and reform, we now have the chance to restore the balance and put the beef back into our security policy. That will give us the confidence that New Zealand is appropriately equipped to play its part with our partners in facing whatever security challenges the 21st century brings.

Chapter 3

The Future of War

Martin van Creveld

The purpose of this chapter is to offer a vision of what future war will probably be like. To this end, it is divided into four parts. First I shall present a brief summary of the most important characteristics normally associated with 'modern' war. Second, I shall show that, in fact, the great majority of wars since 1945 have not shared these characteristics and, to this extent, have not been 'modern' at all; also, that these supposedly 'non-modern' wars have been much more bloody and much more important than the other kind. Third, an attempt will be made to explain the discrepancy involved. Fourth, I shall point out the implications of all this for the future of air forces, navies, armies, and indeed war itself.

I. The Elements of 'Modern' War

To date, the most modern war we have had was the one fought in the Gulf in January-February 1991. When most of us speak of that war as a modern one, it is easy enough to see why. The aircraft and cruise missiles and the precision guided munitions which hit the Iraqis; the satellites which provided intelligence and the various sensors which, focusing on Iraq's radar and communication systems, complemented them; the vast network of computers and electronics which formed the nodes in the gigantic military machine and provided it with command and control and communication - it was the use of these and a great many other technologies which characterised this war, as indeed it does 'modern war' in general. Nor, in the case of the Gulf, was this kind of technology limited to the Coalition forces alone. If only because they relied on hardware that had been sold to them by the developed states themselves, the Iraqis also possessed it and fielded it and used it; albeit to a more limited extent and much, much less effectively.

While technology is a vital component of 'modern' war, it only represents the tip of the iceberg. The principal characteristics of 'modern' war, and the ones which make it all possible, are not technological but political and organisational. Using the Gulf War as a paradigm, the following represents a brief summary of the fundamental qualities of 'modern' war as we have known it during the last two centuries or so; so fundamental, indeed, that they are often taken for granted and overlooked.

First, on both sides of the front, the Gulf War was waged by states. By states, I mean sovereign political organisations which exercise exclusive control over a certain territory. Following a line of analysis that dates back to Thomas Hobbes in the middle of the seventeenth century, Westerners tend to take the primacy of the state as a war-making organisation for granted; so much so that violent conflicts which are conducted by organisations other than states tend to be known by different names, such as civil war, low intensity war, guerrilla, terrorism, and banditry. Yet, even a cursory look at that past, will confirm this has been very far from being the case. During much of recorded, and especially unrecorded history war was waged not by sovereign states but by the various types of tribes which existed in many parts of the world from Europe to South Africa and from the Americas to Australasia. Later, it came to be waged by city states, as in classical Greece and Italy before its conquest by Rome; by various imperial organisations large and small, such as the Assyrian Empire, the Byzantine, Arab and Ottoman Empires, the Aztec and Inca Empires, and the Chinese Empire; by feudal lords such as the ones which dominated both Europe and Japan during long periods of their histories; and even by religious leagues. Some of those organisations were sovereign in the sense that they recognised no superior above themselves, but probably the majority were not. Some possessed exclusive control over a stretch of territory, but others did not. Even so, they only represent a small sample of the various types of political organisation which have existed at various times and places and which occasionally went to war against each other.

Second, and again on both sides of the front, the states involved in the Gulf War were organised on trinitarian lines. The term 'trinitarian' is derived from Clausewitz who, at the end of book I of *On War*, wrote that war is based on a 'remarkable trinity': government, armed forces, and people. This division of labor is one which we today tend to take almost for granted; in fact, however, it is typical of the modern state and was not shared by the majority of previous political organisations. In most of them rulers were also commanders in chief, as when Alexander the Great left his kingdom for ten years on end (he never returned) to fight at the head of the army which conquered Persia and advanced all the way to India thousands of miles from home. In others, notably tribes and ancient city states including both Athens and Rome, there were no civilian populations at all except for old men, women, and children.

Under this division of labor it is the government which directs the war, the armed forces which fight and die, and the people who pay and suffer. Though it is not impossible to find parallels in the remote past, in its modern form the system originated in the second half of the seventeenth century; since then it has become so well established that any deviation from it is commonly regarded as a war-crime. For example, we no longer take civilians as prisoners of war; nor do we deport and resettle them *en masse*, a practice which in the past was often used by Imperial organisations in particular. On the other hand, we no longer engage in treacherous feasts where enemy leaders are first lulled into a false sense of security and then put to death, as is recorded, for instance, in Xenophon's *Anabasis*. Nowadays, when civilians are deliberately targeted by military operations we speak of atrocities; when rulers are killed, of assassination.

Third, it is only the fact that the war-fighting entities on both sides were states; and that the states in question were constructed along trinitarian lines, which made it possible to deploy and operate the kind of technology mentioned above. Both because of the expense involved and for other reasons - for example, the sheer space that it takes up - the only organisations capable of fielding modern technology are states with regular, uniformed, bureaucratically-managed, armed forces. Had we still been living in a world of feudal barons, they could not have maintained and operated even a small fraction of the technology in question even if they could afford it. Let alone do city states, or tribal organisations, have this capability.

This aspect of the matter also has an obverse side. On the one hand, states are the only entities capable of deploying and operating modern military technology as exemplified by that which was used in the Gulf; on the other, it was only because the enemy also consisted of a state and was organised on trinitarian lines with regular armed forces that the technology was as useful as it was. As experience in Algeria, Vietnam, Afghanistan, Lebanon, Somalia and countless other places shows, had the enemy consisted not of a state and its regular armed forces but of guerrillas and terrorists, then much of the technology in question would have been all but useless. It might, indeed, have been counterproductive, given the more or less indiscriminate nature of many of the most powerful weapons as well as their impact on the environment, the civilian population, and the media.

Fourth, it is the fact that modern war is technological which is responsible for its enormous logistic demands. As most experts will be aware, the vast majority of supplies required in modern war are not those which sustain the lives of soldiers. Instead they are those which are consumed or expended by machines; in other words spare parts, ammunition, fuel, engineering materials, and the like. It scarcely has to be pointed out that these items can neither be harvested from the fields nor plucked from the trees. Nor, given the extremely fine tolerances to which they are manufactured and the constant need for fresh supplies of them, is it usually possible to take them away from the enemy except as a makeshift measure.

As a result, modern warfare is based on lines of communication. Whereas earlier commanders, so long as the country was fertile, could usually roam where they would and 'eat whatever there is to eat before moving somewhere else' (Frederick the Great), since about the second half of the eighteenth century it has become absolutely necessary to have a steady stream of vehicles shuttle from base to front and from front to base. Covering the area often known as 'the zone of communications', and forming part of a vast organisation, they carry forward every kind of supply required by the forces while at the same time evacuating the sick, the wounded, and any prisoners that may be taken. Such lines of communication are typical of modern warfare including, of course, the Gulf. In wars pre-dating the middle of the eighteenth century they did not exist in the same form - and, indeed, considering the primitive nature of the means of transportation available at that time, could not exist.

Finally, since modern war requires lines of communication to link the consuming front with the producing homeland, those lines are apt to be cut. Indeed, from the time of the Swiss military writer Antoine Jomini on, the essence of strategy (nowadays often known as operational art) consisted of precisely that - get behind the enemy and cut his line of communication so as to sever him from his base and face him with the choice between battle, retreat, and starvation. So it was during the Napoleonic Wars from 1796 to 1815; so, to adduce but a few examples, it was in 1861-65, 1866, 1870-71, 1914-1918 (when it did not succeed), 1939-1945, 1950, 1956, 1967, 1973, and 1980-1989 (when neither side succeeded in pulling it off, resulting in attrition warfare much like that of 1914-1918). So, too, it was in the Gulf. Indeed it is arguable that, to the extent that 'operational art' was present at all in the Gulf, it consisted precisely of the famous 'Hail Maria' manoeuvre initiated by General Norman Schwarzkopf. And what was that manoeuvre aimed at if not at cutting the Iraqi's line of communication?

To sum up, 'modern war' consists of an entire series of elements, all of which are linked to each other. Its operative tool is strategy, which almost always means movement in two-dimensional space and an attempt to get behind the other side's lines of communication; conversely, a war in which this is not possible is either 'not war', as World War I was in the eyes of some of the generals who waged it, or else known as a 'war without fronts', as in Vietnam. Those lines of communication are not accidental but are made necessary by the nature of modern supply, the overwhelming majority of which consists of factory-manufactured items. This fact in turn is dictated by the technological nature of modern war, which itself both presupposes trinitarian armed forces and, what is more remarkable still, an enemy who is organised along roughly similar lines. Finally trinitarian armed forces, like the form of warfare in which they engage, are themselves the characteristic product of the political entity known as the modern state. Had it not been for that entity, then almost none of the above would have applied in the same form.

II. War since 1945

While the outline of 'modern' war might be clear enough, even the most cursory examination of post-1945 warfare will show that the great majority of wars were not of this kind. In fact, according to my statistics, since then there have taken place approximately one hundred wars; of these, however, fewer than twenty were fought by states on both sides. To proceed in chronological order, the world witnessed the First Indo-Pakistani War and the first Arab-Israeli War, both of which were fought in 1947-49. Then came the Korean War (1950-53), the Suez Campaign (1956) and the Indian-Chinese War (1962). The second Indo-Pakistani War took pace in 1965 and was closely followed by the 1967 Arab-Israeli War. Then came the so-called War of Attrition (1969-70), the Third Indo-Pakistani War (1971) and the

1973 Arab-Israeli War. 1977-78 saw a war between Ethiopia and Somalia, 1979 witnessed the Chinese invasion of Vietnam, 1982 was marked by the Falklands War and the Israeli clash with Syria over Lebanon. Since then, we have only had the Iran-Iraq War between 1980-88 and the Gulf War; purists might add the 'war' which took place between Ecuador and Peru during the early weeks of 1996. During the same period, a much larger number of wars which took place were against or between organisations which were not states. Even a short list of these wars would occupy more space then is available here; suffice it to say that they took place on most continents (except for Australia and North America) and affected the lives of very many people. Examples are the above mentioned ones of Algeria, Vietnam, Afghanistan, Lebanon, and Somalia. However, almost as many others could be adduced as there are 'developing' countries around the globe; and indeed some developing countries have had not one but a whole series of such wars. Nor, to be blunt, are developing countries alone with their troubles. Since 1945 numerous West European countries have witnessed terrorist struggles on their territories. While some of these struggles have been much too small to deserve the appellation 'war', others been both fairly bloody and politically not insignificant. For example, Britain has had far more people killed by the Irish Republican Army than in the Suez and the Falklands put together! And this is to say nothing of the vast blood-lettings that have taken place inside some of the republics of the former USSR (Armenia, Tajikistan, Azerbaijan, Georgia, Chechnya) and Yugoslavia.

As our classification implies, in so far as these wars were not fought between states they do not correspond to the type described in part I of this essay. Not only that, they differ from state-centred wars in numerous other ways as well. In the absence of states, there can be no regular armies either. For example, if the Soviets in Afghanistan *had* been fighting against a regular army it is conceivable they would have made short shrift of the 'rebels'. The absence of regular armies in turn implies the lack of a clear 'trinitarian' distinction between them and the government on the one hand and the people on the other. Not having regular armies, the organisations in question are incapable of fielding large amounts of modern military technology; in fact they are often remarkably deficient in this respect. Not having large amounts of modern military technology, however, also implies that they are very hard to cut off from their virtually non-existent bases, and indeed those who have tried to do so have almost always come to grief.

Looking at the forces involved in these wars, and particularly at the primitive nature of the technology they employ, the commanders of regular armed forces often tend to be dismissive of them. The contempt is totally unjustified; if only because, in terms of casualties, 'small' and 'low intensity' non-trinitarian wars tend to be *much* more bloody than trinitarian ones which are fought between states. For example, in the Gulf - to-date, the most modern armed conflict that we have - it was initially estimated that some 150,000 Iraqis had died. Later that figure was revised downward to perhaps 20-30,000; but then even the original one is smaller than the number who lost their lives in, to pick just one example, the former Yugoslavia. In other cases the discrepancy is much larger still. Between 300,000 and 1,000,000 people are said to have died during the Algerian War, as opposed to no more than a few hundred British soldiers in the Falklands. Millions lost their lives in Afghanistan, in Vietnam, and in Biafra, as against only hundreds of thousands even in the largest conventional interstate conflicts such as the one which took place between Iraq and Iran in 1980-1988. Perhaps the only post-1945 war which came even close to matching these so-called 'low intensity' or 'sub-conventional' conflicts was the one waged in Korea between 1950 and 1953. Which, at the time of writing, is already almost five decades in the past.

As Clausewitz also wrote, however, war is not a game in which the outcome is decided by the number of rounds played or points scored. Instead it is 'the continuation of politics by other means', which in the present context means that its outcome must be judged in political terms. Let us, then, engage in a brief comparison of the political consequences of the two types of war, interstate-trinitarian and intra-state, non-trinitarian.

Since 1945, when World War II came to an end, there has scarcely been a single case when any international border was moved by as much as an inch by means of interstate war. Remarkably enough, this even applied in 1947-48 when a country - Palestine - was cut in half by the first Arab-Israel War; however, when the Jordanians annexed the West Bank the only two states that ever recognised their occupation of the West Bank were Britain (which was running Jordan at the time) and Pakistan. Elsewhere, *all* interstate wars ended with a return to existing borders - in other words, with a stalemate of some sort since when the guns fell silent and the smoke cleared away both of the belligerents were not only there but in control of their own former territories. Even in the one case when a return to the old borders did not occur, i.e. that of Israel following the 1967 war, there was no way in the world in which the occupiers could get their possession to be recognised.

From time immemorial, the desire to occupy additional territory has been one of the prime objectives for which war has been waged. If post-1945 states have failed to do so, this was not due to any accident but to a clear agreement among states that such use of force is impermissible. This agreement is enshrined in the Charter of the United Nations as the most subscribed-to document in history. Since it was first established in 1946 the prohibition has been confirmed and amplified several times; at the time of writing it forms perhaps the one international law which can claim universal validity. No wonder, then, that attempts to violate it have been remarkably few and far between. Even less frequently have they been successful.

During the same period, i.e. 1945-97, non-state, non-trinitarian armed conflicts have led to political change all over the globe. Literally entire continents, hundreds of millions if not billions of people, found themselves living under different regimes as a direct result of such wars. Very few of these wars involved the use of massive, regular, armed forces; let alone of large amounts of advanced military hardware of the kind which was deployed in the Gulf (and, much less effectively, by the Israelis in Operations 'Reckoning' and 'Grapes of Wrath' against the Hizbullah guerrillas in Lebanon). Judged by this criterion - the only one which is in some sense 'correct' - the difference between the two kinds of war can only be called monumental.

When the last colonies - those of Portugal - went free in 1975, it was felt by many people that an era in warfare had come to an end.[1] Having had one defeat after another inflicted upon them, the most important armed forces of the 'developed' world in particular heaved a sigh of relief; gratefully, they felt that they could turn back to 'ordinary' soldiering, by which they meant preparing for wars against armed organisations similar to themselves on the other side of the Iron Curtain. In fact, however, the hoped for respite did not materialise. At the time these lines are being written there are approximately twenty wars being fought all over the globe from the Sudan to East Timor and

1   Walter Laqueur, *Guerrilla: a Historical and Critical Study* (Boston: Little, Brown, 1976), p. 404 ff.

from Algeria to Sri Lanka. *All*, without a single exception, are of the kind which we have called non-trinitarian, and *none* is fought by states on both sides.

III. Enter Nuclear Weapons

The factor which accounts for the paradox, and which explains why large scale warfare between important states has become almost as rare as the dodo, is nuclear weapons. For the first time in history, they have created a situation whereby the link between victory and survival has been severed; supposing a viable second-strike force on the other side, it is now possible for a belligerent to 'win' a war *and* face nuclear annihilation at the same time. An argument might even be made that, the more complete the victory, the greater the prospects of this happening. This is because a belligerent who is looking utter defeat in the face - as, for example, Hitler did in 1945 - may well decide to push the nuclear button by way of getting his final revenge. Or, indeed, fall upon it as his command and control arrangements collapse and desperate subordinates lash out on their own.

The first two states to find themselves virtually secure against large scale military attack by other states were, of course, the United States and the Soviet Union. Now it could be argued that no two great powers were ever more likely to fight each other than those two scorpions in a bottle; for forty years after 1949, they glowered at each other across the Iron Curtain, engaging in 'brinkmanship', testing each other's resolve in numerous crises large and small, and doing their best to outflank each other by gaining some sort of control over the less developed parts of the world. Countless doctrines were formulated, and an almost infinite number of wargames held, whose objective was to find ways in which nuclear weapons could be used for 'warfighting' without at least risking the end of the world. To make such 'warfighting' possible the number of weapons and their range and accuracy were increased many times over, whereas their explosive power increased up until 1961 but tended to decline after that. At the end of it all it was necessary to admit failure, and a significant reduction in the two countries' nuclear armaments soon followed.

Next, the scorpions' close allies - NATO and Japan on the one hand, the Warsaw Pact on the other - became almost as secure against large scale attack as they themselves. To be sure, and in spite of the commitment of a large number of troops, the US never succeeded in convincing their European partners that they would *really* sacrifice New York and Washington D.C. for Hamburg or Frankfurt or Paris or London. Although the Communist system of dictatorship meant that Warsaw pact countries were more able to present a monolithic bloc to the outside world, it is difficult to imagine that similar doubts did not affect people in East Germany and Poland and Czechoslovakia and Hungary. In the end, though, it did not matter. Faced with the possibility that any attack - even the smallest one conducted with conventional weapons - might escalate and escape political control, not even a figure as forbidding as Stalin dared put whatever plans for war he may have had to the test.

The next region in which nuclear weapons created peace was north east Asia. The Soviet-Chinese alliance, which was forged after Mao Zedong took power in 1949, was probably at its strongest in 1956-57 when events in Hungary meant that the Cold War was at its worst. However, already by 1958 Soviet ruler Nikita Khrushchev, by his own subsequent account,[2] had begun to develop his doubts. By 1963, at the latest, the two countries were clearly at loggerheads as each one announced that the other had abandoned the true doctrines of Marx and Lenin and proclaimed itself leader of the Communist camp. By the late sixties, relations had deteriorated to the point where there took place armed skirmishes along the common border in a region where China re-claimed huge territories absorbed by Tsarist Russia during the nineteenth century. By 1969-1970, there was much talk of full scale war; not only did the Soviets engage in a massive buildup of their far-eastern forces, but they are alleged to have sounded out the US concerning the possibility of a first strike against China's nuclear installations.[3] Nothing came of it, however, and the risk of nuclear war finally forced the two countries to repress their differences. Once Soviet ruler Leonid Brezhnev had died, tensions eased. In one of his last acts before leaving power in 1991, Gorbachev even signed a border-treaty with China and thus seems to have put an end to the dispute for the time being.

Further south on the Asian continent, India and Pakistan had given vent to their mutual hatred for each other by fighting no fewer than three wars between the time they were established in 1948 and

2   N. S. Khrushchev, *Khrushchev Remembers* (London: Deutsch, 1971), p. 255 ff.

3   *New York Times*, 19 August 1969; H. A. Kissinger, *The White House Years* (Boston: Little, Brown, 1979), pp. 183-84.

1971.[4] By 1974, though, the Indians had exploded their so called 'peaceful nuclear weapon'; whereas on the other side of the border prime minister Zulfikar Ali Bhutto, taking over after his country's debacle in 1971, reportedly vowed to have his countrymen 'eat grass' so as to achieve the same feat. Though Bhutto himself was removed from the scene in 1977, by the late seventies reports about Pakistani progress in the nuclear field were multiplying and by the early eighties there could be little doubt left that they, too, were in possession of a bomb.[5] In this case, too, the outcome was stalemate; one which was interrupted only by the occasional shell which both sides continued to lob at each other across a remote glacier and, twice, by the Pakistani Army opening fire upon its own people as groups of them threatened to march across the border into Kashmir and thus threatened to create a situation that might escalate and bring about a nuclear conflict that neither side, for very good reasons, wanted.

Finally, since 1945 there has been no region around the world where passions ran as high, and hatreds as deep, as in the Middle East. Between 1947 and 1973 the result was no fewer than five major wars: that of 1947-49, the 1956 Suez Campaign, the 1967 Six Day War, the so-called 'War of Attrition' of 1969-70, and, of course, the October 1973 War itself. Since then, however, in that part of the world large scale warfare also appears to have become a thing of the past. In 1982, it is true, Israel launched a mini war against Lebanon (which included a clash with the Syrians in the Beq'a Valley). The original idea had been to launch an 'operation' which was directed against the PLO and would be over in 48, or 72, hours. When, contrary to the promises of defence minister Ariel Sharon, it developed into a war, so much taken aback was Israeli prime minister Menachem Begin that he went into a depression, resigned, entered his house, and literally never came out again until he died.

The fact that, since 1945, the introduction of nuclear weapons has always resulted in a nuclear peace - even though the road to that peace

4   Since, in the mid-1960s, the Indians were clearly approaching a nuclear capability, it is even possible that the second (1965) Indo-Pakistani conflict was caused by the Pakistani desire to settle over Kashmir before this would happen. Cf. P. K. S. Namboodiri, ' Perceptions and Policies in India and Pakistan', in K. Subrahmanyam, ed., *India and the Nuclear Challenge* (New Delhi: ABC, 1986), p. 222; also M. van Creveld, *Nuclear Proliferation and the Future of Conflict* (New York: Free Press, 1993), pp. 79-80.

5   Cf. R. R. Subramanian, *India, Pakistan, China, Defence and Nuclear Triangle in South Asia* (New Delhi: ABC, 1989), pp. 46-7 and *passim*.

was often scary, as in Cuba in 1962, the Middle East in 1973, and between India and Pakistan during the crisis in their relations in 1990 - does not, of course, constitute an absolute guarantee for the future. As J. F. C Fuller once wrote,[6] one does not eradicate the causes of war by wiping out cities; in many regions where nuclear weapons are present, strong mutual hatred remains as does the potential for miscalculation, unintended escalation, and so forth.

On the other hand, fifty years' experience is not something which ought to be dismissed out of hand. It seems to indicate that, so far, wherever nuclear weapons have made their appearance, large scale conventional warfare has tended to die down and disappear. This was true both when the belligerents were located on separate hemispheres, as in the case of the USA and the USSR, and when they shared a common (and extremely densely inhabited) border as in that of India and Pakistan. It was true regardless of underlying cultural attitudes: that is to say, regardless of whether those who developed and obtained the bombs were god-fearing Americans, or godless communists, or Buddhists claiming to represent ahisma (non-violence), or Moslems preoccupied by Jihad, or Jews possessed of a Holocaust complex, or whatever. It also applied regardless of whether the available means of delivery were simple or complex, few or numerous, balanced (in the sense that there were roughly equal forces on both sides) or not. However much they may have been tempted, reputed madmen such as Stalin and Mao ended by not using the nuclear weapons at their disposal; but neither did such enlightened statesmen as Presidents Dwight Eisenhower (whose Secretary of State, after all, invented the term 'brinkmanship') John Kennedy, and Richard Nixon. Ultimately, paralysis even took hold in those cases where possession of the bomb was not declared as in the case of both Israel and Pakistan. In each case, and as George Orwell had predicted as early as 1949, the outcome was not all out armed conflict but, at worst, occasional incidents, warfare by proxy, and, ultimately, stalemate.

IV. Implications

The implications of this are perfectly clear. Confronted with the availability of nuclear weapons, which were first developed during World War II, large-scale interstate war is a phenomenon which is slowly but surely being squeezed below the historical horizon. To be

6   *Armaments and History* (New York: Scribner, 1945), p. xxxx.

sure, the process has been neither easy nor smooth. Since 1945, even in regions and between countries where nuclear weapons made their presence felt, there have been plenty of crises and scares. Nor should one overlook the wars between non-nuclear states which, as in the Middle East and South Asia, went on fighting to their hearts' contents.

By 1970, if not before, it had become clear that any state capable of building modern conventional armed forces - of operating, say, a number of armoured divisions or maintaining a flotilla of major warships - would also be capable of developing a nuclear programme. To judge by the experience of some countries, indeed, building nuclear weapons was actually easier than producing some advanced conventional ones; as indicated by the history of China, India, Pakistan, and, of course, Israel. To focus on the experience of the last-named, Israel according to the most recent accounts appears to have built its first nuclear weapon in 1967.[7] It was only a decade later, however, that Israel unveiled its first tank, the Merkava I, and even then sixty percent of the parts (including the engine and the transmission) had to be imported from abroad. From then until the present day, Israel has not produced a first line fighter aircraft; while its latest model missile boats, the 1,250 ton Saar IV, are being built for it in American shipyards.

As a result, even in those regions where inter-state warfare was able to continue more or less as before, its size has undergone a dramatic change. Much as the subject has been discussed in works of fiction - whose popularity may well indicate that nuclear weapons alone prevented it from happening - there has been no repetition of World War II when all the world's great powers went to war against each other. During that conflict, six out of seven capitals were either occupied (Paris, Rome, Berlin, Tokyo) or subjected to heavy bombing (London, Moscow); a number of them even suffered both. Since then, is it an accident that not a single one of the world's major capitals has witnessed major warfare unfold within a thousand miles from it?

Conducted as it has been by, or against, third or fourth class states, the size of military operations has also declined. For example, in 1991 the entire Western World combined brought to bear half a million troops against Iraq; not an inconsiderable figure, to be sure, but dwarfed by, say, the three and a half million soldiers with whom Hitler invaded the Soviet Union in 1941 or the four million which

7   S. Peres, *Battling for Peace* (London: Weidenfeld and Nicolson, 1995), p. 167.

Eisenhower ended up by having under his command. Whereas World War II saw several campaigns swinging back and forth over a thousand miles or more, as happened on Germany's Eastern front, in North Africa, and also in the Pacific, since then there has been *no* case in which any armed force was able to advance more than, say, 200 miles in territory which either belonged to the opponent or had been occupied by him.

Judged in terms of the number of major weapons systems, the decline in the scope of conventional interstate war has been more dramatic still. In 1944, the US is said to have procured no fewer than 100,000 military aircraft; in 1995 it procured exactly 127, including transports and helicopters. Similarly, when World War II ended, the US had almost 100 aircraft carriers compared with around 12 today, some of them reportedly so old and subjected to so many modifications that they can barely float. The trend in most other countries has been roughly similar. For example, when Mrs Margaret Thatcher took over in 1979 she promised to set right two decades of neglect and re-arm Britain; when she left Downing Street fourteen years later, the number of Royal Air Force squadrons had been cut by one third.

Nor is it true, as the proponents of airpower are especially fond of arguing, that the quantitative decline is being made up for by qualitative progress. That modern weapons systems are much more powerful and, in particular, much more accurate than their World War II predecessors is, of course, entirely indisputable. It is also indisputable, though, that such calculations only pertain to the ability of x aircraft armed with z missiles to 'service' targets which are *undefended.* Once the defences are taken into account, there is in fact no reason whatsoever to believe that modern weapons systems are more capable *in relation to each other* than were those of previous periods. Aircraft against aircraft, ship against ship, and tank against tank, their relationship is much what it has always been; to judge by some previous historical periods in which the number of main weapons systems also declined even as their quality went up - as happened, for instance, to multiple-oared warships during Hellenistic times and to armoured knights during the late Middle Ages - diminishing quantities represent a typical sign that they may, indeed, have reached the end of their viability.

Since on the one hand, any country capable of building only semi-advanced conventional weapons should be capable of building nuclear weapons; and since, on the other, conventional weapons are only marginally useful in non-trinitarian, interstate, conflicts, it is no wonder that these weapons are being squeezed out. This process, of course, does not apply to the same extent to different countries around the world, nor are the three principal armed services affected to an equal degree. From one country to another, much will depend on geographical situation, perceived threats, strategic plans, and so forth. In each of the three services, it is probably the heaviest weapons and weapons systems that will be the first to go; as is confirmed by the fact that, according to an a recent article in the *Economist*, during the years since 1990 the global market for them has declined by no less than 44 percent.[8]

According to the same *Economist* article, 'with some 30 small wars constantly on the boil, demand for light weapons has rattled on like a vintage Gatling gun'. Many of them are copies of models first introduced by leading arms-producers such as the US, the former USSR, and Israel; they are being produced in such places as Pakistan and Croatia. They range from hand-grenades and submachine guns through mortars and heavy machine guns all the way to armoured cars and personnel carriers; equally brisk is the trade in devices which are used in anti-terrorist operations such as security fences, metal detectors, and the like. Indeed, the point has now been reached where, faced with various internal threats, several developed countries already now have more people employed by the security industry than there are soldiers in the uniformed armed forces. As for many developing countries, the internal threat is such that their armed forces have never been able to turn their attention exclusively outward in the first place.

To sum up, the roughly three hundred year period in which war was associated primarily with the type of political organisation known as the state - first in Europe and then, following the latter's expansion, in other parts of the globe as well - seems to be coming to an end. If the last fifty years or so provide any guide, future wars will be overwhelmingly of the type known, however inaccurately, as 'low intensity'. Both organisationally and in terms of the equipment at their disposal the armed forces of the world will have to adjust themselves to this situation by changing military doctrine, largely jettisoning heavy military equipment, and becoming more like the police. And, in fact, in many places that process is already well under way.

8   *Economist* (London) 25 June 1997, p. 76.

Chapter 4

The Role of Military Force in International Security

Michael Quinlan

Let me start with two quotations from United Kingdom Prime Ministers. First quotation : 'Mine is the first generation able to contemplate the possibility that we may live our entire lives without going to war or sending our children to war'. Second quotation : 'I do see fresh opportunities of approaching this subject of disarmament opening up before us, and I believe they are at least as hopeful as they have been at any previous time. It is to such tasks, the winning back of confidence, the gradual removal of hostility between nations until they feel they can safely discard their weapons, that I would wish to devote what energy and time may be left to me'.

Admirable words, in both instances. The speakers were, respectively, Tony Blair, 1997; and Neville Chamberlain, 1938.

The juxtaposition is perhaps unfair, and I would not want to overstate the warning message I am, by implication, conveying. Mr Blair's language was careful - '... contemplate the possibility that we may ...'; and there are great differences between the two settings, including one crucial difference - the nuclear difference - upon which, at risk of unpopularity, I shall expand a little later. But I begin in this way in order to underscore that defence is not about high and hopeful visions; it is essentially in the insurance business; and defence planners must accordingly be in some degree professional pessimists. The tasks which need to shape military provision, or at least the core of it, have to be derived not from what we would like to see happen, nor even necessarily from what we think is most likely to happen; they need to flow from, in shorthand, what we think to be the most disagreeable and testing scenarios that are not too improbable to merit the cost of insurance. Now there is obviously a whole nexus of awkward judgements called for in the application of that criterion, and I shall not try to explore them all. But I want to offer four general comments which seem to me to bear upon its application.

Comment number one: the world is an uncertain place, and political change can come fast. The astonishing speed and totality of the Soviet Empire's collapse is a vivid reminder of that; and history has plenty of other examples equally dramatic yet a great deal less benign. But high-quality military capability takes many years to build, or to rebuild if lost; the timescales of most defence provision far exceed the reach of political prediction. It would have occurred to no-one in my old field of work, when the requirement for the Vulcan bomber was framed soon after World War II, that the only operational use it would ever see would be the bombardment of Stanley airfield thirty-six years later. Even our Naval Staff planners of the 1960s, desperately keen to think up scenarios which would require the use of aircraft carriers, never thought of the recovery of the Falklands. Our decision to acquire the Trident missile system was made in 1980; the first operational submarine carrying it went to sea in 1995.

Comment number two: defence provision, unlike most other sorts of insurance, can have the bonus effect of actually reducing the probability of the disagreeable events against which it guards - it can deter them. But the trouble with deterrence is that if it succeeds its relevance to the success can rarely be proved. It seems to me pretty likely that if a cohesive NATO with a full spectrum of armament had not existed the Soviet Union would have been more apt, at some time or another during the forty years of the Cold War, to take disagreeable and risky actions - for example over Berlin - which might have started a slide into war, 1914-style; but that is a proposition about alternative history, inherently unprovable. Were those mostly-unused Vulcans I just referred to useful in some degree in helping to prevent the Cold War hotting up, or were they just primitive sacrifices to ensure that the sun rose the following day? Questions like that are hard enough looking backward; looking forward - which is, alas, the direction in which defence planning has to be done - they can be harder still.

Comment number three: armed conflict is something about which the participants can get quite agitated. It is not normally an activity refereed within rules and entered upon in a spirit of gentility and sweet reason. It therefore has a propensity to escalate - not automatic, of course, and there are factors which push the other way, but not negligible. If we are minded to get involved in such conflict, whether as contestants or as some sort of external moderator, we need to be pretty careful not to do so unless we have the capability and the will to stay with the task even if it all gets a good deal rougher, in scale or breadth or weaponry or intensity, than when it started. The wreck of Yugoslavia, and the shifting tasks of intervening forces there have given us some harsh reminders about that.

Comment number four: the developed democratic open-society world is highly prone to over-estimate the degree to which everyone in the world thinks as we do, and perceives interest and risk in the same way as we believe they rationally ought to. Some of you may know of a stimulating book called *The Great Illusion*, in which Norman Angell argues very vigorously that money spent on massive military provision is foolish, because the interdependence of modern economies is so extensive and compelling as to make war between major powers clearly absurd. Angell wrote the book in 1908. Rather more recently, I recall a former Diplomatic Service colleague telling me about his work in the late 1950s on Allied contingency planning related to Berlin. The planners knew that the Soviet Union faced acute problems with a massive migratory haemorrhage through Berlin from East Germany, and they speculated on what options might be taken. They thought up all sorts of imaginative possibilities. One that did occur to them, but which they were minded to dismiss as too crude even for the Russians, was simply to build a high wall down the middle of the city. People in countries like Britain and New Zealand regularly underrate the power of greed, hatred, stupidity, fear, jealousy or ignorance to motivate leaders, especially those who have different values and are not answerable to electorates or reminded of reality by critical oppositions. We underrated the crudity of General Galtieri in 1982, and that of Saddam Hussein in 1990. The eventual outcome demonstrated to both those leaders that they had made a mistake, and I both hope and believe that we have thereby helped to reduce the future likelihood that other such people might make other such mistakes. But I would not wish to wager global security on any assumption that we have reduced the likelihood to a permanent zero - still less on an assumption that it would remain at zero if the rest of us dispensed with the evident military capability for proving that international aggression is indeed a mistake.

So far, I may seem to have been transmitting, at least by implication, a highly conservative message about military force in international affairs. I do think we need - by the very nature of what security is about - to be wary, though in my lexicon that is not a synonym for conservative. But let me now start qualifying the conservatism. There are real changes, and of a kind not likely to be swiftly reversed, both in relative probabilities and importance within the diverse range of challenges we may have to tackle by military means, and in the methods and instruments for doing the tackling.

It is, I fully accept, now very hard to assign any significant probability to scenarios in which the homelands of developed countries - save possibly in just one or two special instances - come under serious threat of direct military attack in the old-fashioned sense. That has of course been true for New Zealand for over half a century, and it seems to me plainly true now for the United Kingdom, the United States and most if not all other members of the European Union. But as *Desert Storm* illustrated, we do all continue to regard it in principle as appropriate that such countries should maintain the possibility (I put it no higher) of intervening, if necessary by force, to correct what we see as unacceptable situations elsewhere in the global scene. We have proper interests in reducing the incidence, the span and the severity of conflict wherever we can - interests deriving from economic concern about trade, for example; from political concern because of the risks of displacement or contagion; and from a degree of moral concern, I would argue, because of our underlying values and the expectation of our peoples that we should not simply stand aside when intolerable events happen in terms of those values. It seems to me plainly right, and generally accepted amongst our publics, that we should not absolutely forswear the option of taking military action for such reasons. But for the great majority of those UN members who are in a position to bear some share of responsibility in this way outside their own borders, far the greatest likelihood of military involvement relates now to making a contribution to collective effort in conflict situations not matching the classic model of interstate war. The probabilities of that classic model, aside perhaps from a few special arenas, have indeed sharply diminished, and are unlikely to surge again unless either gross global economic misfortune generates pressing new incentives, or else the dismantling of military force or the decay of political will among those who are in effect ring-holders in the international system recreates attractive opportunities for the ill-motivated to go to war. IFOR and SFOR in Bosnia are surely more probable types for the future than *Desert Storm* in the Gulf.

If intervention of this kind - whether peacekeeping or peacemaking - is to be the predominant model for the use of armed forces, questions then arise about what sorts of armed forces. I have already offered, indirectly, one part of an answer to the 'what sort?' question, in suggesting that even in lower-level conflict the interveners will often need to have at their disposal higher-level power of something like a classical kind in order either still to cope if conflict does escalate, or else - and of course preferably - to help deter it from escalating; again, consider the former Yugoslavia. But below that tier of capability, what are the key characteristics? This is not the occasion, nor have I the expertise, to offer detailed description; but I suggest that three features of equipment and three of training take on a higher relative salience than they had in what we used to think of as 'normal' war.

The first equipment feature is the ability to acquire targets more discriminately, and hit them more exactly, if we do get to any sort of shooting. In sub-war operations, and under the eye of CNN, the explanation that we didn't really mean to hit the children's school or the refugee camp next door becomes less and less admissible. The second equipment feature is the ability to collect and then to analyse the best possible intelligence in confused and ambiguous situations (and we need, by the way, to break the habit some have of regarding 'intelligence' as a dirty word in UN activities). A third equipment feature : we need the kit and the procedures to communicate immediately and clearly up, down and between what may be pretty heterogeneous force components yet without making an avoidable hash of coherent patterns of command and control.

On the training and preparation side, in addition to the ability to use effectively the kit I have been talking about, my three emphases are these. First, on the ability to fit forces of different nations together - to inter-operate and to pool strengths rather than weaknesses. Second, on the ability to manage public presentation and explanation as an integral part of the task, not an add-on or distraction; public acceptance both on the ground and back home are cardinal to the entire contributory role. Third, on training forces, right down to the level of the individual, to operate with good sense and restraint, but without simply abdicating involvement, in murky and sometimes downright unfair situations. UK forces have had to learn about that, sometimes the hard way for all concerned, in Northern Ireland; and even Canada, with a long and honourable record in peace-keeping, had in Somalia an uncomfortable reminder that highly-professional armed forces do not automatically do well in tasks of this kind. I do not want however to make the activity sound like an up-market police role. This is still a business for armed forces, at least in anything like the tradition our countries share of the distinction between the soldier and the policeman; it requires formed bodies of people under precise command, equipped with and ultimately prepared to use sophisticated lethal force in combat conditions. And let me append to that one other observation before I remove myself from the ground which Mats Berdal will be covering far more expertly. It is not just the armed forces themselves that need trained skills in order to function appropriately in complex situations of dangerous conflict short of war. The entire apparatus of management and control within which they operate, from political leadership downwards, needs to understand and face the constraints and the imperatives of reality. The humiliation of the Netherlands battalion at Srebrenica a year or two ago, deployed in a situation where they were close spectators at intolerable events in which they had neither the capability nor the authorisation to intervene, carries warnings about that.

A last point, of a wider kind. The situations we are here considering are very rarely of a clearcut old-style win-or-lose kind; and it follows that we cannot count on their having conveniently tidy exit points. These tasks can drag on far longer than was hoped at the outset - look, for example, at the UN forces now well beyond their twentieth anniversary in Cyprus. Interveners, whether individual states or groupings, need to have both the military and the political stamina to see the job through.

Now who is going to provide all this spectrum of graduated force, both the low-level apparatus and the various degrees of back-up needed to sustain it and if necessary bail it out; that is, the straight war-fighting capability needed if Saddam Hussein does not after all prove to be the last of the line among old-fashioned state aggressors? I am taking it as my central assumption that we are thinking primarily in terms of responsibility falling collectively upon the international community, whether in UN structures or at least with UN legitimation. But the UN, like the Pope as perceived by Stalin, does not have any divisions, at least not of the military kind. The forces have today to come, as in *Desert Storm,* from nation states, and I see no real likelihood of changing that substantially.

It would carry me beyond the proper scope of my theme to consider at length just who should contribute what to military capability in support of global order; but I should like to offer some brief incidental comment.

It seems to me almost incontrovertible, whether we like it or not, that the key provider of heavyweight force - the military lender of last resort to the international community, as it were - is the United States. I would suggest two reasons why there is basically no alternative to the US. The first point is mostly about resources and technical capability. The projection of military force far from home - and that is what we are talking about - has become a highly demanding task. Modern military technology has put in the hands of quite small and poor states, and indeed sometimes of non-state actors, weapons which can make life very difficult for lightweight long-distance interveners. (It is worth considering, indeed, how even with the United States so fully involved the *Desert Storm* coalition could have done the job if it had not had those massive and well-found bases available in Saudi Arabia.) There are some kinds of military capability, like long-range airlift and satellite reconnaissance, which scarcely exist at all (leaving aside perhaps the decaying ex-Soviet inventory) except in US hands; and there are other kinds which exist elsewhere only in much smaller amounts and lower quality. A united Europe no doubt could in theory rectify all this; but the political probability of its spending the money to do so is effectively zero. And my second point is a political one. The United States, for all the peculiarities of its constitution, is ultimately a single international actor, able to act with a coherence and decisiveness that no coalition, whether permanent or *ad hoc*, can truly match in the use of force. The result is, as we have seen in the Bosnian wreck, that people like Slobodan Milosevic, Radovan Karadzic and Ratko Mladic simply do not believe that the international community is really serious unless the United States commits forces to back up political involvement. I see no likelihood that that reality will dependably change.

What may well change, however, is the form which high-level military force is likely to take. There is a substantial and still-developing debate in the United States - it has not yet, so far as my awareness goes, taken equal general hold in Europe or elsewhere, though interest is rising - about what is shorthanded as RMA : the Revolution in Military Affairs. By that is meant the idea that the convergence of modern technologies, especially in the information field, will confer upon the United States the ability to apply force with such speed and precision, and on the basis of such huge advantage over an adversary in timely and detailed knowledge of exactly what is happening in the conflict arena, that events like the crude clash of armoured forces on the battlefield are rendered obsolete - military superiority can be imposed surgically and conclusively by massive technological capability. And some enthusiasts argue that the long-term effect of all this, as it spreads around the world, will extend beyond how military conflict is conducted to whether it can or need be conducted at all.

I am nowhere near having the knowledge to explain this materially further, still less to evaluate it. At risk of sounding like a First World War cavalry officer decrying the significance of the tank, I will admit to some wariness about just how radical or rapid the transformation might be. I have a lingering scepticism, fuelled partly by memories of President Reagan's 'Star Wars' initiative in its original Astrodome form, about propensities towards technological utopianism. Complex innovations in war do not always work out, amid the stresses and surprises of conflict, quite in accordance with peace-time prediction. But the appropriate posture is one of listening carefully; for sometimes technology does have a truly transforming effect that calls for different ways of thinking.

And that brings me, at last, to nuclear weapons. Various events in the past year or so have amplified the call to abolish these entirely. I need not recapitulate all the events, but the Report of the Canberra Commission published in August 1996 is a high-profile example. Can we realistically plan - and if we can, should we? - for a world in which all nuclear armouries have been dismantled?

I propose to reverse logical order by telling you first what conclusion I offer on that question, and then explaining how I get to it. In brief, I regard a nuclear-weapon-free world as a legitimate long-term aspiration. I draw, however, a clear distinction between aspiration and practical policy. I believe it unwise, and potentially indeed downright damaging, to confuse the two. I do not regard nuclear abolition as a sensible aim to designate now for practical policy.

There are, first, huge difficulties about political feasibility. It is fantasy to suppose that Russia and France - to take just the two most obvious examples of likely resistance - will give up their nuclear arsenals in any world remotely like the one we actually live in. We may wish that current nuclear powers saw their interests differently, and that they thought about these issues in the same way as the Canberra Commission's members do. But they are not going to; and to base policy upon any expectation that they will would be rather like basing our policy now towards China on an expectation that its rulers will be converted to open pluralist democracy.

Partnering that barrier is the obstacle of verification. Precisely because of their unique importance, any comprehensive ban on nuclear weapons would have to be policed to very rigorous standards. It is certainly possible, as the Canberra Commission report shows, to describe an international verification system which would meet such standards pretty well, provided that all significant states agreed both to submit to it and to come down with compelling force on anyone who breached it. But the likelihood of their so agreeing and acting is minimal. Countries like China and Iran are not going to convert themselves into fully-open societies, obedient to international norms as seen in the West, just to satisfy the needs of a nuclear verification regime. Consider how hard it has been to verify the prohibition of weapons of mass destruction in Iraq, a modest-sized developing country that could be treated as defeated, friendless and in disgrace. Consider even, the fuss the United States Congress has made about accepting the verification requirements of the Chemical Warfare Convention. We can of course postulate all these and other such difficulties out of existence; but that is not policy-making.

But I am not arguing against a policy goal of nuclear abolition merely on the ground that key players are too obstinate or unwise to accept it - though even if that were so it might still have to be reckoned with as a fact of international life. The deeper fact however is that purported abolition would be an attempt to impose an outcome against the grain of reality - an attempt to treat what is ultimately a symptom as though it were the underlying ill.

What we have to grasp, at bottom, is that nuclear weapons have brought about their own RMA - Revolution in Military Affairs - and probably the most fundamental one in history. Their effect has been to carry the power to destroy off the end of the scale; and that is something fundamentally different from the effect of any other class of weapon. We cannot sensibly hope therefore to manage them in the same sort of way as we seek to manage other special classes of particularly disagreeable weapons, like gas or biological agents or land-mines. Indeed, one of the reasons why the verification provisions of the prohibitions on chemical and biological weapons are not a safe model for a prohibition on nuclear weapons is that the major powers have felt able to accept imperfections in BW and CW verification precisely because the overshadowing power of nuclear weapons would prevent any serious violator getting away with exploiting such a breach - that was certainly the case with the poorly-verified 1975 BW convention, on which the Soviet Union undoubtedly cheated. *Ex hypothesi*, a nuclear ban would have no similar ultimate underpinning. But the main point is more fundamental. Because they provide effectively infinite force, nuclear weapons have generated the *reductio ad absurdum* of military conflict between advanced states. That, in my opinion, is both a highly salutary fact and an ultimately irreversible one, because it is knowledge-based and knowledge cannot be forgotten. We might consider - though the Canberra Commission's long report does not seem anywhere to have considered - what is to happen if, in a world of purported nuclear abolition, major states do come again to blows over grave issues where neither is prepared to lose. Will they trust a hated adversary not to recreate nuclear weapons as an insurance against defeat? It should be recalled again that war is not a rule-based competition overseen by umpires. We cannot securely re-rationalise major warfare between developed states, even if we wanted to.

What nuclear weapons did during the Cold War was to fix deeply in the minds of both sides the reality that, however abrasive their differences might be, the differences had to be managed in a way that did not risk any drift into war. I do not know what hard tests the twenty-first century may set us; but to take just two examples, I believe that both the rise of China towards superpower status and the evolution of Russia will be more safely accommodated if it remains the case that military conflict is an option utterly excluded. And the exclusion rests today upon nuclear weapons; it cannot rest anything like as securely upon economic interest, or upon political regulation.

Political regulation brings me back to my point about the distinction between aspiration and policy. I do not at all desire or accept that large nuclear armouries should be with us for the rest of human history, even though the knowledge is ineradicable. But the path towards a world in which their contribution to sealing off the option of war is no longer needed has to be a fundamental political path, not an arms control path - just as the ending of the Cold-War confrontation reflected a fundamental political event, not an arms-control deal. The nuclear abolitionists like the Canberra Commission postulate - they have to postulate - massive changes in political stances and attitudes. Those changes may be deeply desirable; but they cannot be created just by a crusade for nuclear abolition - abolition has to be effect, not cause.

Let me make clear, finally, that in opposing abolition as a current policy goal I am not saying that the status quo is either inevitable or tolerable. There have already been massive changes in the nuclear-weapon scene, and there is a large and diverse agenda of further change that ought to be pursued - about numbers, about verification, about control and safety, about proliferation. But the agenda is in no way dependent upon an abolitionist commitment; indeed, such a commitment might in some respects impede it, for example by importing pretexts for delay, avoidance or condition-making, and by diverting diplomatic effort.

In conclusion, I think the likelihood of old-style interstate conflict has indeed greatly declined; but we are not yet in a position safely to base our military provision on the assumption of its disappearance, and to attempt to do so might actually work against the assumption. We need however to be alert to what may prove progressively to be big shifts in how higher-level insurance provision can best be shaped. We need also to focus proportionately more attention on the demands - often complex and awkward - likely to be made upon military capability at lower levels of applying force. And we can tackle a constructive nuclear agenda without supposing it useful to espouse an abolitionist policy that is neither feasible nor necessarily desirable unless and until we first manage massively to change the whole global political environment.

Chapter 5

UN Peacekeeping and the Use of Force: No Escape from Hard Decisions*

Mats Berdal

Introduction

The traditional or 'classic' understanding of peacekeeping derives largely, though not exclusively, from the experience of United Nations field operations during the Cold War. Although the term itself does not appear in the UN Charter, a general consensus concerning its essential character gradually emerged in the course of the thirteen operations that were launched between 1948 and 1987. Peacekeeping came to denote a distinctive form of third-party intervention aimed at avoiding the outbreak or resurgence of violence between warring parties. Field operations usually involved the deployment of lightly equipped military personnel whose task it was to control violence by means *other* than enforcement or counter-violence. To this end, the activities of peacekeepers were governed by three closely related principles: host-state consent; minimum use of force except in self-defence; and impartiality as the determinant of operational activity.

Since the early 1990s, the specificity associated with the term 'peacekeeping' has largely been lost both in public and in much of the academic debate surrounding the role of the UN in the field of security. The choice of 'peacekeeping' to describe the activities of UN forces in the midst of the war in Bosnia between 1992 and 1995, undoubtedly contributed to this development. Indeed, the experience of UNPROFOR led many to conclude that the resort to peacekeeping only served to mask divisions among outside powers about the nature of the conflict, and, more generally, reflected a basic lack of moral

* The author would like to thank Michael Pugh for very helpful comments on an earlier draft of this chapter.

resolve on the part of the 'international community' in the face of an increasingly disorderly and violent international system.[1] There is no doubt that the tasks given to the UN in Bosnia - the growth and increasingly contradictory nature of which are traceable in a paper mountain of Security Council Resolutions and Presidential Statements - did, in effect, serve as a substitute for a more coherent policy towards the conflict. This chapter is concerned with what is seen as an important consequence of this experience, namely, that the 'lessons of the necessary conditions for UN peacekeeping seem to have been forgotten; and all the alternative possibilities under the Charter ignored.'[2] As Rosalyn Higgins noted in one of her lectures for the Hague Academy General Course in International Law: 'UN peacekeeping, together with collective measures under Chapter VII of the Charter, appears to be entering a period of deep incoherence.'[3]

Higgins observations suggest that behind the technical and jargon-laden debates that characterise much of the current writing on the 'utility' and 'future of peacekeeping', lies a question of wider significance: when should collectively legitimised military action be taken, and what *form* should such action assume, in conflicts that originate *within* states but often 'spill-over' or directly involve neighbouring states ? The debate which this question has generated is often referred to as the 'peacekeeping doctrine' debate, though, as indicated above, it touches on much broader issues than military doctrine narrowly conceived. It is with this broader set of issues that this chapter is principally concerned. It is divided into three parts.

The first part briefly examines the evolution of peacekeeping after the Cold War, focusing on changes in the *scale*, *scope* and *context* of UN field operations. The second part looks more closely at the

---

1   As a result of its association with major policy failure, it may well be that the history of the term 'peacekeeping' will be similar to that of 'appeasement', a word which, as D.C. Watt notes, used to refer to a policy of 'defusing conflict [but took] on the meaning of purchasing peace for one's own interests by sacrificing the interests of others'. The fiercest critics of UN policy in former Yugoslavia have, of course, drawn parallels between the policies themselves; i.e. they have viewed 'peacekeeping' as a modern-day version of 'appeasement'. D.C. Watt, 'Churchill and Appeasement', in *Churchill*, edited by R. Blake and Wm. Roger Louis (Oxford: OUP, 1993), p. 200.

2   Rosalyn Higgins, *Problems and Process: International Law and How We Use It* (Oxford: Clarendon Press, 1994), p. 181.

3   Ibid.

implications of these changes as they relate to the issue of the use of force. Specifically, it asks whether the basic distinction between consent-based operations and enforcement should be abandoned in favour of an approach that envisages a 'spectrum' of military responses to contemporary conflicts. Finally, in part three, some general lessons regarding the UN and the use of force are identified.

I. UN Peacekeeping after the Cold War

'Classical peacekeeping'

Although the Cold War paralysed the workings of the Security Council as the organ entrusted with 'primary responsibility for the maintenance of international peace and security',[4] it did not spell a complete end to the UN's role in the field of security. What emerged instead was peacekeeping, originally conceived by Dag Hammarskjold, Secretary-General from 1953 to 1961, as a tool with which to develop the function of 'preventive diplomacy'. Specifically, Hammarskjold argued that a peacekeeping deployment could help to prevent Great Power rivalry in areas of local conflict from developing into wider and, in all likelihood, more dangerous international conflicts. Peacekeeping thus represented a functional adjustment on the part of the UN to an international political system dominated by global rivalry and the ever-present threat of war between two power blocs.

The precise tasks of UN peacekeepers during the Cold War period varied considerably and almost always involved more than simply patrolling a static cease-fire line between belligerents.[5] As noted above, however, the defining characteristics of peacekeeping crystallised early on. The requirement of host-state consent for the deployment of a force; the commitment to impartiality in relation to all disputants and the 'prohibition against any *initiative* in the use of armed force',[6] all combined to give peacekeeping its specific character

4   UN Charter, Article 24 (1).
5   For the best analytical discussion of the varieties of peacekeeping experience, though not confined to the UN, see Alan James, *Peacekeeping in International Politics* (London: Macmillan/IISS, 1990).
6   A/3943, Summary Study of the Experience Derived from the Establishment and Operation of the Force: Report of the Secretary-General, 9 October 1958 (henceforth, 'A/3943, *Summary Study*'), para. 178.

and, it should be stressed, limited scope. The *Summary Report* produced by the Secretary-General following the establishment of the first UN Emergency Force in the Middle East in 1956 (UNEF I) spelled out the crucial implication that followed from these principles: peackeepers 'should not be used to enforce any specific political solution of pending problems or to influence the political balance decisive to such a solution'.[7]

The UN and the End of the Cold War

The passing of the Cold War contributed to a climate of optimism and expectations around the UN not seen since the founding conference in San Francisco in 1945. Between 1988 and early 1992, the organisation's role in helping to defuse conflicts that had previously been fuelled and exacerbated by East-West tensions, appeared to confirm the view that, increasingly, the UN would be able play a more central role not only in the containment but also in the resolution of conflicts. In 1989-90, UN peacekeepers successfully supervised the transition from South African rule to independence in Namibia. Between 1988 and 1991, UN observers were involved in monitoring the withdrawal of Cuban troops from Angola and Soviet troops from Afghanistan. Throughout the same period, slow but steady progress in the Central American peace process was aided by the activities of two UN observer groups. Finally, the willingness of the US to use the UN as the source of legitimation for enforcement action against Iraq during the Gulf crisis, raised expectations further about the future place of the organisation in the field of international peace and security. In terms of the actual changes that have taken place in UN peacekeeping practice, it is useful distinguish between *scale*, *scope* and *context*.

Scale, Scope and Context of Post-Cold War Peacekeeping

Scale

Between 1948 and 1987, 13 operations were launched by the UN; since 1987, more than 20 new operations have been launched. In January 1988, the annual UN budget for peacekeeping was calculated at 230.4 million US dollars; by late 1994 preliminary projections put the figure at 3.6 billion. Since 1988, the number of soldiers deployed

7 Ibid., para. 167.

in the field has increased from 9,500 to a high of 78,000 in 1994. At the same time, the group of troop-contributing countries has grown from 26 to nearly 80 and now includes all five permanent members of the Security Council. This rapid expansion has, not surprisingly, placed serious strains on the UN machinery for planning and supporting operations, as well as on the executive direction of peacekeeping. Deficiencies in areas such as logistic support and procurement; command, control and intelligence; training and specialised personnel (especially engineering and communications), have all, at various times, been cruelly exposed on the ground. The apparent inability to reform the financial, personnel and, above all, procurement procedures governing UN field operations, has been and continues to be a source of deep frustration to troop-contributing nations and outside observers. Nevertheless, given the scale of expansion and the organisational base from which rapid adaptation has had to be effected, the ability of the UN secretariat to adjust (or, rather, to improvise) is perhaps more impressive than is usually suggested.[8]

Scope

This is especially the case if one considers that the changes in peacekeeping practice have not only been quantitative in nature: UN field operations have also become far more complex in their composition and multi-faceted in their objectives. Large civilian elements are now routinely deployed alongside soldiers in the field and, as a result, the traditional functions of peacekeepers have evolved. Military elements have been given a greater number of *support* roles aimed at promoting the objectives of other mission components, specialised UN agencies and non-governmental organisations. One such role has been the provision of theatre-level logistics for non-military elements of a mission. A second, and more controversial, role has been the attempt to establish 'secure environments' for non-military tasks to be carried out.

It is precisely in terms of the range of tasks given to peacekeepers, that UN practice has changed most markedly after the Cold War. Eight categories, several of which overlap and none of

8   I have discussed some of these issues more fully in 'Reforming the UN's Organisational Capacity for Peacekeeping', in *A Crisis of Expectations: UN Peacekeeping in the 1990s*, edited by Ramesh Thakur and Carlyle Thayer (Boulder: Westview Press, Inc., 1995).

which is entirely self-contained, may briefly be identified as having crystallised in recent years:

(1) electoral support;
(2) repatriation of refugees/displaced persons and humanitarian assistance;
(3) demining activities;
(4) observation and verification of cease-fire agreements, buffer zones, foreign troop withdrawals and human rights compliance;
(5) preventive deployments;
(6) the separation of forces, their demobilisation and the collection, custody and/or destruction of weapons;
(7) establishing secure conditions for the delivery of humanitarian relief;
(8) disarming combatants, especially paramilitary forces, private and irregular units.[9]

The last three of these - weapons control measures, the protection of humanitarian activities and the disarmament of combatants - have been the most complex and controversial of all of the UN's post-Cold War activities. The difficulties encountered in each case have been intimately linked to the third area of change alluded to above, namely, the *context* of UN peacekeeping.

Context.

The *Summary Report* produced by the Secretary-General following the UNEF deployment in 1958 referred to a 'rule' of peacekeeping that precluded 'the employment of United Nations elements in situations of an essentially internal nature'.[10] To the extent that this ever constituted a 'rule' of peacekeeping, it has clearly been abandoned. Although UN forces were drawn into the internal conflicts and politics of Congo in the early 1960s (ONUC), and were later deployed in a 'civil war' context in Southern Lebanon (UNIFIL) and Cyprus (UNFICYP), the shift towards UN involvement in intra-state conflict has been a particular feature of the post-Cold War period.

9 These categories are drawn from and discussed more fully in my paper *Whither UN Peacekeeping?* Adelphi Paper 281 (London: Brasseys/IISS, 1993), pp. 12-25.
10 'A/3943, *Summary Study*', para. 166.

Since 1992 alone, nine out of 11 new UN operations have been related to an intra-state conflict. In many of these, the operational environment in which forces have been deployed has been highly volatile, complex and prone to sudden escalation in levels of violence. In Bosnia and Somalia, peacekeepers often worked with only limited consent from warring parties, while front lines and legitimate political authorities were often hard to identify. Indeed, a distinguishing feature of the conflicts where the UN has become involved has been 'the collapse of State institutions, especially the police and the judiciary, with resulting paralysis of governance, a breakdown of law and order, and general banditry and chaos.'[11] The steep rise in the number of casualties from UN peacekeeping operations since 1992 is grim testimony to this change in operational circumstances.

It is against this background— significant changes in the scale, scope and, above all, the context of UN field operations — that the debate about 'peacekeeping doctrine' or, as I have suggested more broadly, the use or threat of use of force must be placed.

II. Peacekeeping Doctrine and the Use of Force

The debate over peacekeeping doctrine has centred on the issue of whether or not it is sensible to predicate operational concepts, planning and training on the assumption that a 'middle-ground' or 'spectrum' of military activity exists between consent-based peacekeeping and enforcement based on traditional war-fighting doctrines. It needs to be stressed here that there is no disagreement over the fact that the *operational environment* in which peacekeepers have found themselves in recent years is far more complex, volatile and dangerous than in the past. Although advocates of a spectrum approach occasionally seem to imply otherwise, very few would dispute that the conflicts in which the UN has increasingly become involved are 'messy' and operationally demanding. Disagreement centres on the role and utility of military force in responding to such situations.

In brief, proponents of a new approach 'beyond peacekeeping but short of all-out warfighting'[12] maintain that a peacekeeping force need *not* be guided by the requirement of *consent* from the parties to a

---

11   'Position Paper Of The Secretary-General On The Occasion Of The Fiftieth Anniversary Of The United Nations', A/50/60-S/1995/1, 3 January 1995 (Supplement to An Agenda for Peace).

12   John Gerard Ruggie, 'The UN and the Collective Use of Force: Whither or Whether ?' *International Peacekeeping*, Vol. 3, No. 4 (Winter 1996), p.1.

conflict. The reason for this, in the words of Richard Connaughton, is that 'consent and impartiality are too fragile to serve as a fulcrum around which a sensible doctrine can be built'.[13] Instead, a military force that is properly equipped, trained and governed by the appropriate operational concepts can engage in various intermediate 'levels' of enforcement.[14]

It is a view which explicitly challenges the British Army doctrine of *Wider Peacekeeping* published in early 1995 and which firmly rejects the 'spectrum approach', identifying instead 'two basic categories of activity ... peacekeeping (including Wider Peacekeeping) and enforcement'.[15] Although, the publication of *Wider Peacekeeping* appeared, for a time, to have decisively shifted the doctrinal debate in favour of a more conservative approach, renewed attention has been given recently to 'middle-ground' options.[16] Indeed, according to Michael Pugh, 'the emerging doctrines of peace support operations in the United Kingdom, United States, France, and in NATO, represent a common shift towards a military spectrum approach, in which peacekeeping and peace enforcement are part of a range of military options'.[17]

The sources of this shift are varied and are themselves a subject of considerable interest. In Britain, the shift is still tentative and a debate is on-going as to whether 'peace enforcement' is doctrinally distinguishable from 'war fighting'. The first draft of a new doctrine for Peace Support Operation does suggest, however, that a shift in favour of the spectrum approach is taking place.[18] Acceptance of the idea that military actions can be calibrated along a spectrum of enforcement is evident in the draft's claim that identifying 'the

13   Richard Connaughton, 'Time to clear the doctrine dilemma', *Jane's Defence Weekly*, 9 April 1994.

14   John MacKinlay and Jarat Chopra, *A Draft Concept of Second Generation Multinational Operations* (Providence RI: The Thomas J. Watson Jr. Institute for International Studies, 1993), pp. 4-5. The meaning of *consent* is, of course, at the heart of the docrine debate and is discussed below.

15   Army Field Manual, *Wider Peacekeeping*, Fifth Draft, chapter 2.

16   For the influence of *Wider Peacekeeping* on US Army thinking, see *FM 100-23 Peace Operations*, HQ Department of the Army, December 1994, p. 13.

17   Michael Pugh, *From Mission Cringe to Mission Creep? - Implications of New Peace Support Operations Doctrine*, Forsvarsstudie No. 2/1997 (Oslo: Institute for Defence Studies, 1997), p. 12.

18   Ibid., p. 13. See also Army Field Manual, Peace Support Operations, First Draft, 1996 (henceforth AFM PSO, 1. Draft) .

similarities and differences between consent based peacekeeping, combat capable but impartial peace enforcement and other *less restrained partial enforcement operations* or war [are] critical to selecting the most appropriate force profile and approach to the conduct of operations'.[19] In the US, the manner in which the UNPROFOR mission in Bosnia finally gave way to a new NATO-led mission (IFOR), especially through the air bombing campaign in September and August 1995, has shaped much of the debate on the use of force in peace support operations. It is in France, however, that the idea of a distinct category of operations between peacekeeping and enforcement which still somehow falls short of war-fighting, has been taken up most keenly. It merits, therefore, more detailed scrutiny.

Is there a middle-ground ? - The French concept of 'peace restoration'

It was the failure of the international response to the unfolding tragedy in Rwanda in 1994 which led the French military to question what is still at the heart of the British doctrine of 'Wider Peacekeeping': that no middle-ground or spectrum of military operations exists between peace-keeping and enforcement. While still highly critical of the US army mode of operation in Somalia, especially its excessive reliance on superior firepower as a means of minimising casualties, the French military has identified 'peace-restoring operations' (*restauration de la paix*) as a third category for which its armed forces have to be prepared. The declared aim of such operations would be to restore security for civilian populations in conditions of civil war and mass violence by using coercive measures under Chapter VII of the UN Charter, though *without* formally designating an aggressor or prejudging the political outcome of the conflict in question. To convey the basic idea behind the notion of 'peace-restoring' operations, the term 'active impartiality' is sometimes used by French officials responsible for doctrine development.[20]

Though not specifically referring to French thinking, John Ruggie expresses a broadly similar view. Force, he notes, could be 'used

19   Ibid. pp. 3-9, para. 27 (my emphasis).
20   Private interview. 'Operations of this type', according to an aide-memoire on the subject submitted to the UN Secretary-General, 'contain risk of escalation' and it is a risk that has to accepted. The notion of 'escalation dominance' is implicit therefore in the French concept. See also 'Supplement to An Agenda for Peace, aide-memoire by France', A/50/869, S/1996/71, 30 January 1996, UN Document.

impartially, meaning without *a priori* prejudice or bias in response to violations of agreements, Security Council mandates, or norms stipulated in some other fashion'.[21] A similar view can be found in the British Army's first draft of its Peace Support Operations doctrine (PSO), where 'peace enforcement' is not equated with 'war' but defined as 'coercive operations carried out to restore or maintain peace in situations of chaos, or between parties who may not all consent to intervention and who may be engaged in combat activities, in order to help create the conditions for diplomatic and humanitarian activities to support political goals.'[22] It is the impartial nature of 'peace enforcement operations' which 'separates them from other traditional enforcement operations'.[23]

The central question raised by the apparent shift, most evident in French military thinking, in favour of a 'spectrum' approach is whether it represents an advance in doctrinal development; whether it really reflects a clearer understanding of the challenge posed by collectively legitimised military action, and the *form* that such action should assume, in contemporary conflicts ?

The notion of 'peace restoration' as presented by French doctrine staff is superficially appealing, but only in the abstract. Indeed, the spectrum approach is flawed in important respects. If adopted uncritically as a basis for planning and deployment, it carries with it considerable risks. Three difficulties merit special mention.

In the first place, and as Michael Pugh has perceptively observed, the fact that 'conflict environments are grey and messy' does not automatically suggest that the solution is to locate 'peace support operations on a spectrum of force'.[24] Indeed, by doing so one is likely to 'encourage the notion that there can be military fixes of deep-rooted political problems, a notion that may be exacerbated by the pressure for quick exit strategies'.[25] There is, in other words, a danger that faith in doctrinal innovation - not unlike faith in technological 'fixes' and breakthroughs - may obscure, or at least redirect the focus of attention away from, the importance of maintaining a firm link

21 Ruggie, 'The UN and the Collective Use of Force', p. 14.
22 AFM PSO, 1. Draft, chapter 1, p. 1.
23 Ibid., pp. 1-3 (para. 11).
24 Pugh, *From Mission Cringe to Mission Creep?*, p. 22.
25 Ibid. As Pugh pointedly adds, 'concerns about grey area operations cannot be dismissed as a case of academics wishing the world were a less messy place. On the contrary, an appreciation that situations are messy and volatile, leads to a concern that interventions do not create more mess in the long term'.

between the employment of military force and the long-term political objective which the use of force is intended to serve.

The second difficulty flows from the first: the idea that a 'peace restoring' operation can clinically apply force to manipulate the behaviour of various parties on the ground *without* designating an enemy while, at the same time, assuming that such action will not prejudge the political outcome of the conflict, is to seriously underestimate the impact of outside military action on the local balance of military, political and economic interests in the kind of complex intra-state situations discussed above. A warring faction which is militarily and politically disadvantaged by the actions of a 'peace restoration' or an 'impartial peace enforcement' mission, will take little comfort from not having been formally designated an *enemy*. [26] Similarly, the assurance that military action directed against a party or faction will not prejudge the political outcome of the conflict, is unlikely to make much of an impact if the action itself is not clearly linked to a broader political strategy aimed at bringing the conflict to an end. The British Army draft of its new Peace Support Operations stresses that in peace enforcement '...force actions should be driven by events'.[27] This may be a case of unfortunate drafting, but it does highlight a very real danger inherent in the entire spectrum approach.

Finally, those who believe in the feasibility of disinterested and politically neutral 'peace restoring operations' may be overestimating the purity of the motives of those charged with restoring the peace, while underestimating the variety of different motives - including political power imperatives and domestic considerations - that influence and constrain governments in their decisions regarding the deployment and use of military force. The clearest example of this is *Operation Turquoise* in 1994 and it is a case of particular interest since it was also the one which inspired the French military to formalise a doctrine for 'peace restoration' operations. [28]

---

26   The first draft of the British Army doctrine for Peace Support Operations discussed above, appears to acknowledge as much by referring to the '*inevitable* accusations of partiality that will be made by all parties at some stage in the operations'. See AFM PSO 1. Draft, pp. 3-5 (my emphasis).

27   Ibid.

28   Events in Bosnia in 1993 offer another good example. Those, especially in the US, who have argued in favour of 'active impartiality' as a means of dealing with violations of agreements and resolutions, usually, and with good reason, refer to the failure of the UN to respond to Bosnian Serb military actions against Bosnian Government forces in 1993 as an instance where

Although formally authorised by the Security Council, *Operation Turquoise* - launched by the French military between 14 June and 21 August 1994 and which provided a security zone for Hutu civilians and remnants of the FAR in the south-west of Rwanda - was not only a disinterested humanitarian effort but looked to many (especially to the parties on the ground) as the creation of a 'safe area on to which the toppled Rwandan government could fall back'.[29] As with previous French interventions in Africa, the operation appeared to confirm Alain Rouvez's perceptive comment that 'the fine line between a purely humanitarian intervention and a regime-stabilisation operation is sometimes difficult to draw.'[30] This view has since been reinforced by incontrovertible evidence that French support to the FAR did not stop with onset of the genocide. When an international embargo was imposed against Rwanda on 17 May 1994, at least five French shipments of arms were later documented by *Human Rights Watch* to have been delivered to the genocidal regime .[31] Rather than providing

force should have been used more readily. 'Active impartially' as envisaged above, however, would also have required forceful action to be taken against Bosnian Croat forces who, with the active support of Franjo Tudjman, launched a brutal war against the Bosnian Government in Central Bosnia in 1993. For a variety of reasons, however, the US government was not prepared to sanction military action against Croat forces. This in itself, one might legitimately argue, ought not to have prevented forceful action from being taken against Bosnian Serb aggression. Aggression is aggression. The point here is merely that such action would *not* have amounted to politically neutral and disinterested 'active impartiality'. To pretend otherwise would have been to disguise a very different reality.

29   'France and Africa: Dangerous Liaisons', *The Economist*, 23rd July 1994, p. 19.

30   Alain Rouvez, 'French, British and Belgian Military Involvement', in *Making War and Waging Peace: Foreign Military Intervention in Africa*, edited by David R. Smock (Washington, DC: US Institute for Peace, 1993), p. 36.

31   *Rearming with Impunity: International Support for the Perpetrators of the Genocide*, Human Rights Watch Arms Project, Vol. 7., No. 4, May 1995, pp. 6-7. See also the important book by Gerard Prunier, *The Rwanda Crisis: History of a Genocide* (London: Hurst and Company, 1996), especially chapters 7 and 8. The nature of French involvement does raise a very serious question about the deeper meaning of Admiral Jacques Lanxade's suggestion in 1995 that *Operation Turquoise* provided a 'very positive balance sheet'. Admiral Lanxade offered this view as the head of the French joint chiefs (quoted in Mel McNulty, 'France, Rwanda and Military Intervention: a Double Discrediting', *International Peacekeeping*, Vol. 4, No. 3 1997).

a model for future operations, *Operation Turquoise* highlights dangers inherent in 'peace restoring' operations.

If the 'spectrum approach' is unsatisfactory, what are the lessons to be learned from the experience of UN field operations since 1992 ?[32]

Peacekeeping, the Use of Force and the Necessity of Choice

There can be little doubt that UN peacekeeping activities since 1992 have exposed major deficiencies in existing structures for mounting, managing and sustaining field operations. This does not mean, however, that the distinction between consent-based and essentially non-threatening activities on the one hand and *enforcement* on the other, should be lightly abandoned. The basic reason for this was succinctly spelled out by the UN Secretary-General in 1995. 'The logic of peacekeeping', he stressed, 'flows from political and military premises that are quite distinct from those of enforcement; and the dynamics of the latter are incompatible with the political process that peacekeeping is intended to facilitate.'[33] This is not to suggest that *consent* , especially in the kind of operational environments discussed above, is an absolute quality. Nor does it rule out the use of force by peacekeepers. It does mean, however, that the primary task of a peacekeeping force is to build local support and seek to enlarge the margin of consent that exists on the ground. It is this conscious promotion of consent - as reflected in the operational methods and procedures of soldiers on the ground - which distinguishes peacekeeping from enforcement. Above all, these two very different sets of activities must not, as happened in Somalia in the summer of 1993, be combined in *one* operation. To do so is to invite the political and military *destabilisation* of the environment in which forces are deployed.[34] That would be a disaster for the forces concerned.

> Together with other pieces of evidence, McNulty's article, which draws on original field research, shows clearly how French policy has been instrumental in exacerbating and prolonging conflict in Central Africa in the 1990s, with deeply tragic consequences.

32   For a number of 'non-military' implications of a spectrum approach that reinforce my scepticism, see Pugh, *From Mission Cringe to Mission Creep?*

33   S/1995/1, 3 January 1995, para. 33.

34   As the *Supplement* also points out, 'nothing is more dangerous for a peacekeeping operation than to ask it to use force when its existing composition, armament, logistic support and deployment deny it the capacity to do so'. Rosalyn Higgins puts it even more forcefully: 'to speak of the

If these are the painful lessons of UN 'peacekeeping' in the 1990s, what are the implications regarding the use of force ? The first point to stress is that to reassert the distinction between consent-based activities and enforcement is not, as it is often portrayed, tantamount to opposing enforcement *per se*. On the contrary, it only makes the choice of instrumentality starker by stressing that in a number of cases, peacekeeping *will not* be appropriate and hard decisions regarding the use of force will have to be made. By identifying 'peace enforcement' as an area of activity distinct from war-fighting, one in which 'escalation dominance' can supposedly be maintained, advocates of the spectrum approach are, whether intentionally or not, allowing governments to avoid hard decisions about the implications of deploying military personnel. While the advocates of 'grey area' and 'robust' operations usually see these as progressive developments from an earlier and more timid approach to complex emergencies, governments, judging from the record of Bosnia, see them as a way of limiting involvement, of avoiding the kind of decisions which the nature of the conflict may call for.

There is a further consideration here and again it was highlighted by events in Bosnia. It is this: it is possible to move from peacekeeping to enforcement but a decision to do so must reflect a deliberate choice. An important implication in terms of future operations is that a military force which is *initially* deployed for peacekeeping purposes must possess a degree of operational flexibility - in terms of manpower, mobility and equipment - that will allow it to support the transition to, and if appropriate engage in, enforcement. That some of these lessons have already been absorbed by the British Army was perhaps suggested by the plans drawn up for a Multinational Force in Zaire in December 1996 (*Operation Purposeful*). It envisaged the deployment of a combat-ready and mobile brigade which, in the event that it had been deployed, would have been able to protect itself, escalate and, if the political decision was taken, withdraw from theatre.

Where does all of this leave *Wider Peacekeeping*, the document which has provided the point of reference for much of the debate about the use of force in peacekeeping in recent years ?

need for more muscular peace-keeping simply evidences that the wrong mandate has been chosen *ab initio*.' Rosalyn Higgins, 'Peace and Security: Achievements and Failures', *European Journal of International Law*, Vol. 6, No. 3, 1995, p. 459

Wider Peacekeeping: *fundamentally flawed ?*

The criticisms levelled against *Wider Peacekeeping* as 'an unhelpful irrelevance' and a 'fudge' have concentrated on the difficulties of identifying a clear-cut 'consent divide' in contemporary peacekeeping operations.[35] Focus on this aspect of the doctrine was no doubt reinforced by General Michael Rose's use of the term 'Mogadishu line' which gave the misleading impression that consent was indeed to be viewed as an absolute quality. In fact, *Wider Peacekeeping* makes it quite clear that consent is usually far from absolute. Instead, the doctrine involves, in the words of Allan Mallison, 'a judgement that there is sufficient consent with which to begin working, with the prospect that judicious activity, at the strategic, operational and tactical level, will extend that consent'.[36] There is very little in the experience of recent operations to suggest that the underlying emphasis in *Wider Peacekeeping* on maintaining one broad, but nevertheless fundamental, distinction between consent-based operations and enforcement is in need of upgrading.

This is not to suggest that *Wider Peacekeeping* is a flawless document. To the extent that *Wider Peacekeeping* places an excessive reliance on the virtues of vulnerability on the part of peacekeepers (i.e. in order to accentuate their non-threatening posture), a change of emphasis might be in order. The reason for this has already been alluded to: 'grey and messy environments' place a premium on flexibility and force protection which in turn allows a force, in response to a *political decision*, to move from peacekeeping to enforcement. The tragedy of the UN *Protection* Force in Bosnia was that for much of its deployment it had more than enough to do with protecting itself, let alone those it was ostensibly sent to protect. It was only after it had been reinforced by the Rapid Reaction Force in the summer of 1995 that transition to enforcement became possible.[37]

---

35   Richard Connaughton, 'Wider Peacekeeping - How Wide of the Mark ?', *The British Army Review* no. 111, p. 57.

36   Allan Mallinson, 'Wider Peacekeeping - An Option of Difficulties', *The British Army Review* no. 111. Mallinson's article is a thoughtful, convincing and carefully argued response to Richard Connaughton's assertion that *'wider' peacekeeping* is a 'dangerous nonsense'.

37   The move to enforcement was also aided, of course, by the fact that points of military vulnerability - such as the weapon collection points throughout Bosnia - had been abandoned.

But there is a further reason why *Wider Peacekeeping* remains an incisive and useful document for thinking about the requirements of peacekeeping. The document explicitly stresses the need to make choices. To that extent, it is anything but a 'fudge' and its implications make uncomfortable reading for political decision-makers. The distinction between two categories of activities does not imply that:

... a UN force could not or should not undertake peace enforcement operations from the outset if that is demanded by analysis of the mission and conditions on the ground. Nor is it to suggest that a deployed Wider Peacekeeping contingent would necessarily be unable to transit to such operations. Transiting to peace enforcement, however, should be a deliberate, premeditated act, taking account of the risks involved, and matched by the appropriate force levels, equipment and doctrine .... The choice must be made, at the outset, of which course of action is going to be followed. Once that *political* decision has been taken, then practitioners on the ground must act consistently with it, peacekeeping and peace enforcement cannot be mixed....[38]

There is no escape from hard, and what for many governments have proved to be morally uncomfortable, political choices. The experience of UN field operations in the 1990s has shown all too clearly that decisions made in the name of practical and political compromise; policies of the lowest common denominator; mixing peacekeeping with 'elements' of enforcement; all these contain within them the potential for disaster.

III. Conclusion

In terms of future peacekeeping operations, the principal implication of the arguments put forward in this paper is that much more careful consideration must be given to the choice of instrumentality for intervening in a conflict. The record of post-Cold War peacekeeping is far from being all bleak and one clearly should not base an analysis of future options exclusively on the case of Bosnia. The overall lesson of Bosnia is, however, very important: for most of its time in the former Yugoslavia, the UN served the 'international community' by acting as a substitute for lack of agreement and coherent policy towards the

38   Army Field Manual, *Wider Peacekeeping*, Fifth Draft, chapter 2.

conflict. As suggested in this chapter, one may legitimately ask whether peacekeeping was ever the right instrument to be applied to the particular case of the former Yugoslavia.[39] A comprehensive review by the UN of its entire operation in May 1995, regarded as 'unhelpful' by key Council members,[40] accurately spelled out the situation in which the UN had gradually been placed:

> UNPROFOR remains deployed in a war situation where, after more than three years, there is still no peace to keep. Its position is further complicated by the fact that its original peacekeeping mandate, which cannot be implemented without the co-operation of the parties, has gradually been enlarged to include elements of enforcement, which cause it to be seen as a party to the conflict. .... As a result of these contradictions, UNPROFOR, now finds itself obstructed, targeted by both sides, denied re-supply, restricted in its movements, subject to constant criticism....[41]

To ensure that situations such as these are not repeated, member states, unable to agree among themselves about the basis for international security, should encourage the organisation to strengthen its ability to mount, manage and sustain a broader range of consent-based operations. Many of the tasks listed above, notably electoral support activities and humanitarian relief operations, have in fact been carried out far more effectively by the UN than by some of the regional organisations that have engaged in similar activities. Difficult judgements about the level of consent needed to carry out tasks will have to be made and, in some cases, enforcement will be the only appropriate response to particular circumstances. Enforcement, however, is more likely to be organised by coalitions of the willing or, indeed, unilaterally. It should not be ruled out for this reason.

39   For a persuasive argument along these lines see Rosalyn Higgins, 'The New United Nations and former Yugoslavia', *International Affairs* 69: 3 (1993).
40   Private interview.
41   Report of the Secretary-General Pursuant to Security Council Res. 982 and 987, 30 May 1995, pp. 33-34.

Chapter 6

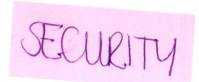

Whose Security? Re-imagining Post-Cold War Peacekeeping from a Feminist Perspective

Dianne Otto

Introduction

Feminists have utilized a range of strategies to analyze matters of international security.[1] One strategy is to look for silences and gaps in the mainstream discourse, to think about what is not being articulated and to ask where the women are, so as to bring to the fore issues of gender that had previously been erased.[2] A related strategy is to examine whether apparently neutral policies and programmes have gender-differentiated impacts and to thereby lend a transparency to those who are actually benefiting from the way neutrality is understood.[3] A third strategy is to examine who has access to and participates in decision-making in order to problematize the narrow, masculinist interests represented by those who have the power to determine security priorities.[4] A fourth approach is to critique the

1   Hilary Charlesworth and Christine Chinkin, 'Violence Against Women: A Global Issue' in Julie Stubbs, ed., *Women, Male Violence and the Law* (1994), p. 13; Kathleen Barry, 'Female Sexual Slavery: Understanding the International Dimensions of Women's Oppression' (1981) 3 *Human Rights Quarterly*, p. 44; Judith Gardam, 'A Feminist Analysis of Certain Aspects of International Humanitarian Law' (1992) 12 *Australian Yearbook of International Law*, p. 265; V. Spike Petersen, 'Security and Sovereign States: What is at Stake in Taking Feminism Seriously?' in V.S. Petersen, ed., *Gendered States: Feminist (Re) Visions of International Relations Theory* (1992), p. 31.
2   Cynthia Enloe, *Bananas, Beaches and Bases: Making Feminist Sense of International Politics* (1989). Enloe asks the question 'Where are the women'?
3   Rhonda Copelon, 'Intimate Terror: Understanding Domestic Violence as Torture', in Rebecca Cook, ed., *Human Rights of Women* (1995), p. 116.

conceptions of gender that are being produced by the dominant discourse in order to highlight discursive strategies for resisting the production of gender and other hierarchies. I draw something from all of these approaches in answering the question of *whose* security is of primary importance in the post-Cold War era.

Security is one of those slippery concepts which can take us in contradictory directions. Security goals can be used to reinforce an oppressive *status quo* or they can be a means of promoting liberating outcomes which challenge the *status quo*. We have seen this paradox played out in domestic legal responses to girls who are at risk of sexual abuse by members of their families or from within their communities. All too often their lack of security is addressed by removing the young women from their homes and communities and housing them, for their own *protection,* in institutions which we call *secure* but which are in fact little more than prisons. Analogous protective[5] measures have been adopted in post-Cold War responses to threats to international security in the creation of *secure* spaces like the safe havens in Northern and Southern Iraq, and the partitioning of the former Yugoslavia along ethnic lines. This approach restricts the liberties of those whose security is threatened and has the corresponding effect of allowing the threatening or dominating behaviour to continue outside the boundaries of the protective enclosures. The outcome, which passes for a form of peace, is the defence of the *status quo* of global power distribution. This outcome is disguised by cogent arguments which talk of the need to *protect* the vulnerable while, in reality, they justify an intensification of militarization.

Alternatively, security measures can be aimed at the aggressor, at addressing the underlying causes of the insecurity, with the result of

4   Hilary Charlesworth, 'Transforming the United Men's Club: Feminist Futures for the United Nations' (1994) 3 *Transnational Law and Contemporary Problems,* p. 421; Dorinda Dallmeyer, ed., *Reconceiving Reality: Women and International Law* (1993).

5   There is a considerable body of feminist analysis of 'protective' approaches to women taken by legal discourse. The effect is to disempower and control women and to reconfirm the dominance of men. See Natalie Hevener, 'An Analysis of Gender-based Treaty Law: Contemporary Developments in Historical Perspective' (1986) 8 *Human Rights Quarterly,* p. 70; Rebecca Cook, 'The Elimination of Sexual Apartheid: Prospects for the Fourth World Conference on Women', *Issue Papers on World Conferences*, no.5, American Society of International Law (1995).

enhancing, rather than curtailing, the liberties[6] of those at risk. With respect to girls at risk of sexual abuse, this involves removing and punishing the perpetrators of the abuse and embarking on community education campaigns which build a culture in which girls are empowered and communities are committed to ensuring their safety. In the global context, this approach requires an understanding of security as something more than the absence or the containment of armed conflict, as many feminists have argued.[7] Such an approach is suggested in the words of the former United Nations Secretary General Boutros Boutros-Ghali when he says, in his *Agenda for Peace*, that addressing the security crises of the post-Cold War world requires 'our utmost effort to enhance respect for human rights and fundamental freedoms, to promote sustainable economic and social development for wider prosperity, to alleviate distress and to curtail the existence and use of massively destructive weapons'.[8] A liberatory approach to security is obviously much more difficult because it necessitates directly addressing issues of domination and involves acknowledging the ways in which the most powerful states and economic interests contribute to global insecurities.

It is possible to find support for both protective and liberating approaches to global security in the *UN Charter*. The *Charter* clearly defers to the *status quo* of world power distribution in the way that the Security Council is constituted and endowed with primary responsibility for the maintenance of peace and security.[9] In so doing, the *Charter* conceives of security protectively, in realist terms, as an outcome of the maintenance of the existing world order. However, the *Charter* also suggests a liberating approach in the links it asserts between equality, self-determination, overall socio-economic cooperation and respect for human rights, and the achievement of

6   I am using the term 'liberty' in its broad sense to include not only civil and political liberties but also economic, social and cultural liberties.

7   J. Ann Tickner, *Gender in International Relations: Feminist Perspectives on Achieving Global Security* (1992), pp. 54-66. Tickner argues that security is multidimensional and is as much about economic security, social justice, sustainable development and environmental security as it is about military security and national interest.

8   Boutros Boutros-Ghali, *An Agenda For Peace* (1992), para. 5. This report was prepared by the Secretary General at the invitation of the first meeting at the level of Heads of States and Government held by the Security Council in January 1992.

9   *UN Charter*, arts. 23(1), 24 (1), 27.

world peace.[10] While the Cold War approach to global security was clearly protective in seeking to maintain the balance of power that East/West *detente* relied upon, are there some indications that this approach may be shifting in the post-Cold War era? Might we interpret the increasing use of peacekeeping forces, at least in the first few years of the new era, as a sign of a more liberating shift? What gender identities are being produced by these shifts? These are the questions I want to address.

I begin with a brief overview of the changes in the way that security is officially understood in the post-Cold War environment and the dramatic increase in peacekeeping activities that has accompanied this change. Second, I advance a feminist critique of these developments focusing on three aspects: the increased powers assumed by the Security Council; the extension of militarism to ever more local forms; and the neo-colonial overtones of many peacekeeping efforts. Third, I suggest that from a feminist perspective some aspects of these developments are potentially positive. In particular, I suggest that peacekeeping is, in some ways, a strategy of demilitarization; that there is some evidence that militarized gender identities are in a process of renegotiation; and that Boutros Boutros-Ghali's stated commitment to addressing the underlying causes of global insecurity might be something to build upon. I conclude that global security, in the sense of enhancing the liberties of those whose security is currently or potentially at risk and addressing the primary causes of that insecurity, is still a long way from realization but that post-Cold War peacekeeping could make important contributions to such a goal.

Security and Peacekeeping post-Cold War

The protective Cold War approach to security, which buttressed the bipolar *status quo,* conceived of global security in military and state-centred terms. It relied on guarding the territorial integrity of sovereign states from superpower expansionism and upholding the principle of non-intervention in the internal affairs of states, even in the face of massive human rights violations.[11] This approach to security did not even purport to address the underlying causes of global insecurity on

10   Ibid. arts. 1(3) and 55.
11   For example, the Idi Amin regime in Uganda, the Pol Pot Khmer Rouge in Kampuchea and the Indonesian invasion of East Timor.

which superpower dominion relied. Even the UN's decolonization agenda served the interests of the Cold War powers by producing postcolonial elites with allegiances to one or the other version of Europe, despite their attempts at non-alignment.[12] Indeed, the Cold War concern with racial discrimination as a threat to international peace, particularly in Southern Africa,[13] while immensely significant, was consistent with superpower agendas. The concern with racial inequalities did not, for example, extend to the indigenous peoples of the world. Issues of gender or sexuality discrimination and persecution were never considered important enough to be the basis of an international dispute, revealing the commitment of both sides of the East/West divide to a global narrative of the subjugation of women and to hetero-normativity,[14] notwithstanding the different forms that male domination takes in different cultural and ideological contexts.This gender and sexuality *blindness* occurred despite overwhelming evidence that, as many feminists have observed, 'the most common form of violence in our [global] society is violence against women by men'. [15]

Although the *Charter* makes no specific reference to peacekeeping, it was invented during the Cold War as a strategy of *detente* in the face of the Security Council deadlock. The enduring image of Cold War peacekeeping is that of policing the separation of belligerents, usually by interposing third-party troops between warring states to patrol safe buffer zones and to monitor ceasefires.[16] Three

12 Dianne Otto, 'Subalternity and International Law: The Problems of Global Community and the Incommensurability of Difference' (1996) 5 *Social and Legal Studies,* p. 337.
13 Southern Rhodesia SC Res 217, 20 November 1965; International Convention for the Suppression and Punishment of the Crime of Apartheid, GA Res 3068, 30 November 1973 art. 1(1) recognizes apartheid as 'a serious threat to international peace and security'.
14 Dianne Otto, Wayne Morgan and Kristen Walker, 'Rejecting (In)Tolerance: Critical Perspectives on the United Nations Year for Tolerance' (1995) 20 *Melbourne University Law Review,* p. 192.
15 Christine Chinkin, 'Women and Peace: Miltarism and Oppression' in Kathleen Mahoney and Paul Mahoney, eds., *Human Rights in the Twenty-First Century: A Global Challenge* (1993), p. 405, at p. 410 quoting B. Roberts 'Reclaiming the Discourse: Feminist Perspectives in Peace Research' in D. Russell, ed., *Exposing Nuclear Phallacies,* p. 278.
16 The first operation of this kind was the UN Emergency Force (UNEF) established by the General Assembly in 1956 to supervize the cease-fire in the Middle-East following the Suez crisis. There followed the 1964 UN Force

primary peacekeeping principles were defined during this period: that there be a strict separation between peacekeeping and peace-enforcement; that a necessary precondition was the consent of the warring parties; and that peacekeeping forces be neutral or impartial with respect to the dispute, which was understood to exclude troops from the five Security Council veto powers.[17] In sum, the Cold War security agenda safeguarded a dualized world order that depended on a multitude of economic and social inequalities and relied, for its legitimation, on hierarchical constructions of both gender and race. It was a protective approach to security.

Perhaps the most significant change precipitated by the end of the Cold War was the new consensus in the Security Council. Many expected that this would result in a reduction in threats to world peace, less armed conflict and vastly improved international security. However, despite optimistic predictions, there has been a dramatic increase in armed conflict in the new uni-polar world, particularly in what are ostensibly civil disputes.[18] These conflicts are often accompanied by a total collapse of institutions which provide the means of state and local governance, they frequently revolve around religious or ethnic differences and involve unusual cruelty which often targets women.[19] Further, the main casualties are civilians[20] which

in Cyprus (UNFICYP) following conflict between Greek and Turkish Cypriots, the UN Disengagement Observation Force (UNDOF) which patrols a buffer zone between Israel and Syria, and the UN Interim Force in Lebanon (UNFIL) which polices the border between Israel and Lebanon. An important exception to this pattern was the UN intervention in the internal conflict in the Congo 1960-64 (UNUC).

17   The three core peacekeeping principles of consent, impartiality and non-use of force were identified by Secretary General Dag Hammarskjöld in 1956. See Ove Bring, 'Peacekeeping and Peacemaking: Prospective Issues for the United Nations' (1995) 20 *Melbourne University Law Review*, p. 55, at p. 56.

18   Of the 32 UN peacekeeping operations established between January 1988 and December 1994, 22 or two thirds have been in response to internal conflicts. Internal conflicts did, of course, occur during the Cold War but they were seldom treated as a threat to international peace and security. The Congo crisis was an important exception.

19   A Stiglmayer, ed., *Mass Rape: The War Against Women in Bosnia-Herzegovina* (1994).

20   The percentage of civilian, as opposed to military, casualties of war has progressively increased since the first World War reaching the level of 90% in 1994. C Lamb, 'The Laws of Armed Conflict' in Hugh Smith, ed., *The Force of Law: International Law and the Land Commander* (1994), p. 1, at p.

has produced large flows of refugees and internally displaced people, the majority of whom are women and children.[21] The dominant discourse about the security issues of the post-Cold War world is a narrative of small-scale crises which could threaten global security unless checked and managed. This has fostered a broader understanding of what might constitute threats to international security and the Security Council itself stated in 1992 that the 'absence of war and military conflicts amongst States does not in itself ensure international peace and security ... non-military sources of instability in the economic, social, humanitarian and ecological fields have become threats to international peace and security'.[22]

The changed conception of international security has had extensive repercussions for peacekeeping activities prompting Boutros Boutros-Ghali to claim, in 1992, that the UN has become 'the world's most active peacekeeper'.[23] There were more UN peacekeeping operations launched between 1989 and 1992 than during the entire preceding forty-three years.[24] Further, the role of peacekeepers is no longer one of *detente*. Instead, they are expected to perform a wider range of tasks in increasingly complex and often dangerous situations.[25] Perhaps the most far-reaching change has been that peacekeeping operations may continue, or sometimes only be established, after peace negotiations are completed in order to assist in the implementation of negotiated settlements[26] or to assume a longer

17   referring to the results of a study reported in United Nations Development Project, Human Development Report (1994).

21   Jacqueline Greatbach, 'The Gender Difference: Feminist Critiques of Refugee Discourse' (1989) 1 *International Journal of Refugee Law,* p. 518.

22   UN Doc S/23500 (31 January 1992), statement issued from the Security Council Summit Meeting.

23   Boutros Boutros-Ghali, 'Remark: Beyond Peacekeeping' (1992) 25 *New York University Journal of International Law and Politics* p. 113, at p. 113.

24   Ibid. p. 114.

25   *Agenda For Peace,* above n. 8, para. 20. Boutros Boutros-Ghali, in his efforts to bring some order to the burgeoning of peacekeeping operations, notes that by 1995 UN peacekeepers were involved in four types of activity: first, in preventative diplomacy and peacemaking by, for example, providing on the ground support for diplomatic missions; second, in expanding the possibilities for the prevention of conflict and the making of peace as before; third, in the implementation and verification of negotiated settlements; and finally, in assisting post-conflict micro-disarmament.

26   This has happened in Namibia, Angola, El Salvador, Cambodia and Mozambique.

term role over a number of years to ensure that the underlying socio-economic, cultural and humanitarian causes of conflict are addressed.[27] To this end, the focus of much peacekeeping activity is now on peace-building: on establishing legal institutions, building democratic polities and governmental structures in states which have 'collapsed'.

But whose security concerns are motivating these endeavours? Is the UN finally addressing the underlying causes of global insecurity by identifying such factors as poverty, environmental degradation, population growth and non-sustainable development as issues of security? Why are there still silences about gender subordination in this new scheme? Has the goal of international security changed from protecting the inequitable *de facto* distribution of world power to one of liberation? Or, to put it in less utopian terms, do these developments open some new possibilities for promoting a more liberatory approach? In attempting an answer to these questions I will examine, first, the ways in which the new security and peacekeeping developments function to reinforce dominating forms of global power and, second, how they also create new conditions for the contestation of militarized notions of gender and security.

Peacekeeping as a Protective Strategy

There are many ways in which security and peacekeeping developments serve to entrench existing global regimes of power which are reliant on the production of narratives of gender which subordinate women. I will focus on three: first, the enormous powers assumed by the democratically unaccountable Security Council in constructing how we understand contemporary threats to international peace and security; second, the blurring of the boundaries between peacekeeping and peace enforcement resulting in an extension of the legitimized use of force in international law and the corresponding normalization of militarism in ever more local forms; and third, the neocolonial effects of many peacebuilding efforts.

27   *Supplement to An Agenda For Peace*, A/50/60-S/1995/1, para. 22. 'Only sustained efforts to resolve underlying socio-economic, cultural and humanitarian problems can place an achieved peace on a durable foundation.'

Security Council Powers

Turning first to the issue of Security Council powers in the post-Cold War UN: this can be thought about in several ways, one of which is its power to construct an authoritative global discourse or *Truth*[28] about global security. In exercising this power, the Security Council has created a new discourse of *global insecurity* which has enabled it to push at the boundaries of its *Charter* powers in a number of ways. For example, the expansion of what might constitute a threat to global security to include social, economic, humanitarian and ecological causes of instability suggests an almost boundless competence of the Security Council to sanction the use of force under chapter VII and not be limited by the principle of state sovereignty.[29] Christopher Greenwood has observed that the requirement that the Security Council determine the existence of a 'threat to international peace and security' before invoking its Chapter VII powers is increasingly treated as a procedural rather than substantive prerequisite.[30] This creates a new sense of the indispensability of the Security Council and legitimates the Council's assumption of a policing role in areas which, as Martti Koskenniemi points out, the *Charter* originally envisaged would fall within the competence of the General Assembly.[31]

Further, despite the new rhetoric of tackling the underlying *causes* of insecurity, the Security Council's discourse of global insecurity functions to resolutely conceal them. One way in which this masking is achieved is by characterizing the majority of contemporary conflicts as essentially civil disputes associated with local ethnic or tribal differences which have random and even primitive origins. This construction suggests, falsely, that civil wars and ethno-nationalist violence present a *new* set of circumstances which necessitate Security

28   Michel Foucault, 'Two Lectures' in Colin Gordon, ed., *Power/Knowledge* (1980), p. 78, at p. 93. Foucault describes knowledge or Truth as the product of a complex of power relations whereby Truth is the product of power and power is exercised by the production of Truth.

29   *UN Charter*, art. 2(7) creates an exception to the principle of state sovereignty when enforcement actions under chapter VII are being applied.

30   Mats R Berdal, 'The Security Council, Peacekeeping and Internal Conflict after the Cold War' (1996) 7 *Duke Journal of Comparative and International Law* 71, 76 referring to Christopher Greenwood, 'Legal Constraints on UN Military Operations', IISS Strategic Comments, 22 March 1995.

31   Martti Koskenniemi, 'The Police in the Temple, Order, Justice and the UN: A Dialectical View' (1995) 6 *European Journal of International Law*, p. 325.

Council action and that the conflicts are somehow outside politics.[32] These discursive manoeuvres blur the fact that the Security Council makes the *political choice* to become involved in internal disputes rather than that it has suddenly become obliged to. The narrative of localized ethnic conflicts also masks the many ways in which global networks of power are responsible for the contemporary disputes which result in various ways from colonialism, neocolonialism, the Cold War itself and, in the current context, the globalization of capital which is deepening the gender, class and race-based disparities in the global distribution of wealth.

Peacekeeping was given a central role in the paradigm of global insecurity, at least initially. The Cold War rules of engagement requiring consensus, impartiality and abstaining from the use of force were officially reaffirmed[33] and underwrote the initial public enthusiasm and moral authority that peacekeepers enjoyed. However, despite their retention, the Cold War peacekeeping principles have been seriously compromised in a number of ways. For example, the Security Council has stretched the principle of the non-use of force except in self-defence beyond recognition to include defence of the humanitarian goals of peacekeeping mandates as, for example, in Bosnia[34] and Somalia.[35] As a result, peacekeepers have used force in efforts to variously protect humanitarian relief operations, to protect civilians in areas designated as safe havens and to prompt the parties to move more quickly towards national reconciliation. The Security Council mandate regarding Haiti also included a confusion of chapter VI and chapter VII functions.[36] Concurrently, the Security Council has consistently reaffirmed the principle of the non-use of force,

32   Peter Rosenblum, 'Save The Tribunals: Salvage the Movement, a Response to Makau Mutua' (1997) 11 *Temple International and Comparative Law Journal*, p. 189, at p. 193.
33   Boutros Boutros-Ghali reaffirmed these principles in 1995. See *Supplement*, above n. 27, para. 33.
34   Berdal, above n. 30, 81. SC Res 836, UN SCOR, 48th Sess, UN Doc. S/RES/836 (1993), para. 9.
35   SC Res 794, UN SCOR, 47th Sess, 2-4, UN Doc. S/RES/794 (1992); SC Res 814, UN SCOR, 48th Sess, 1, UN Doc. S/RES/814 (1993).
36   Robert O. Weiner and Fionnuala Ni Aolain, 'Beyond the Laws of War: Peacekeeping in Search of a Legal Framework' (1996) 27 *Columbia Human Rights Law Review*, p. 293, at pp. 321-323.

hopelessly blurring the distinction between peacekeeping and peace enforcement.[37]
Transgression of the principle of non-use of force has assumed other dimensions as reflected in the reports of rape by peacekeepers in Bosnia, Cambodia and the Gulf;[38] of child sexual exploitation in Mozambique;[39] and of torture of local petty thieves in Somalia. Yet it is surely inconceivable that these activities are consistent with the cardinal principle of the non-use of force. It would seem that defending the physical security of the local population, particularly when they are women and children, does not figure in the security calculus and certainly does not extend to protection from the peacekeepers themselves. In this respect, the new world security order is hardly distinguishable from the gender blind security system of the Cold War years.

The discourse of global insecurity also legitimates the Security Council's exercise of power in its decision-making about which situations constitute a threat to international peace and security and how they will be responded to under chapter VII. We are to assume, as an article of faith, that the Council operates within restraints established by international law and with respect for human rights and fundamental freedoms. Yet Security Council decision-making lacks transparency,[40] can hardly claim to be democratically accountable, and its actions under chapter VII are probably not even amenable to judicial review.[41] The system is so closed, and the Security Council so all-powerful, that there are no mechanisms which provide redress for those (individuals or states) who suffer harm and no means by which local communities might challenge decisions which affect them. As

37   The confusion has been compounded by the Security Council's increasing practice of formulating peacekeeping mandates using their chapter VII powers.
38   Anne Orford, 'The Politics of Collective Security' (1996) 17 *Michigan Journal of International Law,* p. 373 at p. 377. Orford also points out that it was officially acknowledged that 24 US servicewomen deployed in the Gulf were raped or sexually assaulted.
39   Ibid., p. 378. Orford cites Gayle Kirshenbaum, 'Who's Watching the Peacekeepers?', *Ms Magazine* (May-June 1994), p. 12.
40   Ibid., pp. 377-378.
41   W. Michael Reisman, 'The Constitutional Crisis in the United Nations' (1993) 87 *American Journal of International Law,* p. 83; Ruth Gordon, 'United Nations Intervention in Internal Conflicts: Iraq, Somalia and Beyond' (1994) 15 *Michigan Journal of International Law,* p. 519.

Ruth Wedgwood observes, the sense is that we really ought to cherish the Council for what it is doing and worry about the fine points later.[42]

The peacekeeping principle of impartiality illustrates some of the concerns this raises. The Security Council is an unashamedly political body controlled by the veto powers and therefore hardly capable of designing neutral interventions. We have seen neutrality (mis)used, as an excuse for Security Council inaction to disguise its lack of political will, in the Rwandan situation[43] and in Bosnia.[44] Impartiality has also justified the inaction of peacekeepers in the face of disappearances, extra-judicial executions, rape allegations and other serious human rights abuses.[45] Anne Orford points to other disparities between the rhetoric of an impartial Security Council and the realities with respect to women's security. She argues that women are often *less* secure as a result of Security Council actions:

> Security Council actions, including military operations and economic sanctions, have [negatively] influenced the struggle of women to acquire basic sociopolitical rights, improve health and survival, secure freedom from rape and sexual harassment, and establish economic security. Perhaps the clearest examples of gender-differentiated consequences of such actions concern the growing number of complaints of rape by peacekeepers, the harsh effects of economic sanctions on women, and women's status in militarized cultures.[46]

These are hardly neutral outcomes, yet critical views like Orford's are silenced or discredited in the 'warm glow' of the official narratives of the post-Cold War collective security system. It is all too apparent that the new discourse of global insecurity continues to rely on the silences of women and other less powerful groups. The effect is to endorse the Security Council's unaccountable power and self-interest, and to legitimate the way in which the Security Council orders and narrates the world by authorizing military and economic coercion in order to protect, first and foremost, the interests of the global *status quo*.

---

42 Ruth Wedgwood, 'The Evolution of United Nations Peacekeeping' (1995) 28 *Cornell International Law Journal,* p. 631 at p. 631.
43 Rosenblum, above n. 32, p. 192.
44 Berdal, above n. 30, p. 78.
45 Weiner and Ni Aolain, above n. 36, pp. 313-314.
46 Orford, above n. 38, p. 377.

The Extension of Militarism

The post-Cold War blurring of the boundaries between peacekeeping and peace enforcement has the effect of extending the scope of the legal use of force in international law. In eroding the non-violent and non-coercive foundational principles of peacekeeping operations, the Security Council's authorization of the collective use of force to achieve humanitarian goals is expanding what passes for 'military necessity'. Historically, the underlying assumption in the development of laws of war has been that it is possible to humanize war through law by striking a balance between judgments of military necessity and humanitarian considerations. However, when we look more closely at the history of war we see, as Chris af Jochnick and Roger Normand have argued, that 'the development of a more elaborate legal regime has proceeded apace with the increasing savagery and destructiveness of modern war'.[47] Their argument is that law provides a 'humanitarian cover' which legitimizes, and even promotes, unrestrained military responses rather than humanitarian practice.[48] Further, Judith Gardam has argued that the doctrine of military necessity operates to justify or excuse gendered violence and to disguise the interdependence between militarism and male violence against women.[49]

In the post-Cold War context, we can see the pattern of expanding normalization of militarization continuing, in direct contrast to the prognosis of a more peaceful world. The deployment of peacekeeping missions in increasingly dangerous situations has been used to justify the increasing resort of the Security Council to its chapter VII powers.[50] The image of defenceless peacekeepers assembled in the midst of what was essentially a war in Bosnia prompted many calls for more 'robust' or 'muscular' peacekeeping, as Mats Berdal observes.[51]

47   Chris af Jochnick and Roger Normand, 'The Legitimation of Violence: A Critical History of the Laws of War' (1994) 35 *Harvard International Law Journal* , p. 49 at p. 55.
48   Ibid., pp. 56-59.
49   Judith Gardam, 'The Law of Armed Conflict: A Feminist Perspective' in Mahoney and Mahoney, above n. 15, p. 419. See also P Strange, 'It'll Make a Man Out of You' in D Russell, ed., *Exposing Nuclear Phallacies* (1989); Robin Morgan, *The Demon Lover: On the Sexuality of Terrorism* (1989).
50   Bring, above n. 17.
51   Berdal, above n. 30, p. 76. Support for the idea of more 'robust' peacekeeping is also evinced by proposals that 'peace restoration' become a chapter VI 1/2 activity which would enable intervention without the consent

Even in the comparative safety of the Cambodian peacekeeping operation (UNTAC), Force Commander Colonel John Sanderson noted, with concern, the passion with which the use of force by peacekeepers was espoused.[52] The dilemmas thrown up by the contradictions of using force in connection with peacekeeping have even led to suggestions that a 'rapid reaction force' of qualified troops be made available to the UN Secretariat,[53] an idea which is completely outside the collective security system envisaged by the *Charter*. In sum, peacekeeping has helped to create the conditions for heightened political tolerance of the use of armed force under the auspices of the UN.

In tandem with the blurring of peacekeeping and peace enforcement, the expansion of NATO, the build-up of national and regional defence forces around the globe[54] and the continuing threat of nuclear weapons provide further examples of the way in which military thinking has been normalized in the post-Cold War period. Christine Chinkin defines militarism as 'the belief system that upholds the legitimacy of the military control that the State exercises and the assumption that military values and policies are conducive to creating an orderly and secure society'.[55] As many feminist theorists have argued, citizenship and identity in a militarized framework are built on the masculine archetypes associated with war and the, corresponding, feminization or subjugation of non-military social identities and functions. Male domination and militarism are therefore interdependent.[56] In this paradigm women are maternalized in that their primary responsibility is to reproduce soldiers[57] and, along with other targets and victims of war, women are reified or reduced to

of the warring parties but still fall short of full scale resort to the use of force.

52 John Sanderson, 'Peacekeeping and Peacemaking: A Critical Retrospective' (1995) 20 *Melbourne University Law Review* p. 35 at p. 41.

53 *Supplement*, above n. 27.

54 Cynthia Enloe, *The Morning After: Sexual Politics at the End of the Cold War* (1993), pp. 28-30.

55 Chinkin, above n. 15, pp. 405-6.

56 Enloe, above n. 2.

57 Morgan, above n. 49, chapter. 8. Morgan describes the pressure on Palestinian women in refugee camps to have children who will become the next generation of fighters for Palestinian self-determination.

objects which makes it possible for them to be killed, humiliated and raped in the course of legally and morally justifiable wars.[58] To extend the legality of the use of force in international law is to deepen the militarization of international society which is to underscore a global construction of gender that affirms male dominance and its corollary of female subordination. Post-Cold War peacekeeping has proved to be an effective means of re-militarization rather than de-militarization, and of promoting the normality of militarism at ever more local levels. The gender identities produced legitimate women's secondary citizenship and make the gendered consequences of armed conflict more acceptable and less visible.

New Forms of Colonialism

The third aspect of recent peacekeeping developments which supports global regimes of inequitable power is its resemblance to colonialism. The idea that states have 'failed' and need direction and expertise to assist with post-conflict peace-building is, potentially, a new assertion of European superiority and a new version of Europe's global 'civilizing mission'. Indeed, as Orford points out:

> Collective security texts create a context of fear of disorder, difference, and tribalism, in which increased military and economic intervention in the affairs of developing states is legitimized to create a ruthlessly 'ordered' world.[59]

The suggestion to reactivate the Trusteeship Council, which was established by the *Charter* to assist strategic colonial territories to achieve independence, is an example of the revitalization of European paternalism and assimilationism. The proposal invokes the neo-colonial belief that non-European peoples need to be educated into accepting the ways of modernity before they will be capable of assuming the responsibilities of statehood and sovereignty.[60] The dogged determination with which the colonial boundaries in Africa are defended - admittedly an extremely complex issue - is a further

---

58 Chinkin, above n. 15, p. 410; Ann Scales, 'Militarism, Male Dominance and Law: Feminist Jurisprudence as Oxymoron?' (1989) 12 *Harvard Women's Law Journal,* 25, 26; Ninotchka Rosca, 'Effects of Militarism and State Violence on Women and Children' in Mahoney and Mahoney, above n. 15, p. 237 at p. 238.

59 Orford, above n. 38, p. 404.

60 Otto, above n. 12, pp. 351-352.

example of the Eurocentrism of the security agenda. There have been some attempts by Southern states to resist more radical UN intervention in internal conflicts, and to oppose further expansion of Security Council powers, because of concerns about Northern imperialism.[61]

Post-conflict peace-building involves a large cast of outside actors including civilian police, human rights experts, election monitors, and other specialists and advisers. It is highly likely that almost all of these actors work uncritically within their own frameworks which are based on masculinist and European norms. While the peace-building language of democratic institution building and the rule of law does not *inevitably* lead to the imposition of western political and legal forms, the hegemonic grip of the West is not easily resisted. The emphasis on elections, for example, assumes that centralized and representative forms of democracy make sense to diverse local communities.[62] Further, Western forms of democracy and the common law system involve dualistic thinking and are essentially adversarial in form. They do not lend themselves to the expression of a multitude of positions and viewpoints, let alone to conciliatory styles of negotiating such differences or to consensual outcomes.

It must also be remembered that masculinist and racialized gender identities are deeply embedded in neocolonial encounters between the North and the South. The exotic and exploitable 'woman' who emerges from Edward Said's deconstruction of the Orientalism of the West[63] is in danger of being reinvented in the peace-building process. It is all too easily overlooked that western-style democracy disproportionately empowers men; that human rights protections as currently constructed are based on masculinist, European standards; and that economic development is, in many ways, colonialism in its most recent guise.[64] There is little doubt that the elites of the global *status quo*, including post-colonial elites, stand to benefit most from the establishment of European-style governmental and legal institutions in non-European states. Therefore international security in the post-

61   Berdal, above n. 30, p. 91 referring to discussion in Sally Morphet, 'The Influence of States and Groups of States on and in the Security Council and General Assembly, 1980-94' (1995) 21 *Review of International Studies*, p. 435.
62   Dipesh Chakrabarty, 'Modernity and Ethnicity in India' in David Bennett, ed., *Multicultural States: Rethinking Difference and Identity* (1997).
63   Edward Said, *Orientalism* (1978/1995).
64   Chakrabarty, above n. 62.

Cold War era, despite promising a liberating new world order, may prove to be nothing more than new clothes for the same old dominating Emperor.

In sum, the post-Cold War discourse of global insecurity, and the peacekeeping developments that have accompanied it, have a vast potential to do no more than re-privilege and re-legitimate dominating forms of global power and a world order that continues to rely on hierarchical constructions of gender, race and other diversities. The cooperative endeavours of the unchecked self-interest of the Security Council to authorize the collective use of force in response to an expanding catalogue of potential threats to international peace and security, the extension of the legitimate use of force in international law, the corresponding intensification of the militarized character of the global order, and the neocolonial overtones of peacebuilding mandates, lay the foundations for a protective, rather than liberating, approach to global security.

Reimagining Peacekeeping as a Liberating Strategy

At the same time as having the ability to reinforce the power of global elites, the increased mobilization and expanding functions of peacekeeping forces have some potentially transformative effects. This potential lies largely in the different attitude and approach that peacekeeping requires of military personnel at all levels of the military hierarchy in conducting 'operations other than war'. Second, it also lies in complementary shifts and blurrings of the archetypal gender roles, traditionally associated with militarism, by the increasing number of women and openly gay men employed in the armed forces, at least in the West. And third, the liberatory potential of peacekeeping lies in the commitment, albeit rhetorical so far, to addressing the underlying causes of conflict.

The 'Attitude' of Peacekeeping

First, there is no doubt that peacekeeping involves an altogether different logic than peace enforcement. As Colonel Sanderson has described it:

> Peacekeeping is based on the consent of all the parties involved, including that of the peacekeepers. This requires that peacekeepers, for their own protection, make an overt display of impartiality to establish their credentials as 'honest brokers' in

the process. This display is totally different from the display required for enforcement, which is warlike and concentrated to establish seriousness of intent.[65]

In a detailed study of the training needs of peacekeepers undertaken in 1993-1994, researchers Barry Blechman and Matthew Vaccaro describe the peacekeeping 'mind-set' as a 'tuning down' of the attitude required for traditional military operations.[66] They suggest that combat troops who have been deployed in peacekeeping operations need 'a little refresher training ... before getting back to their previous level of aggressiveness'.[67]

Blechman and Vaccaro found there were many tasks undertaken by troops engaged in peacekeeping which required specialized peacekeeping training, and that often the effective performance of these tasks was critical to the success or failure of the peacekeeping mission. The tasks they found were *not* covered in traditional military training included: controlling crowds in an appropriate manner, administering humanitarian relief, negotiation skills, validating compliance with negotiated agreements, preventing refugee flows and establishing and/or administering a criminal justice system.

The study identified further skills which were not *adequately* covered by existing training such as interacting with civilians, liaising with foreign forces, applying the laws of war and using loudspeakers.[68] Blechman and Vaccaro identified a third category of skills which needed *modification* in the peacekeeping context. They detail two examples in particular. First, the task of 'seizing and clearing a building' in combat conditions involves taking control of the building with guns blazing, a method clearly inconsistent with the restraint expected of peacekeepers. Second, military marksmanship training does not equip soldiers with the specialized shooting skills

65   Sanderson, above n. 52, p. 39
66   Barry M. Blechman and J. Matthew Vaccaro, 'Training For Peacekeeping: The United Nations' Role', The Henry L Stimson Centre, Report n. 12, (July 1994), p. 2.
67   Ibid.
68   Ibid., pp. 3-4. Other tasks identified as needing greater emphasis than was given in traditional military training were: applying the rules of engagement, guarding operations, counter mine operations and convoy security.

they need to discriminately target snipers who are, for example, using a civilian crowd for cover, without killing innocent bystanders.[69]

I have gone into some detail here in order to make the point that the logic of peacekeeping is significantly different to that of military combat operations. This is underscored by the tardiness of the US armed forces to provide *any* peacekeeping training because, as Blechman and Vaccaro found, they were fearful that it 'would degrade that unit's warfighting utility'.[70] Even states like New Zealand, who today identify the primary purpose of their armed forces as assisting in peacekeeping missions, are completely resistant to the idea that peacekeeping training might actually replace basic military training. At best, peacekeeping training is viewed by military establishments as an add-on to training for combat rather than a replacement. Even so, it seems clear that peacekeeping forces are learning to respond to conflict situations by using an array of peaceful, or minimally forceful, dispute resolution techniques. Further, they are applying these techniques with a broad range of non-military personnel including civilians, NGOs, government officials, non-military members of peacekeeping missions and civilian police, as well as with the disputing parties and multi-national peacekeeping forces.

The developments in military training and practice, although emphatically secondary to the war-oriented and protective military discourse, potentially have far-reaching implications. Although these developments have taken place *within* a military framework, and therefore could hardly be considered *de-militarized,* they could assist in reversing the hitherto intractable trumping of humanitarian considerations by military necessities. They could change the ways in which militaries understand themselves and lead to a reimagining of the militarized world order so that it is no longer dependent on notions of dominating masculinities and subordinate femininities in order to legitimate sending soldiers to war.[71] They could raise the profile and increase the capabilities of chapter VI actions so that chapter VII eventually becomes redundant.

69   Ibid., p. 4. They also identified training in the use of force, interactions with NGOs, disarming belligerents and civilians and static defences as needing modification.
70   Ibid., p. 10.
71   Rebecca Grant, 'The Quagmire of Gender and International Security' in V. Spike Petersen (ed), *Gendered States: Feminist (Re)Visions of International Relations Theory* (1992), p. 83 at p. 91.

Renegotiating Militarized Constructions of Gender

The archetypal militarized male gender roles are also undergoing a process of change because of a second important shift: the increasing participation of women, and of openly homosexual men, in the regular armed forces of many states. As Cynthia Enloe argues, Cold War militarism relied on the idea that *real* men were those who were prepared to kill for their country, which required that women were barred from killing for their country.[72] The new female and gay presences within a previously exclusive male and heterosexual domain, transgress the clarity of earlier militarized male and female gender roles and suggest that a new relationship might be developing between the patriarchal state, and women (including lesbians) and gay men. By extension, this could help to lay new foundations for the way that global security is understood, achieved and maintained. I am not suggesting that mere presence of women and gay men in the military will alter the militaristic world order, because it is the structures themselves, and the gender identities that they produce, which need to change. Rather, I am proposing that disruptive presences might be an initial step towards more fundamental structural change.

I am also not suggesting that women and/or gay men are *inherently* more predisposed towards the peaceful resolution of disputes or *intrinsically* more likely to take an anti-militaristic position than heterosexual men.[73] To understand peacefulness as a feminine quality, in the context of a militaristic and patriarchal world order, is to unwittingly repeat the derision of non-militarized peace as unmanly. As bell hooks says,

> while these may be stereotypical norms that many people live out, such dualistic thinking is dangerous; it is a basic ideological component of logic that informs and promotes domination in Western society. Even when inverted and employed for a meaningful purpose, like nuclear disarmament, it is nevertheless

---

72   Enloe, above n. 54, p. 17.
73   The view that women take a more caring and connected approach to the resolution of conflict is supported by the work of Carol Gilligan, *In A Different Voice: Psychological Theory and Women's Development* (1982).

risky, for it reinforces the cultural basis of sexism and other forms of group oppression.[74]

Alternatively, it is important to recognize that the institution of the military plays a central role in constructing what we understand to be characteristics of masculinity and femininity. As Enloe suggests, we must ask what new masculinities and femininities are being produced in the post-Cold War peacekeeping environment. Is UN peacekeeping reshaping what we understand to be 'real men' in a way that disengages masculinity and femininity from militarism? What strategies can we employ to assist in breaking the nexus between the maintenance of gender, sexuality and other dominating hierarchies, and the military?

Addressing Underlying Causes

Finally, and very briefly, the emphasis, of Boutros Boutros-Ghali on the necessity that peacekeeping strategies address the root causes of global conflict, also opens some more liberating possibilities. The realization of these possibilities depends in large part on the extent to which the local communities, which are supported by peacebuilding operations, are able to determine the form and content of their political and legal institutions. It is essential to enable space for the assertion of non-militarized notions of citizenship, by which I mean citizenship which is not founded on violence.[75] Addressing the underlying causes of global insecurity also depends on the political commitment and will of the UN membership to address the gendered distribution of power globally, to change the inequitable distribution of wealth within the North and between the North and the South, and to demilitarize their discourse of peace and security.

Liberatory change also involves transforming ourselves so that we interrogate our own participation in global militarism, refrain from the use of violence in every part of our lives and resist militarized conceptions of gender, race, sexuality and other differences. I also cautiously agree with Koskenniemi's suggestion that achieving global security involves empowering the more democratic General Assembly to play a central role in peace-building and thereby reducing the scope

74   bell hooks, 'Feminism and Militarism: A Comment' (1995) 3 & 4 *Women's Studies Quarterly,* p. 58 at pp. 59-60.
75   Stephanie A. Levin, 'Women, Peace, and Violence: A New Perspective' (1992) 59 *Tennessee Law Review,* p. 611 at p. 616.

of the Security Council's powers, even though the Assembly has not proved to be any less masculinist than the Council. His strategy opens another dimension to the relentless convergence of state interests and subordinating narratives of gender, that feminists must also tackle. Which leads me to stress the critical importance of local and transnational women's movements and solidarities, in the struggle to address the underlying causes of global insecurity. In total, this is an ambitious project - a feminist reimagining - which has, at least, some post-Cold War rhetorical support from the highest levels of the UN bureaucracy.

Conclusion

The claim by Boutros Boutros-Ghali that the UN has become the world's most active peacekeeper in the post-Cold War period is something which it might reasonably be expected that feminists would welcome and support. Principles like the non-use or minimal use of force, consent of the parties, respect for human rights, democratic processes and the rule of law, the development of military expertise in the use of non-lethal methods and weapons, even the broader definitions of what might constitute threats to international peace and security seem to, in some ways at least, respond to many feminist critiques of global militarism. But do these principles simply cloak the same global elites in a newly palatable legal and humanitarian disguise?

An examination of *whose* security is at the forefront of the contemporary security agenda indicates that little of substance has changed. Global security is still dependent on the vagaries of power politics, on a militarized commitment to the use of force and on subordinating narratives of gender, race and sexuality hierarchies. The imperative of global security, even in its peacekeeping form, remains the coercive containment and silencing of the dissent produced by the inequitable world order. While some signs of a more liberating approach have accompanied the post-Cold War intensification of militarism, these are as yet embryonic and uncertain. We need a theory of peacekeeping that enables us to build on these shaky foundations towards a non-military calculus, a non-dominating discourse of global security and a liberating discourse of gender, race and sexuality.

Chapter 7

Fighting for Survival: Environmental Decline, Social Conflict, and the New Age of Insecurity

Michael Renner

The events in Rwanda and Zaire during the past four years serve as powerful testimony for a long-ignored but increasingly obvious fact: violent conflict occurs much less frequently between sovereign nations now than it does within countries. Almost none of the major armed conflicts in the 1990s has been unambiguously country-against-country.

The temptation for the world's 'major powers' is to ignore these kinds of conflicts as much as possible, even in the event of genocide, as happened in the case of Rwanda in 1994. But the outside world neglects these conflicts at its own peril. As we now know, the Rwandan tragedy had an enormous spillover effect on neighbouring Zaire - a country that, due to its size, commands much greater attention than does tiny Rwanda.

The argument that I wish to present here is that the nature of 'security' has been transformed. A powerful preoccupation with traditional 'national security' concerns has led decision-makers in many countries to neglect other dimensions of security that may be much more relevant to their constituents' well-being, and hence to the social and political stability that is crucial if internal conflicts are to be avoided. (See Table 1.) Today, humanity is facing a triple security crisis: the effects of environmental decline, the repercussions of social divisions and stress, and the dangers arising out of an unchecked arms proliferation that is a direct legacy of the Cold War period.

Security in the Post-Cold War Era

Far from the traditional image of war with opposed national armies, the 'battlefield' in today's violent conflicts can be anywhere, and the distinction between combatants and noncombatants is blurred. The fighting is done as often by guerrilla groups, paramilitary forces, and vigilante squads as by regular, uniformed soldiers. Child soldiers are by no means an uncommon sight. Civilians are often not accidental victims but explicit targets of violence, intimidation, and expulsion. By some rough estimates, civilians accounted for half of all war-related deaths in the fifties, three quarters in the 1980s, and almost 90 percent in 1990. Humanitarian relief supplies are frequently delayed and used as bargaining chips.[1]

As many countries teetering on war are actually engaged in hostilities, a pattern of endemic political violence has emerged. Analysts are finding a growing privatization of security and violence - in the form of legions of private security guards, the proliferation of small arms among the general population, and the spread of vigilante and 'self-defence' groups. A culture of violence, in which vicious responses to social problems are the norm, has taken root in many countries.[2]

The post-Cold War era is increasingly witnessing a phenomenon known as 'failed states' - the implosion of states like Rwanda, Yugoslavia, and others. But these are only the most spectacular examples of the pressures and vulnerabilities currently affecting many countries. It is just that some states, for the present at least, are managing to cope more successfully than others with such underlying forces.[3]

Several countries are among the ranks of what James Rosenau calls 'adrift nation-states'. That is, situations where one or more of the following conditions is likely to be present: the economy is being depleted; the state is unable to provide anything like adequate services

1   Share of civilian victims from Ruth Leger Sivard, *World Military and Social Expenditures 1989* (Washington, D.C.: World Priorities, 1989), and from Ernie Regehr, 'A Pattern of War', *Ploughshares Monitor* (December 1991).

2   Dan Smith, *War, Peace and Third World Development*, Human Development Report Office, Occasional Papers No. 16, UNDP, New York (1993); Michael T. Klare, 'The Global Trade in Light Weapons and the International System in the Post-Cold War Era', in Jeffrey Boutwell, Michael T. Klare, and Laura W. Reed, eds., *Lethal Commerce: The Global Trade in Small Arms and Light Weapons* (Cambridge, Mass.: American Academy of Arts and Sciences, 1995); Christopher Louise, *The Social Impacts of Light Weapons Availability and Proliferation*, Discussion Paper No. 59, U.N. Research Institute for Social Development Geneva (March 1995).

3   See, for example, Gerald B. Helman and Steven R. Ratner, 'Saving Failed States', *Foreign Policy* (Winter 1992-93).

to its citizens; grievances are disregarded and political dissent is repressed; the social fabric is unravelling; and the political leadership is unable to cope with growing tensions among different ethnic groups, regions, and classes, or it plays different groups off against each other in an effort to prolong its rule.[4]

In short, an amalgam of forces is at work. But the media and many other observers now almost habitually ascribe the outbreak of civil wars and the collapse of entire societies to just one factor: the resurfacing of 'ancient ethnic hatreds' revolving around seemingly irreconcilable religious and cultural differences.

Of course, ethnic tensions do play some role. Roughly half of the world's countries have experienced some kind of inter-ethnic strife in recent years. A 1993 study for the U.S. Institute of Peace found 233 minority groups at risk from political or economic discrimination. These groups encompassed 915 million people in 1990, about 17 percent of the world's population.[5] Ethnic, religious, cultural, or linguistic divisions will likely dominate the perceptions of the protagonists themselves, partly because political leaders in divided societies see playing the ethnic card as an essential way to capture and maintain power.

Yet it is important to examine the underlying stress factors that produce or deepen rifts in societies, particularly since ethnic distinctions often lie dormant for long periods of time. Disputes are often sharpened or triggered by glaring social and economic disparities. These are potentially explosive conditions exacerbated by the growing pressures of population growth, resource depletion, and environmental degradation.

Together, these conditions can form a powerful blend of insecurities. Accompanied by weak, nonrepresentative political systems that are increasingly seen as illegitimate and incapable of attending to people's needs, these pressures can lead to the wholesale fragmentation of societies. As people turn to ethnic, religious, or other identity-based organizations for assistance and protection, 'other'

4   James N. Rosenau, 'New Dimensions of Security: The Interaction of Globalizing and Localizing Dynamics', *Security Dialogue* (September 1994).

5   Half of all countries experienced ethnic strife - from U.N. Development Programme (UNDP), *Human Development Report 1994* (New York: Oxford University Press, 1994); other data from Ted Robert Gurr, *Minorities at Risk: A Global View of Ethnopolitical Conflicts* (Washington, D.C.: U.S. Institute for Peace Press, 1993).

groups tend to be regarded as competing and threatening, and whatever bonds may have held societies together in the past grow more tenuous. In such circumstances, the easy availability of armaments, especially those of small calibre, increases the temptation to 'resolve' disputes by violent means.

What I will do here is provide a brief overview of environmental and social pressures, illustrate some examples of conflicts in which these pressures have played a role, and then suggest some policy recommendations.

Environmental Pressures

The depletion and deterioration of natural systems has become an important source of insecurity and stress in many societies. Desertification, soil erosion, deforestation, and water scarcity are worldwide phenomena that make themselves felt in the form of reduced food-growing potential, worsening health effects, or diminished habitability.

A major threat to the economic well-being of many countries is land degradation. The plowing of highly erodible land, the salinization of irrigated land, the overgrazing of rangelands, and the loss of arable land, rangeland, and forests to expanding urban and industrial needs have all contributed to this. Although the immediate reasons may be found in inappropriate practices or inefficient technologies, land degradation often is the result of social and economic inequities.

According to U.N. Environment Programme (UNEP) estimates at the beginning of the 1990s, some 3.6 billion hectares, about 70 percent of potentially productive drylands worldwide, are affected by desertification. One third of all agricultural land is lightly degraded, half is moderately degraded, and 16 percent strongly or extremely degraded. Some 400 million poor people live in rural, ecologically fragile areas of the developing world characterized by land degradation, water scarcity, and reduced agricultural productivity.[6]

6   Desertification is defined by UNEP as 'land degradation in arid, semi-arid, and dry subhumid areas resulting mainly from adverse human impacts'; Günther Bächler, 'Desertification and Conflict: The Marginalization of Poverty and of Environmental Conflicts', Occasional Paper No. 10, ENCOP, Bern, Switzerland (March 1994); percentage of degraded agricultural land from L.R. Oldeman, International Soil Reference and Information Centre, Wageningen, Netherlands, private communication with Gary Gardner, Worldwatch Institute, Washington, D.C., September 21, 1995.

Currently 65 percent of the agricultural land in Africa, 45 percent in South America, 38 percent in Asia, and 25 percent in North America and Europe is affected by soil degradation. (See Table 2.) Among the soil erosion crisis areas are the Horn of Africa, eastern Iran, large patches of Iraq, the northwestern and northeastern corners of the Indian subcontinent, Central America, the Amazon basin, and several parts of China.[7]

Because of population growth and unequal land distribution, large numbers of small peasants are cultivating highly fragile areas, such as steep hill sides and patches cleared out of rain forests, that are easily susceptible to erosion and the soils of which are quickly exhausted. In Rwanda, for example, half of all farming took place on hillsides by the mid-1980s, when overcultivation and soil erosion led to falling yields and a steep decline in total grain production. In Mexico, more than half of all farmers eke out a living on steep hill slopes that now account for one fifth of all Mexican cropland.[8]

Water, like cropland, is a fundamental resource for human well-being. It is essential for food production, health, and economic development. Yet in many countries it is an increasingly scarce resource, under threat from both depletion and pollution. Countries with annual supplies in the range of 1,000-2,000 cubic metres per person are generally regarded as water-stressed, and those with less than 1,000 cubic metres are considered water-scarce. About 230 million people currently live in the most water-scarce countries, but more than 700 million people live in nations whose per-capita supplies

---

7   L.R. Oldeman, International Soil Reference and Information Centre, Wageningen, Netherlands, private communication with Gary Gardner, Worldwatch Institute, Washington, D.C., April 12, 1996; crisis areas from Astri Suhrke, 'Pressure Points: Environmental Degradation, Migration and Conflict', in Occasional Paper No. 3, Project on Environmental Change and Acute Conflict, American Academy of Arts and Sciences and University of Toronto (March 1993).

8   Mexico from Norman Myers, *Ultimate Security: The Environmental Basis of National Security* (New York: W.W. Norton & Co., 1993); Rwanda from Valerie Percival and Thomas Homer-Dixon, 'Environmental Scarcity and Violent Conflict: The Case of Rwanda', The Project on Environment, Population, and Security, American Association for the Advancement of Science and University of Toronto (June 1995); Rwandan yields and grain production from U.S. Department of Agriculture, Economic Research Service, 'Production, Supply, and Distribution' (electronic database), Washington, D.C. (November 1995).

are at or below the level where food self-sufficiency is problematic.[9] (See Table 3.)

Many rivers and aquifers, and not just in countries with acute water scarcity, are overexploited. Excessive withdrawal of river and groundwater leads to land subsidence, intrusion of salt water in coastal areas, desiccation of lakes, and eventual depletion of water sources. Aquifer depletion due to overpumping is occurring in crop-growing areas around the globe, including the United States, Mexico, China, India, Thailand, northern Africa, and the Middle East.[10]

Another problem is waterlogging and salinization brought about by poor water management. Salt buildup in the soil is thought to reduce crop yields by about 30 percent in Egypt, Pakistan, and the United States. Data are sketchy, but it is estimated that about 10 percent of irrigated cropland worldwide suffers4 from salt accumulation.[11]

The already observable degradation of the earth's soil and water resources is likely to be compounded by climate change. Changing precipitation patterns, shifting vegetation zones, and rising sea levels caused by global warming threaten to disrupt crop harvests, inundate heavily populated low-lying coastal areas, upset human settlement patterns, imperil estuaries and coastal aquifers with intruding salt water, and undermine biological diversity.

River deltas and coastal areas around the globe likely to be strongly affected by global warming include the Yangtze, Mekong, and Indus in Asia; the Tigris and Euphrates in the Middle East; the Zambezi, Niger, and Senegal in Africa; the Orinoco, Amazon, and La Plata in South America; the Mississippi in North America; and the Rhine in Europe.[12]

River deltas and other low-lying coastal areas most at risk from sea-level rise are precisely the places with some of the densest human settlements and the most intensive agriculture. UNEP anticipates that sea level rise, along with amplified tidal waves and storm surges,

9   Sandra Postel, *Last Oasis: Facing Water Scarcity* (New York: W.W. Norton & Company, 1992).

10   Ibid.; Sandra Postel, 'Forging a Sustainable Water Strategy', in Lester R. Brown et al., *State of the World 1996* (New York: W.W. Norton & Company, 1996).

11   Postel, op. cit. note 9.

12   William K. Stevens, 'Scientists Say Earth's Warming Could Set Off Wide Disruptions', *New York Times*, 18 September 1995.

could eventually threaten some 5 million square kilometers of coastal areas worldwide. Though accounting for only 3 percent of the world's total land, this area is home to more than a billion people.[13]

Global warming's impact on agriculture - through rising seas, higher or more variable temperatures, more frequent droughts, and changes in precipitation patterns - is thus a major concern. Given already existing water shortages, agriculture in arid and semiarid areas is particularly vulnerable to climate change. Studies suggest that Egypt's corn yield may drop by one fifth and its wheat yield by one third, while Mexico's rain-fed maize crop may be reduced by as much as 40 percent.[14]

To summarize, the human security implications of degraded or depleted lands, forests, and marine ecosystems, intensified by climate change, are manifold: heightened droughts and increasing food insecurity; reduced crop yields that force farmers to look for work in already crowded cities; environmental refugees from coastal areas seeking new homes and livelihoods elsewhere, possibly clashing with hostile host communities; the disruption of local, regional, and possibly national economies; and the soaring costs of coping with the dislocations. ✗

Social Pressures

In addition, many societies have to contend with increasing social conflict, and indeed, social and environmental factors sometimes interact closely with each other. Juan Somavia, the Secretary General of the 1995 World Social Summit, observed that 'We have less insecurity in the military sphere and more insecurity in the personal and community spheres. We have replaced the threat of the nuclear bomb with the threat of a social bomb'.[15]

---

13 Myers, op. cit. note 8; Chapter 9, 'Coastal Zones and Small Islands', in Robert T. Watson, Marufu C. Zinyowera, and Richard H. Moss, eds., *Climate Change 1995: Impacts, Adaptations and Mitigation of Climate Change: Scientific-Technical Analyses* (Cambridge, Mass.: Cambridge University Press, for the Intergovernmental Panel on Climate Change, 1996).

14 Thomas F. Homer-Dixon, 'Environmental Scarcities and Violent Conflict: Evidence from Cases', *International Security* (Summer 1994); Myers, op. cit. note 8.

15 Quoted in Barbara Crossette, 'Despite the Risks, the U.N. Plans a World Conference on Poverty', *New York Times*, 23 January, 1995.

Measured by a traditional yardstick, the world is getting steadily richer from year to year. Since 1950, the gross global product has grown from $3.8 trillion to $20.8 trillion (in 1987 prices), far outpacing the population growth rate. Statistically speaking, the average person has thus grown richer.

Yet the benefits of economic growth are very unevenly distributed. The gap between rich and poor has grown to tremendous levels, both globally and within many individual countries. Worldwide, the richest fifth of the population now receives 60 times the income of the poorest fifth, up from 30 times in 1960.[16]

Perhaps more importantly, gaps exist within countries, and they seem to be growing in many nations. There is a 'Third World' of impoverished communities even within the richest countries, just as there is a 'First World' of wealthy enclaves within poorer ones. Rising inequality, marginalization, and the resulting societal rifts and fractures can be found around the globe. (See Table 4.)

Latin American countries have long displayed the most unequal income distribution in the world. The growth of GNP, foreign investment, and other macroeconomic indicators in Latin America has been impressive in recent years. But with few exceptions, income distribution in the region remains highly skewed, with close to half the population living in poverty.[17]

Income inequality has also risen sharply in many countries in Eastern Europe and the former Soviet Union. And it has not spared some of the richest countries: in the United States, the ratio between the top 20 and bottom 20 percent went from 4:1 in 1970 to 13:1 in 1993.[18] The nations of South-East Asia are one of the few exceptions: income distribution in India, Malaysia, Singapore, Hong Kong, and Taiwan has improved (though it has deteriorated in China, Bangladesh, and Thailand).[19]

16   Global ratio from UNDP, op. cit. note 5.
17   Nathaniel C. Nash, 'Latin Economic Speedup Leaves Poor in the Dust', *New York Times*, 7 September 1994; U.N. Economic Commission for Latin America and the Caribbean, *Social Panorama of Latin America 1994* (Santiago, Chile: 1994); 'Mexico and Latin America: Poverty and Integration', *NAFTA and Inter-American Trade Monitor* (Institute for Agriculture and Trade Policy, December 1995).
18   United States from David Dembo and Ward Morehouse, *The Underbelly of the U.S. Economy* (New York: Apex Press, 1995).
19   UNDP, *Human Development Report 1996* (New York: Oxford University Press, 1996).

The growing gap between rich and poor, conspicuous wealth in the midst of misery and hardship for the poor, and growing economic uncertainty for portions of the middle class, generate discontent and resentment, fuelling social conflict. But conflict does not necessarily take place across the class spectrum. Those who struggle to get just a few crumbs from the pie frequently see themselves in competition with others who are equally hard-pressed.

The beleaguered part of the middle class often perceive the less well-off to be the source of their troubles - ostensibly by competing for the same scarce jobs and by burdening social services. Under such circumstances, people sometimes organize and mobilize in ways that are intended to benefit the immediate group they feel loyal to, rather than the community at large. It is the splintering and breakdown of communities that may be the most worrying trend in terms of the potential for social conflict and violence.

In most developing countries, where agriculture is a mainstay of the economy and key to people's livelihoods, land distribution is an indicator as important as the distribution of wealth. It, too, tells a story of immense imbalances. (See Table 5.) On the whole, Latin American land tenure patterns are much more inequitable than those found in Asia and Africa. Brazil has one of the most lopsided patterns of land distribution: the top 1 percent of landowners control 45 percent of the arable land, while the bottom 80 percent have to make do with 13 percent.[20]

In many countries, small farmers are losing access to credits, extension services, and other forms of support, such as guaranteed prices, as governments favour the larger cash crop producers (who are typically more oriented toward lucrative export markets and non-staple and perhaps even non-food crops).

Unequal and insecure land tenure, the marginalization of small-scale agriculture by cash-crop operations, and still-high rates of population growth, are combining to cause increasing landlessness. In 1981, an estimated 167 million households worldwide (938 million people) were landless or near-landless; that number is expected to reach nearly 220 million by the end of the 1990s. Large numbers of peasants feel compelled to migrate to more marginal areas, such as hillsides and rain forests, where the limited fertility soon makes them move on. Others turn to seasonal or permanent wage labour on large

20 Brazil from Myriam Vander Stichele, 'Trade Liberalization - The Other Side of the Coin', *Development + Cooperation* (January/February) 1996.

agricultural estates, or end up seeking new livelihoods in already crowded cities.[21]

Marginalized peasants may have little choice but to join the trek to urban areas. It would be one thing if those displaced could find jobs in cities and towns. But by and large a sufficient number of jobs, particularly jobs that pay a living wage, do not exist. Indeed, one reason for rising inequality and poverty - and a major threat to social cohesion and stability - is found in what some observers have termed the global jobs crisis. Out of the global labour force of about 2.8 billion people, at least 120 million people are unemployed, while 700 million are classified as 'underemployed'. That is a misleading term because many in this category are actually working long hours but receiving too little in return to cover even the most basic of needs.[22]

Perhaps most unsettling is the reality of large-scale youth unemployment, which virtually everywhere is substantially higher than that for the labour force as a whole. High rates of population growth and the resulting disproportionately large share of young people in many developing countries translate into much greater pressure on job markets there. The world's labour force is projected to grow by almost 1 billion during the next two decades, mostly in developing countries hard-pressed to generate anywhere near adequate numbers of jobs. The uncertain and frequently negative prospects that many young adults face are likely to provoke a range of undesirable reactions: they may trigger self-doubt and apathy, cause criminal or deviant behavior, feed discontent that may burst open in street riots, or foment political extremism.[23]

Unemployment, underemployment, the threat of job loss, and the spectre of eroding real wages are challenges for many workers across

21   Alan B. Durning, *Poverty and the Environment: Reversing the Downward Spiral*, Worldwatch Paper 92 (Washington, D.C.: Worldwatch Institute, November 1989).

22   Ray Marshall, 'The Global Jobs Crisis', *Foreign Policy* (Fall 1995); Richard J. Barnet, 'Lords of the Global Economy', *The Nation*, 19 December 1994.

23   International Labour Organisation (ILO), *World Labour Report 1995* (Geneva: 1995); projected growth of global labour force from Hal Kane, *The Hour of Departure: Forces That Create Refugees and Migrants*, Worldwatch Paper 125 (Washington, D.C.: Worldwatch Institute, June 1995); Peter Gizewski and Thomas Homer-Dixon, 'Urban Growth and Violence: Will the Future Resemble the Past?' The Project on Environment, Population, and Security, American Association for the Advancement of Science and University of Toronto (1995).

the globe, though the particular conditions and circumstances diverge widely in rich and poor countries. There is indeed growing concern about the uneven and uncertain impact of economic globalization. (See Table 6.)

Failure to deal appropriately with sharpening social problems could have serious political consequences. People whose hopes have worn thin, whose discontent is rising, and whose feelings of security have been stripped away are more likely to support extreme 'solutions', and it is clear that some politicians stand ready to exploit the politics of fear.

Inequality, poverty, and lack of opportunity are, of course, nothing new. But today's polarization takes place when traditional support systems are weakening or falling by the wayside. In developing countries, there is an erosion of the webs and networks of support and reciprocal obligations found in extended family and community relationships (although these are admittedly often paternalistic and exploitative). In Western industrial countries, the post-World War II welfare state that substituted for or supplemented many family and community support functions has come under growing attack. The social fabric of many societies, whether affluent or destitute, is under greater strain as the paths of rich and poor diverge more sharply, and as the stakes of economic success or failure rise.

Conflicts Based on Environmental and Social Stress

Beyond generating hardships or uncertainty in the daily existence of many people, environmental and social stress factors also can lead to violent conflict. Particularly with regard to water resources, there is potential for conflict between sovereign nations. (See Table 7.)

But on the whole, such conflict is more likely within than between individual countries. This is because the needs and interests of contending groups tied closely to land and environmental resources, peasants, pastoralists, ranchers, loggers and other resource extractors, often remain unreconciled. These contending interests are typically bound up with issues of ethnicity. There is considerable scope for environmental scarcities and social inequities to feed on each other.

Environmental factors are usually but one of a range of reasons for conflict. In the case of Bougainville, however, environmental degradation was the primary cause of conflict. On that island, guerrillas have been fighting a ferocious war of secession from Papua

New Guinea since 1988. The Bougainville Revolutionary Army issued a dramatic declaration in 1990, from which I quote the following:

> Our land is being polluted, our water is being polluted, the air we breathe is being polluted with dangerous chemicals that are slowly killing us and destroying our land for future generations. Better that we die fighting than to be slowly poisoned.

The conflict was triggered largely by the environmental devastation caused by the gigantic Panguna copper mine. Mine tailings and pollutants covered vast areas of land, decimated harvests of cash and food crops including cocoa and bananas, and blocked and contaminated rivers, leading to depleted fish stocks. About one fifth of the island's total land area has been damaged during almost two decades of operations at Panguna.

Of course, factors other than environment came to play a role as well.

> **Economics**: The economic benefits went almost exclusively to the central government and foreign shareholders. Royalty payments to local landholders amounted to only 0.2 percent of the cash revenue of the mine, and compensation payments for land leased and damage wrought were seen as totally inadequate. The concerns and demands of Bougainville's inhabitants were ignored by both the central government and the British/Australian-owned copper company. As discontent built up, local landowners put themselves in the forefront of a sabotage campaign that quickly evolved into a guerrilla war.[24]
>
> **Ethnicity**: The population of Bougainville is ethnically distinct from that of other parts of Papua-New Guinea. Although secessionist aspirations had existed before the Panguna mine opened, it was the conflict over mining's environmental destruction that brought these aspirations to the forefront.

As the Bougainville case demonstrates, resource extraction and large-scale infrastructure projects often create two types of burdens. First, they lead to massive displacement of local populations because

24   Volker Böge, 'Bougainville: A "Classical" Environmental Conflict?' Occasional Paper No. 3, ENCOP, Bern, Switzerland (October 1992).

they disrupt traditional economic systems or render areas uninhabitable. Second, the environmental burden is disproportionately borne by these populations, even as they derive few, if any, economic benefits from these projects. Typically, the affected populations are minority groups, indigenous peoples, and other vulnerable and impoverished communities such as subsistence peasants or nomadic tribes.

Indigenous groups in Nigeria's delta region face a threat quite similar to that of Bougainvilleans. Among them, the Ogoni have waged a peaceful campaign demanding an environmental clean up and a fairer share of the economic benefits of oil production. Frequent oil spills, natural gas flaring, and leaks from toxic waste pits have exacted a heavy toll on soil, water, air, and human health. Much vegetation and wildlife has been destroyed; many Ogoni suffer from respiratory diseases and cancer, and birth defects are frequent. Despite huge oil revenues, the area remains impoverished. The military government responded to the Ogoni campaign with massive repression that destroyed several Ogoni villages, killed 2,000 people, and uprooted 80,000 more. The crackdown culminated in November 1995, when nine Ogoni activists were executed despite international protests.[25]

The expected devastating impact of the gigantic Sardar-Sarovar dam project in India's Narmada river valley has also triggered intense opposition from affected communities. Close to 100,000 hectares of arable land would be flooded or lost to irrigation infrastructure. Aside from detrimental environmental and health consequences, the project is estimated to displace 240,000-320,000 people. The benefits would go to a small number of wealthy export farmers, while those displaced would include the Adivasi, an indigenous group. Marshalling broad international support, project opponents eventually compelled the World Bank to withdraw its crucial financial support. Some construction continues, but prospects for the project are uncertain.[26]

25   Peter B. Okoh, 'Schutzpatronin der Ölkonzerne', *Der Überblick* (March 1994); Steve Kretzmann, 'Nigeria's "Drilling Fields": Shell Oil's Role in Repression', *Multinational Monitor* (January/February 1995); Geraldine Brooks, 'Shell's Nigerian Fields Produce Few Benefits for Region's Villagers', *Wall Street Journal*, 6 May 1994; Howard F. French, 'Nigeria Executes Critic of Regime; Nations Protest', *New York Times*, 11 November 1995.
26   Volker Böge, 'Das Sardar-Sarovar-Projekt an der Narmada in Indien-Gegenstand ökologischer Konflikts', Occasional Paper No. 8, ENCOP, Bern, Switzerland (June 1993); 'Water in South Asia: Narmada River Fact Sheet',

In the Sudan, the expansion of large-scale mechanized farming schemes displaced several million small producers. Some lost their land outright in expropriations; others were forced out indirectly by declining soil quality, the blockage of traditional herding routes, and the increasing scarcity of grazing areas. Because Sudan's fragile soils were rapidly exhausted, mechanized farming kept claiming fresh lands, a southward march seen increasingly by the local population as a hostile incursion. The dispute over mechanized farming was an important contributing factor to the renewed confrontation and civil war between north and south Sudan that broke out in 1983 and continues today.[27]

Table 8 provides an overview of a number of selected conflicts in which environmental factors played a role.

One additional case warrants consideration here: the 1994 Zapatista uprising in the southern Mexican state of Chiapas. This episode illustrates the complex interactions of several stress factors: population growth, environmental decline, the lack of economic opportunities, and the absence of representative forms of governance.

On January 1, 1994, several hundred rebels of the Zapatista National Liberation Army (or EZLN) - a previously unknown force drawn from marginalized peasant and Mayan indigenous communities - seized towns in the eastern and central parts of Chiapas in southern Mexico. In less than two weeks, government troops had forced the EZLN to retreat to inaccessible strongholds in eastern Chiapas, and eventually, the two sides agreed to a series of talks to resolve the conflict. These talks have been unsuccessful so far and indeed remain suspended.[28]

The Zapatista rebellion found wide resonance throughout the country. Citizens in Chiapas and neighbouring states seized dozens of town halls to protest fraudulent elections that kept the ruling party in

Southern Asian Institute, Columbia University, New York, revised version (May 1995); Narmada Bachao Andolan, 'The Narmada Struggle: International Campaign After the World Bank Pullout', in the APC electronic conference igc:dev.worldbank on 6 October 1995.

27   Mohamed Suliman, 'Civil War in Sudan: The Impact of Ecological Degradation', Occasional Paper No. 4, ENCOP, Bern, Switzerland (December 1992).

28   Tim Golden, 'Mexican Troops Battling Rebels; Toll at Least 56', *New York Times*, 3 January, 1994; Tim Golden, 'Mexican Copters Pursue Rebels; Death Toll in Uprising Is Put at 95', *New York Times*, 6 January, 1994.

power. Land-hungry peasants invaded private ranches; some landowners fled, while others counterattacked with hired gunmen.[29] Although Chiapas is rich in natural resources, much of its population derives few benefits from logging, ranching, coffee growing, hydroelectrical and gas production. Although a tiny class of landowners and entrepreneurs is well off, most people, and especially indigenous communities, remain extremely poor, and Chiapas lags far behind the rest of Mexico in terms of education and health services.[30]

Land is one of the key issues in the Zapatista rebellion. The highly unequal land tenure has bedevilled the area ever since Spanish colonialism. A small number of farming and ranching elites control much of the best land in Chiapas and dominate its political system.[31]

In Chiapas, most land struggles are taking place in the eastern half of the state. Virtually uninhabited until the mid-twentieth century, the region, particularly the Lacandón rain forest, attracted waves of peasants fleeing land scarcity, dislocation from dam construction, and persecution during the 1960s and 1970s. They were joined by Guatemalans fleeing civil war in their country. Population in the Lacandón has grown twenty-five-fold since 1960. Peasants in eastern Chiapas are locked into competition not only with each other but also with loggers and ranchers who continue to control the local governments.[32]

As growing numbers of peasants, ranchers, and loggers pressed into the area, the region suffered an enormous loss of forested lands. Tree cover in the Lacandón rain forest declined from 90 percent in 1960 to 30 percent today. The intensive cultivation practices

29 National resonance from Tom Barry, *Zapata's Revenge: Free Trade and the Farm Crisis in Mexico* (Boston, Mass.: South End Press, 1995); takeovers and scrutiny from Tim Golden, '"Awakened" Peasant Farmers Overrunning Mexican Towns', *New York Times*, 9 February, 1994, and from George A. Collier with Elizabeth Lowery Quaratiello, *Basta! Land and the Zapatista Rebellion in Chiapas* (Oakland, Calif.: Food First Books, Institute for Food and Development Policy, 1994).

30 Barry, op. cit. note 29; Collier, op. cit. note 29; Philip Howard and Thomas Homer-Dixon, 'Environmental Scarcity and Violent Conflict: The Case of Chiapas, Mexico', The Project on Environment, Population, and Security, American Association for the Advancement of Science and University of Toronto (January 1996); 'The Mexican Rebels' Impoverished Home', *New York Times*, 9 January, 1994.

31 Barry, op. cit. note 29.

32 Collier, op. cit. note 29; Homero Aridjis, 'Slaves and Guerrillas, Forests and Blood' (op-ed), *New York Times*, 5 January, 1994.

appropriate to the climate and soils of the highlands from which most new settlers came soon exhausted the land, and the peasants were forced to move further into the forest. Meanwhile, ranchers turned forests into grazing lands, sometimes in direct competition with peasants; at other times, moving in after peasants could no longer cultivate the degraded land. The amount of pastureland within the Lacandón doubled during the 1980s. All told, large swathes of eastern Chiapas are now so deforested that the border between Chiapas and neighbouring Guatemala is clearly visible from space. As deforestation and soil degradation march on, land pressures intensify.[33]

Following some substantial redistribution of land in the 1930s, subsequent Mexican governments upheld the rhetoric of land reform but did little to implement it. More so than in other Mexican states, the large landowners of Chiapas have been able to delay or entirely resist land redistribution, or confine it to the least desirable land. In 1992, unresolved land claims and unfulfilled promises in Chiapas accounted for almost 30 percent of the total land reform backlog in all of Mexico. Thus, land distribution continues to be highly unequal.[34]

Throughout southern Mexico, landless peasants concluded that the only way to get land they coveted was to occupy it. Landowners responded to a growing wave of takeovers with violence by unleashing private paramilitary bands. The result was an endless string of local land skirmishes since the early 1970s, in which state and federal governments almost invariably sided with the big landowners.[35]

In 1992, then-President Salinas formally halted land reform, ending a government pledge that had its origins in the founding of the Mexican Republic and, although far from fulfilled, was critical to social and political stability. Embracing world market-oriented agriculture, Salinas in effect disavowed the peasantry as a constituency.[36] One observer commented that this step 'robbed many peasants not just of the possibility of gaining a piece of land, but, quite simply, of hope'. The formal end of land redistribution, together with

33 Collier, op. cit. note 29; decline of Lacandón tree cover from Barry, op. cit. note 29; doubling of pastureland from Howard and Homer-Dixon, op. cit. note 30; border visibility from space from 'The Mexican Rebels' Impoverished Home', op. cit. note 30.

34 Collier, op. cit. note 29; Barry, op. cit. note 29.

35 Barry, op. cit. note 29; Andrew Reding, 'Chiapas Is Mexico: The Imperative of Political Reform', *World Policy Journal* (Spring 1994).

36 Collier, op. cit. note 29; Barry, op. cit. note 29.

the removal of agricultural tariffs under NAFTA, which presented a clear threat to the livelihoods of millions of small-scale farmers, played a key role in propelling the Zapatistas toward armed rebellion.[37] Rural credit went increasingly primarily to cattle ranchers; small commercial and subsistence farmers rarely qualified. By 1990, 87 percent of agricultural producers in Chiapas had no access at all to government credit.[38]

As Mexico went through cycles of deep economic crisis in the 1980s and 1990s, the governing party (PRI) had difficulty maintaining its elaborate system of patronage. Instead of buying peasant loyalty, the central, state, and local governments turned to more coercive and violent measures against opponents.[39]

Elements of a Human Security Policy

Unlike traditional military security, human security is much less about procuring arms and deploying troops than it is about strengthening the social and environmental fabric of societies and improving their governance. To avoid the instability and breakdown now witnessed in countless areas around the globe, a human security policy must take into account a complex web of social, economic, environmental, and other factors.

Although there is much that national governments can do on their own to promote human security, national policies need to be complemented by improved international cooperation. This is true, for instance, in the field of global environmental governance - where the gap between rhetoric and action is growing. The 1995 World Social Summit in Copenhagen recognized, rhetorically at any rate, that poverty, unemployment, and social disintegration are closely linked to issues of peace and security, and that there is an urgent need for a new global commitment, a global social compact, to reduce deep inequities that breed explosive social conditions, fuel ethnic antagonisms, and drive environmental decline.[40]

Among many important measures, I will mention here just a few key proposals.

37 Collier, op. cit. note 29; removal of agricultural tariffs from Reding, op. cit. note 35.
38 Lack of credit access from Howard and Homer-Dixon, op. cit. note 30.
39 Collier, op. cit. note 29.
40 United Nations, 'Report of the World Summit for Social Development (Copenhagen, 6-12 March 1995)', New York, 19 April 1995.

1 One is more effective debt relief. Efforts by debtor nations to service their foreign loans have undermined their economies and increased the strain on an often already frayed social fabric without even getting the countries off the debt treadmill. African governments now spend more than twice as much servicing foreign debts as they do on health and primary education for their people. Debt servicing has also led to environmentally disastrous resource extraction projects that put increased pressure on indigenous peoples and trigger evictions of small-scale farmers and pastoralists. So far, debt relief has been extremely modest in scale.

2 Though hardly a new idea, another measure with multiple benefits is far-reaching redistribution of land. It would help counter the processes that fuel land wars and push the landless into ecologically fragile areas or into urban slums. Redistributing land, guaranteeing secure land tenure, and improving the availability and quality of rural credit and extension services would help increase rural incomes and jobs, and generate greater social stability.

3 Equally important is the provision of credit to the urban and rural poor who are usually denied loans by commercial banks because of insufficient collateral. These micro-loans can help individuals and communities escape the poverty trap, and can generate jobs and income that will help communities gain a more secure footing so that they can again be anchors of society instead of sources of migrants and pools of festering resentment. The number of people served by micro-credit institutions such as banks and cooperatives has risen from 1 million in 1985 to about 10 million now. Following a 'micro-credit summit' in January 1997, there are hopes that a total of $21.6 billion in small credit can be made available by 2005 to 100 million poor people who now are denied loans.[41]

41 Hal Kane, 'Microenterprise', *World Watch* (March/April 1996); Edward A. Gargan, 'People's Banks Help Rescue Poor Indonesians', *New York Times*, 18 February 1996; Patrick E. Tyler, 'Star at Conference on Women: Banker Who Lends to the Poor', *New York Times*, 14 September 1995; Paul Lewis,

4 Since many contemporary conflicts arise within countries, promoting more democratic forms of domestic governance and facilitating the emergence of more pluralistic societies is crucial. While far from being a panacea, the tremendous rise in the number of non-governmental organizations is on the whole an encouraging development.

5 The broad availability of arms means that disputes can easily be transformed into violent conflict. It is time that governments everywhere made a strenuous effort to reverse course: from a permissive and careless attitude toward developing, producing, procuring, and trading arms, we need to move toward constraint. This means adopting meaningful limits on new production, but it also means undertaking an effort to collect and destroy as large a portion of the arms already in circulation as possible.

6 Finance is the last key element in a human security policy. It is time to strike a new balance in our security investments - a balance that curtails the excessive reliance on traditional military means, promotes disarmament and the elimination of surplus arms, and corrects massive social and environmental investment deficits. Policies to prevent social breakdown, environmental degradation, and violent conflict require some substantial upfront investments, but they would cost much less than current reactive security policies. Moreover, they would help avoid the costly emergency measures that arise when societies splinter and disintegrate.

Building an alternative security system, based on far-reaching disarmament, demobilization of soldiers, conversion of arms factories, more effective peacekeeping, and non-violent conflict resolution, might require some $40 billion annually. The global social and environmental investment needs - encompassing such areas as preventing soil erosion, providing safe drinking water, eliminating malnourishment, and providing adequate shelter - will take a larger amount, perhaps some $200 billion annually for several years. This

'Small Loans May Be Key to Helping Third World', *New York Times*, 26 January, 1997.

compares with roughly \$800 billion spent per year on military budgets.[42]

Devoting greater resources to demilitarization, environmental sustainability, and social well-being may be regarded as incurring unwelcome expenses. Yet they constitute a set of highly beneficial, mutually reinforcing, and long overdue investments. Put simply, the choice before humanity is pay now or pay much more later. The cost of failing to advance human security is already escalating.

---

42 For details, see Michael Renner, *Fighting for Survival: Environmental Decline, Social Conflict, and the New Age of Insecurity* (New York: W.W. Norton & Company, 1996).

Table 1. Dimensions and Magnitude of Human Insecurity, Early 1990s[43]

Source of Insecurity	*Observation*
Income	1.3 billion people in developing countries live in poverty; 600 million are considered extremely poor; in industrial countries, 200 million people live below the poverty line.
Literacy	900 million adults worldwide are illiterate.
Land	More than 1 billion people are landless or near-landless; 400 million people in developing countries living on degraded, ecologically fragile lands.
Water	1.3 billion people in developing countries lack access to safe water; more than 700 million people live in countries where per-capita water supplies are inadequate or barely sufficient for food self-sufficiency.
Food	800 million people in developing countries have inadequate food supplies; 500 million of them are chronically malnourished, and 175 million are children under the age of five.
Jobs	120 million people worldwide are unemployed and 700 million more are underemployed.

43   SOURCES: UNDP, *Human Development Report* (New York: Oxford University Press), various editions; U.N. Department of Public Information (UNDPI) factsheets: 'The Faces of Poverty' (March 1996), 'The Geography of Poverty' (March 1996), and 'Poverty: Casting Long Shadows' (February 1996); U.N. Research Institute for Social Development (UNRISD), *States of Disarray: The Social Effects of Globalization* (Geneva: 1995); United Nations, 'Backgrounder – Global Report on Human Settlements Reveals: 500 Million Homeless or Poorly Housed in Cities Worldwide', in the APC electronic conference igc:unic.news on February 9, 1996; Sandra Postel, *Dividing the Waters: Food Security, Ecosystem Health, and the New Politics of Scarcity*, Worldwatch Paper 132 (Washington, D.C.: Worldwatch Institute, September 1996); Alan B. Durning, *Poverty and the Environment: Reversing the Downward Spiral*, Worldwatch Paper 92 (Washington, D.C.: Worldwatch Institute, November 1989).

Housing	100 million urban dwellers worldwide (out of 2.4 billion) are homeless; another 400 million live in inadequate housing.
Preventable Death	15-20 million people die each year due to starvation and disease aggravated by malnutrition; 10 million people die annually due to substandard housing, unsafe water, and poor sanitation in densely populated cities.
Cultural Status	300 million indigenous people in 70 countries are subject to discrimination and marginalization.

Table 2. Causes of Land Degradation, by Region[44]

Region	Degraded Area (billion hectares)	Defores- tation	Over- grazing	Crop- lands	Other
		(percent of degraded land)			
Asia	0.75	40	26	27	7
Africa	0.49	14	49	24	13
South America	0.24	41	28	26	5
Europe	0.22	38	23	29	10
North & Central America	0.16	11	24	57	8
Oceania	0.10	12	80	8	0
World	1.96	30	35	28	8

44   SOURCE: Günther Bächler, 'Desertification and Conflict: The Marginalization of Poverty and of Environmental Conflicts', Occasional Paper No. 10, ENCOP, Bern, Switzerland (March 1994).

Table 3. Selected Water-Scarce Countries, 1990 and 2025[45]

Country	Water Supply 1990	2025
	(cubic metres per person)	
Nigeria	2,660	1,000
Ethiopia	2,360	980
Iran	2,080	960
Peru	1,790	980
Haiti	1,690	960
Somalia	1,510	610
South Africa	1,420	790
Egypt	1,070	620
Rwanda	880	350
Algeria	750	380
Kenya	590	190
Israel	470	310
Jordan	260	80
Libya	160	60
Saudi Arabia	160	50

As reflected in this table, water-scarce countries are mostly found in Africa and Asia (specifically the Middle East); there are few countries that belong in this category in the Americas, Oceania, and Europe (although Belgium, the Netherlands, Hungary, and Malta are included).

45   SOURCE: Derived from Peter H. Gleick, 'Water and Conflict', in Occasional Paper No. 1, Project on Environmental Change and Acute Conflict, American Academy of Arts and Sciences and University of Toronto (September 1992).

Table 4.⁴⁶

Ratio of richest 20 percent
of population to poorest 20 percent
in selected countries

South Africa	45
Brazil	32
Guatemala	30
Senegal	17
Mexico	14
United States	13
Malaysia	12
Zambia	9
Algeria	7
China	7
South Korea	6
Germany	6
India	5
Japan	4

46   SOURCES: U.N. Development Programme, *Human Development Report 1995* (New York: Oxford University Press, 1995); David Dembo and Ward Morehouse, *The Underbelly of the U.S. Economy* (New York: Apex Press, 1995); Reinhold Meyer, 'Waiting for the Fruits of Change. South Africa's Difficult Road to Equality', *Development + Cooperation* (July/August 1996).

Table 5. Land Distribution and Landlessness, Selected Countries or Regions[47]

Country/ Region	Observation
Brazil	Top 5 percent of landowners control at least 70 percent of the arable land; the bottom 80 percent have only 13 percent of the cultivable area.
Peru	Three quarters of the rural population are landless or near-landless.
Central America	Guatemala: 2 percent of farmers control 80 percent of all arable land; Honduras: the top 5 percent occupy 60 percent; El Salvador: the top 2 percent own 60 percent, and almost two thirds of the farmers are landless or nearly landless; Costa Rica: top 3 percent have 54 percent of arable land.
India	40 percent of rural households are landless or near-landless; the 25 million landless households in 1980 are expected to reach 44 million by the end of the century.
Philippines	3 percent of landowners control one quarter of the land; 60 percent of rural families have no or too little land.
South Africa	Even after the end of apartheid, 67,000 white farmers own 87 percent of the arable land and account for 90 percent of agricultural production.
Sudan	An estimated 90 percent of the marketable agricultural production is controlled by fewer than 1 percent of the farmers.

47 Near-landlessness means that a rural family or household possesses too little land to sustain its members' livelihoods with farming alone.
SOURCES: Norman Myers, *Ultimate Security : The Environmental Basis of Political Stability* (New York: W.W. Norton & Company); U.N. Department of Public Information, 'The Geography of Poverty', factsheet (March 1996); Myriam Vander Stichele, 'Trade Liberalization - The Other Side of the Coin', *Development + Cooperation* (January/February 1996); Reinhold Meyer, 'Waiting for the Fruits of Change. South Africa's Difficult Road to Equality', *Development + Cooperation* (July/August 1996); John Prendergast, 'Greenwars in Sudan',*Center Focus* (July 1992).

Table 6. Destructive Growth Processes
and Conflict Potential[48]

Phenomenon	Policies that promote growth ...
Jobless growth	... but fail to generate a commensurate rise in employment (unemployment, job insecurity, competition for jobs)
Voiceless growth	... but suppress unions and human rights (political oppression, lack of democracy)
Ruthless growth	... but fail to invest in human capital and distribute the benefits fairly (poverty and income inequality)
Rootless growth	... but marginalize or eliminate cultural diversity (homogenization)
Futureless growth	... but diminish or destroy the environment (habitability, sustainability)

48   SOURCE: Compiled by author, based on UNDP, *Human Development Report 1996* (New York: Oxford University Press, 1996).

Table 7. International Water Disputes of Varying Intensity, 1980s and 1990s[49]

Body of Water	Countries Involved	Subject of Dispute
Nile	Egypt, Ethiopia, Sudan	Water diversion, flooding, siltation
Euphrates	Iraq, Syria, Turkey	Reduced water flow, salinization
Jordan, Yarmuk, Litani	Israel, Jordan, Syria, Lebanon	Water flow, diversion
West Bank	Israel, Palestinians	Water allocation and aquifer water rights
Indus, Sutlei	India, Pakistan	Irrigation
Brahmaputra, Ganges	Bangladesh, India	Water flow, siltation, flooding
Salween/Nu Jiang	Burma, China	Siltation, flooding
Mekong	Cambodia, Laos, Thailand, Vietnam, China	Water flow, flooding
Aral Sea	Kazakhstan, Uzbekistan, Turkmenistan	Repercussions of shrinking sea, water scarcity, salinization
Paraná	Argentina, Brazil	Dam, land inundation
Lauca	Bolivia, Chile	Dam, salinization
Rio Grande/ Colorado	Mexico, United States	Water flow, salinization, pollution
Rhine	France, Germany, Netherlands, Switzerland	Industrial pollution
Szamos	Hungary, Romania	Industrial pollution
Danube	Hungary, Slovakia	Dam, flooding

49   SOURCE: Michael Renner, *Fighting for Survival: Environmental Decline, Social Conflict, and the New Age of Insecurity* (New York: W.W. Norton & Company, 1996).

Table 8.   Characteristics of Selected

Location	Environmental Change	Social/Economic Factors
SUDAN	Soil depletion through mechanized farming	Displacement of subsistence farmers; export orientation of agriculture
PAPUA NEW-GUINEA (Bougainville)	Massive contamination by copper mining	Destruction of living space; benefits to outsiders only
NIGERIA (Ogoniland)	Massive contamination by oil industry operations	Destruction of living space; benefits to outsiders only
INDIA (Narmada valley)	Narmada dam construction; flooding of arable land impending	Displacement of local population; destruction of indigenous culture; benefits to wealthy farmers only
MEXICO (Chiapas)	Deforestation; soil erosion & depletion; conversion of farmland into rangeland	Unequal land distribution & severe social disparities; austerity & political repression; discrimination against indigenous communities
RWANDA	Scarcity of arable land; overuse of land & tilling of marginal land; steeply falling grain yields	Intense ethnic & political competition; severe economic crisis; lack of non-agricultural jobs; regional favouritism
CANADA/ SPAIN	Overfishing in Newfoundland fishery	Allocation of fish catch disputed; fish industry jobs

Environmentally-Induced Conflicts

Protagonists	Impact	Conduct of Conflict
Government vs. rebel forces; north vs. south	Nationwide	Civil war
Local population vs. central government	Local (war) / National (economic)	Secessionist war
Local population vs. government & oil companies	Local / International public opinion	Nonviolent protests, gov't repression & human rights violations
Indigenous people & international NGOs vs. government & World Bank	Local / International public opinion	Nonviolent protests, government harassment
Peasants vs. big landowners & ranchers; Zapatistas vs. ruling party	Regional / International public opinion	Armed uprising; militarization of region; constant low-level violence & intimidation; intermittent talks
Hutu vs. Tutsi; struggle against dictatorship; extremists vs. moderates	Nationwide / regional spillover / International humanitarian involvement	Civil war; genocide; manipulation of refugee politics
Trawlers vs. government vessels	Inter-state	Scuffles, diplomatic & political conflict

Chapter 8

Geoeconomics in American Foreign Policy

Walter Russell Mead

I. The Post-Cold War Shift

With the end of the Cold War, American analysts and politicians have increasingly shifted their attention from military alliances and the military balance of power to economic issues. In the absence of any new security threat on the scale once posed by the Soviet Union, the emphasis on economic issues is likely to remain and to become more deeply rooted over time.

To be sure, war planning and defence spending go on and will go on. Rogue states and problems like nuclear proliferation will continue to engage United States interests and concern. But, barring new problems, security concerns will recede into the background of Washington planning and domestic policy debates.

They will be replaced by what some call, awkwardly, 'geoeconomics'. This is what people in my home state of South Carolina call a three dollar word, and it means that the United States will be increasingly engaged in the pursuit and defence of its economic rather than its security interests.

There is a tendency to view this as an epochal shift, and some commentators both inside the United States and out maintain that the shift to economic interests means the end of foreign policy consensus in the United States. Others suppose that there will be dramatic shifts in United States policy as economic concerns move to the fore.

In fact, the consequences of this shift may not be as dramatic as predicted. After all, the shift to a largely geoeconomic policy is now almost a decade old. The Cold War ended eight years ago; economic considerations have largely guided United States policy ever since. Furthermore, despite occasional changes in tactics, United States 'geoeconomic' policy since 1989 has been relatively stable.

The differences between the Clinton and Bush administrations on international economic issues have been vanishingly small. This suggests that the policies we have seen since 1989 are likely to survive future presidents drawn from the mainstream of either party.

The purpose of my chapter is to describe this emerging consensus in United States policy and to look at the implications of what seems to be a long term, deeply set trend in the foreign policy of the United States.

For countries like New Zealand, any change in the priorities of as important a power as the United States will have implications. The change in American priorities will give New Zealand new opportunities to build its relationship with the United States while safeguarding key interests; it can also make parts of the traditional relationship less viable.

II. Geoeconomics and diplomacy

In looking at the economic dimension of American foreign policy, it is useful to divide the subject into two: commercial diplomacy, aimed at securing short term trade and business advantages for the United States in disputes with other nations; and economic diplomacy, whose goal is the security of the nation's long term economic interests.

Helping Boeing land a contract is commercial diplomacy; developing an international system of free trade in aviation is economic diplomacy. The distinction is clear in principle, though in some cases - as for example in the long running United States effort to open Japanese markets to foreign goods - the line between the two forms of diplomacy can blur.

The pursuit of commercial diplomacy is both easier and more difficult for the United States than for other countries. It is easier because the United States has such enormous clout - political, military and economic - that American negotiators have an unusually wide choice of instruments that can be used to persuade other countries to grant concessions or make purchases. American commercial diplomacy is difficult because as the world's largest trading economy, the United States has a unique interest in and responsibility for the multilateral trade system. This system is undermined if the United States engages in a too-vigorous pursuit of its lesser interests in bilateral trade issues. Therefore the United States government must continually balance short term advantage against the long term importance of a healthy multilateral system.

It is unfortunately true that the general interest in a healthy multilateral system is often shouted down by the impassioned proponents of a particular special interest. American commercial diplomacy is therefore likely over the long term, as often in the past, to be shaped less by long range considerations than by short term political and economic calculations. It is, however, not unreasonable to hope that over the long run the values of a multilateral trading system will become so thoroughly understood by the American political classes that the temptation to sacrifice the health of the whole system to satisfy a particular lobby will somewhat diminish.

Economic diplomacy is the more interesting area of discussion. Economic diplomacy has a much longer history in the American foreign policy tradition than many observers think, and it plays a much greater role in the formation of contemporary American foreign policy than many understand. Indeed, the fundamental world view that has guided most American statesmen from the 18th century to the present day is based on a view that economic issues are the key to American foreign policy.

Foreign observers often talk about the 'idealism' of American foreign policy. There is certainly a strain of idealism in the American approach to world issues though it is less unique than often assumed, though a New Zealand audience will easily grasp the close connection between American Wilsonianism and British Gladstonianism. But the dominant strain of thought in the formation of United States foreign policy has been something I call American Realism, something that is both similar to and strikingly different from the darker, less economic and more military form of Realism found in Europe.

American Realists are not optimists about human nature. Unlike so many eighteenth century political reformers, the American Founding Fathers were notoriously convinced that mankind was a quarrelsome and greedy race; that, as the psalmist tells us, the human heart is wicked above all things. They did not expect a spirit of generosity and fair play to guide the councils of foreign countries any more than they expected the American political process to be a series of enlightened debates among dispassionate philosopher-kings. In foreign policy as in domestic, American Realists looked to interest as the guide to conduct.

Yet when the American Founders came to consider the foreign policy interests of the United States, they came up with a radically different list of interests than those drawn up in most of the chancelleries of Europe. European powers were surrounded by jealous and powerful rivals, and their relations alternated between war and armed truce. European states were forced to understand their interests primarily in military terms.

The British of course had developed a strategic doctrine that was different from the views of their Continental neighbours. British security could be safeguarded by specialising in the construction of an invincible Navy and by defending the balance of power in Continental Europe, while British prosperity could be enhanced by developing a global trading system. The financial resources created by its trade enabled Britain to subsidise its temporary Continental allies and to keep its Navy up to strength, while skimping on the cost of its Army - maintaining it as a kind of force de frappe under normal circumstances.

Many of the American Founders seem to have thought of the United States as 'the Britain of Britain'. British policy was more commercial and less militaristic than the Continental policies; with an ocean instead of a Channel separating it from the Continent, American policy could and would be more commercial still. Indeed, the importance of trade would define America's security interests. If the United States was isolated from European armies, it was also potentially isolated from European trade. The weakest point of the United States was its sea link across the Atlantic to Europe. Access to trade with the rest of the world would clearly be a paramount American interest; it was an interruption of trade, rather than the loss of territory to great power rivals, that would worry American foreign policy intellectuals through the first 150 years of national independence.

A foreign policy that was fundamentally commercial changed the nature of the American relationship with other powers. Security policy has historically been played like a zero-sum game. If Austria became more secure vis a vis France, France would become less secure vis a vis Austria. There might be occasional happy exceptions to this dismal rule, but in general, a policy of military competition involves states in inevitable conflict. Their interests cannot all be served to the same degree, and every political settlement will leave some power or group of powers unhappy and restlessly intriguing for change.

The zero-sum game of military rivalry played an enormous role in European power politics. The prospects for cooperation among participants in a zero-sum game are not good. Today's temporary ally is tomorrow's mortal foe.

Commercial relations do not work in this way. In commercial transactions it is possible to have both a satisfied buyer and a satisfied seller. Furthermore, economic prosperity is not zero sum. If Austria becomes richer, it can buy more goods from France, and this will make France richer. War, on the other hand, would hurt the economic interests of both nations, interrupting their trade, diverting their resources from productive to military uses, and increasing taxation in both countries.

Unlike Lenin, who saw capitalism as the cause of international warfare, American Realists have seen commerce as, potentially, a cause of peace. The expansion of trade, and the substitution of the win-win strategy of commerce for the zero-sum game of war would become important American aims in the twentieth century. At the end of the Cold War, the traditional structure of American foreign policy has emerged once again.

III. The structure of American geoeconomic interests

If American realism seeks 'win-win' relationships with other countries based on the primacy of economic considerations, that does not mean that American Realists abjure the national interest. On the contrary. The emerging economic diplomacy now reshaping American foreign policy is based on very specific ideas about the national interest and, despite the many vicissitudes of the American policy process, American economic policy is visibly shaped by concern for those interests.

From an economic point of view today, United States interests can be defined in terms of three facts about the nation, with each of these facets of the national interest giving rise to important aspects of American geoeconomic policy.

The United States is a global nation, a 'middle' nation and a service nation. American economic policy today is fundamentally determined by these three conditions and it is likely that they will continue to dominate American policy for many years to come.

To say that the United States is a global nation is not simply to reiterate that American military power is a factor world wide. More profoundly, it is a statement about the nature of American interests. Partly because of geography - what used to be called the 'world island' with long coasts inviting trade with both shores of the great Eurasian world continent - and partly because of the decentralised nature of the American government (and especially the Senate which gives great weight to small states) the United States does not concentrate its energy on any one part of the globe.

However, North America is the home of the largest and third largest trading partners of the United States, (total trade with Canada is $275.6 billion and with Mexico $108.5 billion[1]). Together, the two NAFTA partners accounted for 26.7% of total United States trade. Even so, North America is not as important for the United States as, say, the European Union is to Germany. In 1996 total United States trade with Europe was $318.9 billion and with Asia $505 billion[2]. The United States cannot ignore developments in any of the great market areas of the world. It is condemned to globalism.

It follows that the United States supports the development of a single global economic and trading system and in fact this has been the case throughout American history. We managed very well in the nineteenth century British system, and once Washington understood that the British system had collapsed beyond repair, the United States sought to build a new system of its own. The WTO of today is the descendant of the organisation which the United States sought to create in the 1940s; though torpedoed by a protectionist Congress the vision of WTO lived on, animating first the GATT and then the Uruguay Round that culminated in the revised WTO that now exists.

The United States attitude toward regional blocs has been more complex. Generally United States support for regional blocs such as the European Union and ASEAN has had roots in security concerns. Even so, the United States attitude toward such blocs has always been ambivalent. During the late 1980s, when both European integration and the rise of Japan appeared to be capable of creating closed, tightly integrated economic units, the United States worked to create NAFTA as, in part, a counterweight and bargaining chip. The United States clearly promotes the tendencies within regional blocs that favour regional free trade as a stepping stone to global free trade and is less supportive of attempts to build trade areas that divert trade in the interest of regional unity. Furthermore it has proved to be extraordinarily suspicious of efforts at regional integration that appear to threaten the privileged United States position in various locations. Thus in Europe the United States has consistently sought to defend its

1   Robin Bew, *United States Country Report 1996-1997* (United Kingdom: The Economist Intelligence Unit, 1997), 52.
2   International Monetary Fund, *Direction of Trade Statistics: Quarterly* (June 1997).

position by using NATO as an instrument to insert the United States into the heart of European political deliberations and in Asia the United States has worked against proposals that would have created forums in which Japan had a seat and the United States did not.

There are other ways in which the United States global vocation influences its economic policy. It has been an enthusiastic if not always consistent or open handed backer of such institutions as the World Bank and the IMF that seem able to further the United States agenda of an open global economy. The United States also tends to have a larger perspective on the global economy than its leading European and Asian partners. That is, the European Union is not greatly concerned about growth rates in Asia, and much of Asia sees little impact on its affairs of slow growth in Europe. The United States has a much stronger stake in the prosperity of all the major sectors of the world economy and tends to view the world economy as a single system more, perhaps, than other leading economies.

The global nature of the United States economy and national interest is therefore likely to be displayed in a continuing effort to regulate and stimulate the world economy as a whole. It is likely that the continuing development and industrialisation of formerly poor countries and the global spread of United States corporations will increase this United States tendency in the future. Earlier in the history of the industrial revolution, the expansion of corporations to a national scale led to an increasing emphasis on national economic policy. It is likely that the tremendous growth of internationally integrated corporations in the last twenty years will have far more dramatic effects on the international political picture than we have yet seen.

Companies who produce goods in twelve different countries with inputs coming from fifteen more, and who then aspire to market their products in scores of different national markets constitute an entrenched, powerful and growing lobby for regulation and property rights protection on an international scale. Increasingly, these companies are likely to press also for international policy coordination to improve (that is, to stimulate and, occasionally, to stabilise) macro-economic conditions on a global scale, and the United States, original home for many of the global corporations now spread out across the world, will be responsive to their requests. Central banks and international financial institutions are likely to see continued and intensified United States support for internationally coordinated efforts to improve poor economic conditions in lagging or stagnant regions.

The importance of trade with developing countries will also play a role in keeping the United States focused on stimulating global growth. In 1996, United States trade with developing countries amounted to 45% of total trade, including $271[3] billion of exports. The United States is not only a global nation; it is a 'nation in the middle' - that is to say, in many important areas United States interests are somewhere in the middle between most of the industrial world and most of the developing world.

Thus in western Europe, population is stagnant or declining, with a birth rate in Germany of ten live births per one thousand people and nine births per one thousand people in Italy. In Egypt the birth rate is approximately 30 per thousand,[4] and in Indonesia, it is 24.[5] In the United States it is 16 per thousand,[6] midway between the birthrates of Italy and Indonesia. Add immigration to birth rates, and population is rising faster in the United States than in any member of the European Union and much faster than in Japan.

This trend is also reflected in the age of the population. Americans are, on average, younger than Europeans and older than citizens of the developing world. In 1994 23.3% of the residents of the Netherlands were older than 60 years of age.[7] In Kenya, only 6.5% of the population had celebrated its sixtieth birthday.[8] In the United States, 16.3% of the population is over sixty.[9] Given the difference in birth rates, the United States will continue to have a younger population than its European and Japanese partners for many decades to come.

Demographics have a great deal to do with economic objectives. Aging countries tend to be more concerned with stability; growth is not as much of an issue. Younger countries want to grow. In the future as demographic changes become more marked, countries like Germany and Japan will be even more reluctant to grow than they are now, and even more concerned about currency stability - to conserve the value of the savings on which older people count. At the same time, the aspiring, younger masses of the developing world will want

3   International Monetary Fund, *Direction of Trade Statistics: Quarterly* (June 1997).
4   *World Population Data Sheets*, Population Reference Bureau.
5   *World Population Data Sheets*, Population Reference Bureau.
6   *World Population Data Sheets*, Population Reference Bureau.
7   *Encyclopedia Britannica Book of the Year (1997)* p. 677.
8   *Encyclopedia Britannica Book of the Year (1997)* p. 641.
9   *Encyclopedia Britannica Book of the Year (1997)* p. 793.

an expanding economy even at the risk of inflation that undermines the savings of the elderly.

This split is already visible in international economic policy. The austerity to which Europeans have subjected themselves in the name of the Maastricht agreement is something that neither the United States nor the developing world could tolerate. Since the monetary turbulence of the 1970s and early 1980s subsided, the United States dollar has roughly held its level against gold. By contrast, both the yen and the deutschemark have sharply appreciated against gold while those developing world currencies not pegged to the dollar or the yen have generally depreciated, sometimes sharply.[10]

As populations in the developed world age and population growth continues to slow, it is likely over the long term that the monetary divergence between Europe and the developing world will increase, while the United States will remain in the middle.

Other factors in its domestic political economy demographics incline the United States toward this middle path. One is the structure of production. Unlike countries like Britain and Japan, or even most of western Europe, the United States remains a major commodity producer with large sectors of the domestic economy tied to such activities as mining, gas and oil extraction, the production of non-food agricultural commodities such as cotton and tobacco, as well as conventional agriculture. In 1995 the United States ranked among the top three producers of salt, sulphur, gold, aluminium, and copper.[11] The total of workers employed by mining in all European Union countries in 1994 was 170,000;[12] in the United States, with a total economy smaller than that of the European Union, mining employed over 600,000 people and added $89.4 billion to GDP[13].

Because of the regional distribution of power in the United States Senate, these commodity interests are extraordinarily powerful. Wyoming, an agricultural and mining state with a population of only 453,000, has as many votes in the United States Senate as California, home of Silicon Valley and Hollywood. United States commodity producers can not only exert control in matters affecting their specific

10   Gold Fields Mineral Services, *Gold 1997* (London 1997).
11   Robin Bew, *United States Country Report 1996-1997* (United Kingdom: The Economist Intelligence Unit, 1997), p. 37.
12   BM Coope & Partners, *EuroStat*, DEBA, GEIE.
13   U.S. Department of Commerce, *Statistical Abstract of the United States 1996* 116 ed. (G.P.O. Washington DC, 1996), p. 411.

products; farmers in the European Union and coal miners in much of Europe can do as much. But United States commodity producers are additionally strong enough to help tilt the United States economic policy base toward a more accommodating, easy money stance than can their counterparts in Europe and Japan. In this, the United States is more like Australia or Brazil than like the Netherlands, and it still bears the marks of its role in the colonial period and the nineteenth century as a producer of raw materials in the British world system.

Finally, the entrepreneurial climate and relatively decentralised financial system of the United States reinforce its tendency to prefer a middle monetary and fiscal course between the extremes represented by the European Union and Japan on the one hand, and by the developing world on the other. An entrepreneurial society almost by definition is a society of debtors, busily searching for cheap capital for start up ventures. The United States economy is better positioned to take advantage of low interest rates and suffers more distress when interest rates are high than do the creditor-oriented economies of the other leading industrial powers.

It is not surprising given these considerations that the world economy grew rapidly during the Bretton Woods period when the United States Federal Reserve effectively set world interest rates at the relatively low levels that the United States preferred. Nor is it surprising that the dollar, more loosely managed than the German and Japanese currencies, gradually came under increased pressure in the Bretton Woods era and, since Bretton Woods broke down in the early 1970s, has lost about two thirds of its value against both the mark and the yen.[14] It is also not surprising that developing countries have generally chosen to peg their currencies to the dollar rather than accept the more restrictive straitjackets that long term stability against the mark or the yen would imply.

Thus the world economic policy which the United States, as a global nation, wishes to set can be generally characterised as a looser, more expansionary policy than either the European Union or Japan would prefer on their own. By the same token the policy approach that the United States prefers is generally somewhat more restrictive than many developing countries would prefer. It is likely that over the coming years and even decades we will see the United States maintain this stance by and large and, as the developing economies grow in size and clout, the role of the United States as a 'swing vote' in international economic policy is likely to emerge as a significant asset for United States policy makers.

Finally, United States economic policy reflects a widespread conviction that the future of the United States economy is in the production and distribution of services rather than goods. On both the domestic and international fronts, the United States has now for almost twenty years pursued a steady and generally successful policy of promoting the growth and export of the American service industry.

Domestically the United States led the way in the deregulation of financial services, air travel and telecommunications, three key price bottlenecks for the emerging high value service sector economy. Internationally, the United States has pushed strongly and consistently for the development of a global market that is favourable to trade in services. Whether in the field of intellectual property rights, the push to deregulate international air travel and telecommunications, in attempts to penetrate such markets as the Japanese pension market, or in its efforts to open international trade in services, United States economic policy has by and large consistently favoured the growth and development of international trade in services.

One useful way to understand United States policy is to see the analogy between its contemporary approach to services and its approach to manufacturing earlier in this century. The United States was the first country to develop a mass consumer market; United States based corporations therefore had significant advantages in both manufacturing and, crucially, in marketing and distributing consumer goods to mass populations. United States initiatives to open world trade in manufactured goods after World War Two were supported by companies conscious that these advantages - plus the financial resources they had accumulated thanks to their dominance of the large and lucrative United States domestic market - would enable them to compete aggressively around the world.

In the same way, contemporary United States banks, software firms, franchise operations, telecommunications companies, movie and recording studios and airlines, among others, all believe that they will on balance benefit from a more open trading system. As these companies grow in size - software is now said by some to be the third largest industry in the United States - they become a more powerful force in United States domestic politics and therefore in the formation of American foreign policy. From year to year we are witnessing the development of a large and powerful lobby of competitive, profitable and dynamic companies who are eager to move out into world markets.

IV. Geoeconomic problems

America's roles as a global nation, a nation in the middle and as a service nation all seem destined to become clearer and more important in the coming years. This underlines my prediction that economic interests will continue to shape United States foreign policy in much the same way as we have seen in recent years. While circumstances may change, and the international environment may change as America's negotiating partners develop their own approaches to these issues, it is likely that the underlying strategic shape of America's economic diplomacy will remain similar to what we now see.

I have stressed continuities of concern in American policy, in part because I believe that there is too much talk about a drift in American foreign policy. The discussion of United States post-Cold War policy has not fully taken on board the strong and enduring consensus - sometimes an unconscious consensus in which the underlying common assumptions are so deeply rooted as to be unperceived by those who share them. However it seems clear that there are genuinely problematical areas in United States economic policy and in these areas we can expect evolutions and shifts in policy in coming years.

First is the evolution of the export-oriented development model which has so massively transformed East Asia. This system is one of the great facts of contemporary life, but it is unlikely that it can enjoy continued success along the same line of development. The world has so far been perturbed by the consequences of East Asia's rise; it is likely in the future to be perturbed by Asia's struggles to redefine this model and to shift toward growth strategies based on the development of internal markets.

There are two basic problems for export-oriented growth strategies. The first comes from their continued heavy reliance on state planning. Countries like South Korea and Japan did not rely on communist style central planning, but government played a major role in credit allocation in these and other Asian exporting economies. That works well as long as the conditions persist which made the credit allocation policies useful in the first place, but when political and bureaucratic rigidities prevent rapid shifts in credit policy in the face of changing economic conditions, disaster can and too often does strike.

The second problem is that as more countries adopt export-oriented strategies, and as the economies adopting these strategies grow in size, they begin to bump up against external constraints. Not only are they forced into an ever more vigorous competition against one another, their potential for growth is increasingly limited to the rate of growth in their target markets. The ability of Asia to export cars to the West is ultimately dependent on the size of car markets in Europe and North America, and while a few small countries can grow rapidly selling into that market, there is simply not enough demand in the west to accommodate the growth rates that countries like China, Indonesia and India hope to attain over coming decades.

This unfortunate fact poses huge problems for United States economic policy and perhaps also for strategic policy. It suggests a long term increase in tension between Asia and the West, as well as within Asia both at the level of national and international politics. The success of Asian tiger economies has played an important role in reducing world tensions and smoothing the political path for Asian governments. As that growth slows, we will all face a different and less favourable environment.

It is likely that the United States will need over time to respond with proposals for the international community to finance investments in infrastructure and other programs which can cushion Asia's inevitable shift from export-driven to domestic-led growth.

The second area in which we are likely to see change in United States geoeconomic policy will become manifest as we understand the extent to which the triumph of liberal capitalism, the United States goal, is a profoundly destabilising achievement. It accelerates change and increases stress in the international system. The 'creative destruction' at the heart of capitalism is a dynamic system, and both the creative and the destructive potentials of capitalism are more active in a deregulated, uncontrolled environment. At the extreme, there is new potential for international financial disaster on the scale of the panics that periodically paralysed economic life in the nineteenth century. Far more common, and perhaps no less dangerous in the long run, is the political backlash against capitalism that occurs when industries, regions and economic sectors are devastated by rapid change. While the United States was rich enough and large enough to withstand the shocks of its own transformation in the 1980s - the collapse of manufacturing, the $300 billion savings and loans debacle, the crisis at money centre banks when the Third World debt crisis broke out - other countries are not as happily situated. To a certain degree the very success of United States economic policy creates new dangers in the international system, and unless the United States and the world find ways to cope with these unwanted consequences, the history of the twenty first century may be more tumultuous and bloody than we hope.

Over time, the United States is likely to modify its insistence on rapid economic change as it develops, through sad experience, a more sober appreciation of the costs of too-rapid change.

The third change which looms on the horizon will be forced by the rising power and political focus of international civil society. Globalisation has to date largely been dominated by corporations. Capital is more mobile than labour, and the corporate sector established an effective international presence long before such civil organisations as labour unions, citizen advocacy groups, NGOs and even environmentalists began to establish effective international networks. This created a situation in which international negotiations on subjects like trade and economic liberalisation were less subject to popular pressure than were the deliberations of national governments. The result, so far, has been a tendency for international agreements to deregulate and liberalise without regard for other considerations. The failure to include a green chapter and a social chapter in the charter of the World Trade Organisation is a result of this situation.

It is likely that the comparative weakness of non-corporate civil society at the international level is a temporary phenomenon. A combination of new technologies, the falling cost of international communication, and the gradual increase in international awareness on the part of civil society throughout the world will enable other forces to express themselves more fully and powerfully at the international level. Such issues as worker rights, environmental protection and women's rights will figure more prominently in the emerging international order as the balance is restored. In the end, the United States may once again emerge as a 'middle country', with a position on these issues part way between that of, say, the European Union and ASEAN on many contentious issues. Nevertheless, the international order is likely to become increasingly affected by the views of the critics of unbridled liberalisation.

Chapter 9

Achieving Nuclear Weapon Non-Proliferation and Non-Possession: Problems and Prospects

John Simpson

Introduction

We currently live in an era where, for the first time for half a century, the global elimination of nuclear weapons appears possible, though not yet probable. The five nuclear weapon states, who also happen to be the five permanent members of the UN Security Council (the P-5), have been for the last six years in a relationship other than acute political hostility. Their pressing need for nuclear weapons to ensure their own security is no longer so self-evident as it was prior to 1991. This in itself will not be sufficient to produce the elimination of nuclear weapons: other changes in the perspectives that states and their leaders hold about nuclear weapons will be necessary. But such changes are not impossible. The 'realist' perspective that suggests that a universal, determinist and unchanging logic applies to attitudes and policies towards such weapons is open to question, at the very least.

Even during the Cold War political and military perspectives on nuclear weaponry were not immutable: they changed in significant ways. Forty years ago, many Western analysts and politicians believed that by 1970 the numbers of nuclear weapon states would be in double figures and would continue to rise.[1] Their forecasts were based upon several neo-determinist observations concerning nuclear weaponry and energy. These included the propositions that:

---

1   A representative example of this type of writing is Alistair Buchan's edited volume *A world of nuclear Powers?* (New Jersey: Prentice Hall, 1966). In particular see Leonard Beaton's chapter 'Capabilities of Non-Nuclear Powers' pp. 13-38 which discusses the capabilities of 12 states other than the declared 5 to acquire nuclear weapons.

* as nuclear weapons were the most modern and lethal weapons[2] a state could have in its arsenal, all states with the technical capability to develop and manufacture such weapons, or to acquire them by transfer, would do so. This process would accelerate as supplies of uranium became more widely available and knowledge of how to build them slowly disseminated

* nuclear weaponry would continue to be conventionalised, as fissile material production expanded, and nuclear warheads were deployed on an ever-widening range of delivery systems, and performed more military functions, and

* the energy production and civil engineering applications of fissile materials would continue to expand, and make a meaningful distinction between military and peaceful uses of nuclear energy impossible.

After 1970, an increasing number of states rejected these propositions through their actions of ratifying the Treaty on the Non-Proliferation of Nuclear Weapons (NPT) and negotiating its mandatory INFCIRC/153 safeguards agreement with the IAEA.

Associated with these forecasts were two distinct concepts concerning nuclear deterrence:

* 'pure' deterrence, arising from the strategic use of nuclear weapons, particularly multi-megaton thermonuclear ones, by means of threats of unacceptable damage in a retaliatory strike against cities, and

* 'indirect' deterrence arising from nuclear devices being used to enhance combat potential. These would enable missions to be accomplished which conventional ordnance could not perform, and states with inferior conventional military forces to conduct war on more equal

2 A flavour of this perception can be obtained from the British Official History of the development of nuclear weapons, M.Gowing's *Britain and Atomic Energy, 1939-1945* (London: Macmillan, 1964). Among other statements is one contained in the first report on the Maud Committee, set up to examine the prospects for making nuclear weapons, to the effect that 'no nation would care to risk being caught without a weapon of such decisive possibilities', p. 395.

terms with opponents possessing superior conventional capabilities.[3]

Thermonuclear weapons of theoretically unlimited yield and with the potential to destroy all human life on the planet had become an integral part of this picture in the early 1950s. Although one initial response to them was to distinguish between small and large yield nuclear weapons, and seek to constrain only the latter, the 'Lucky Dragon' incident and growing concern over the medical consequences of fall-out from nuclear testing soon generated international campaigns to ban all nuclear weapons, and led the three existing nuclear-weapon states to contemplate negotiating a series of treaties to constrain, and then terminate, nuclear-weapon development and to dismantle all existing devices. Although this process lead to the partial test-ban treaty (PTBT) of 1963, with hindsight it remains unclear how seriously the participants regarded it or whether they saw it as just another aspect of the diplomatic gamesmanship associated with the Cold War.

The PTBT led its signatories to abandon above-ground testing, and had the side effect of making it more difficult for proliferators to acquire information on the design of advanced thermonuclear weapons. But the next step in the process, a ban on fissile material production for military purposes through a fissile material cut-off treaty (FMCT), was tacitly abandoned in 1964 on the grounds that it was unenforceable. Attention then shifted to an NPT, driven on by the mutual interests in this area of the two superpowers.

Today, not only is the PTBT still in force, but it is in the process of being superseded by a Comprehensive Test Ban Treaty (CTBT) signed in 1996. However, negotiations in the Conference on Disarmament (CD) on an FMCT have become stalemated, nominally over attempts by states in the non-aligned movement (NAM) to insist that progress can only be made on this issue if parallel discussions start on a Nuclear Weapons Convention aimed at eliminating all nuclear weapons. Underlying this conflict is a disagreement over nuclear disarmament strategies. The central issue is whether the process of nuclear-weapon elimination should be one in which an unequivocal political commitment to its completion by the nuclear

3   These terms are taken from Nikolai Sokov, 'Tactical Nuclear Weapons: New Geopolitical Realities or Old Mistakes?' *Yaderny Kontrol Digest* (Spring 1997), pp. 11-14.

weapon states (and by implication India, Israel and Pakistan) through a number of fixed, time-bound steps contained in such a convention is a necessary first step, and some would appear to be arguing a sufficient one, to guarantee the achievement of a nuclear-weapon-free world - the 'blueprint' approach.

The alternative position is to regard nuclear-weapon elimination as an 'incremental' process, which by necessity will have to be conducted within a flexible and adaptive framework of actions and changing perceptions. The key objectives in this process are to sustain the downward trend of weapon numbers; to minimise the risks of accidental or unintended use of existing weapons; to change existing perceptions of the utility of nuclear weapons; and to construct an effective regime to safeguard the materials removed from dismantled weapons. Only when this low salience world is reached will it be useful and realistic to negotiate seriously on the discrete steps necessary to achieve the elimination of nuclear weapons, through a nuclear weapons convention. And until that world is reached, the motives of those seeking to achieve it, whether they are to sustain arsenals at a low level or abolish them, are not central to the nuclear disarmament process. Indeed, without such mixed motives, movement towards a disarmed world will probably stall.

The sincere disagreement between those arguing for the 'blueprint' and the 'incremental' approach to nuclear elimination also serves to mask another, less obvious, reality: that while stalemate persists in nuclear disarmament *negotiations*, movement has been occurring and continues to occur in the nuclear-weapon states on a *process* of nuclear disarmament. This process - technologically, economically and doctrinally driven - is almost totally divorced from events in both bilateral and multilateral negotiating forums. Indeed the current situation over nuclear disarmament contains five distinct, and arguably contradictory, elements:

* the reduction of current stockpiles of quick-reaction nuclear forces to probably no more than 2000 warheads globally, with large numbers of additional warheads in reserve or storage. In the case of the Russian Federation, this is paralleled by degradation in its capability for regeneration of forces and obtaining early-warning of attack which, coupled with concerns over its command

and control arrangements, has generated fears that it may be relying upon a fire-on-warning operational doctrine

* the lack of significant movement in negotiations on further disarmament measures because of both disagreements over disarmament strategies and the lack of willingness of the American Senate and the Russian Duma to ratify existing bilateral agreements

* the existence of divisions of responsibility and lack of co-ordination between the United Nations and the semi-autonomous regime secretariats and executive organs responsible for dealing with weapons of mass destruction (WMD), which generate problems for implementation and uncertainties over how cases of non-compliance will be dealt with; and

* the linkages between the non-proliferation regime and progress in the nuclear disarmament process, both in reducing dissonance between disarmament and non-proliferation objectives, and in ensuring that the disarmament process itself does not contribute directly to nuclear proliferation.

The remainder of this chapter will start by sketching the development of the existing nuclear non-proliferation regime, and identifying its current problems and the options for resolving them. It will then explore further the existing situation in the nuclear weapon states, and the nature of the new environment into which their policies of nuclear weapon possession are leading them, and particularly how this affects their traditional thinking about nuclear weapons and the political objective of nuclear disarmament. Finally, it will attempt to explore how the contradictions between the non-proliferation and non-possession norms inherent in the existing non-proliferation regime might affect the possibilities of achieving further progress in nuclear non-proliferation and disarmament.

Nuclear Weapon Non-proliferation and Non-possession Norms

In the early 1960s, as writers on nuclear deterrence in the United States started to emphasise the dangers of nuclear escalation ladders,[4] they also recognised that control over any superpower nuclear exchange would be crucially dependent upon the concentration of decision-making concerning it in the hands of the leaderships of the US and USSR. At the same time, the break with China led the USSR to accept that the problem of nuclear weapons was not confined to capitalist weapons, but could also emanate from communist ones as well. The consequence was a coincidence of interests between the US and USSR to prevent additional states acquiring nuclear weapons. This was so strong that it survived all the vicissitudes of the later years of the Cold War. This mutuality of interests was expressed through:

* US policies to provide functional substitutes for national nuclear-weapon stockpiles through both extended deterrence guarantees and arrangements to transfer US nuclear weapons to allies for use on their own delivery systems in the event of hostilities

* USSR policies to deny access to nuclear weapons to its allies by refraining from similar wartime transfer arrangements and to take back nuclear fuel supplied to allies for their civil power reactors

* US policies to constrain the enthusiasm for disseminating civil research and power reactors generated by its 'Atoms for Peace' initiative of 1953, and to transfer responsibility to the International Atomic Energy Agency (IAEA) for providing assurances that transferred plant and materials were not being diverted to military purposes; and

* their co-chairmanship of the multilateral process which produced agreement in 1968 on a text of a Treaty on the Non-Proliferation of Nuclear Weapons (NPT).

The signing of the NPT in 1968, and its entry into force in March 1970, represented a sea-change in expectations concerning nuclear proliferation. It was based on several practical assumptions and one

4   The most famous of these texts was Herman Kahn's *On Escalation* (Maryland: Penguin, 1965).

normative one, linked to a series of rules for behaviour that flowed from them. The practical assumptions were that:

* the self-interest of the nuclear weapon states would prevent them transferring complete nuclear weapons to other states in peacetime, or disseminating their design information, materials and technology to non-nuclear weapon states
* the Treaty provided an acceptable security substitute to nuclear-weapons for those non-nuclear weapon state parties capable of acquiring them, and reduced the nuclear dangers facing those incapable of doing so
* an IAEA safeguards system could be implemented which would offer timely warning of any diversion of materials from declared nuclear facilities in non-nuclear weapon states, and thus both provide assurance to other parties of compliance with the NPT and deter clandestine nuclear-weapon programmes based on diversion of materials from existing facilities
* the existence of the IAEA safeguards system would allow non-nuclear weapon states to develop all aspects of nuclear energy, providing it was to be used only for peaceful purposes or military propulsion
* only nuclear explosive devices supplied by existing nuclear-weapon states under internationally agreed and verified arrangements were to be used in civil engineering projects, and
* regional non-proliferation organisations would be supportive of the global regime, and should therefore be encouraged.

The normative assumption was that:

* nuclear weapons had to be regarded as weapons of mass destruction, irrespective of their yield, design or role, and as such there was an absolute need to ban their possession, acquisition and use.

Existing nuclear weapon states implicitly recognised the incompatibility between their possession of such weapons and this general norm by undertaking to pursue negotiations in good faith to cap the numbers and halt development of such weapons, and then to reduce and eliminate them.[5] However, given the specific role played by nuclear weapons in 'indirect' deterrence in Europe and elsewhere this was paralleled, but not conditioned, by the undertaking to pursue negotiations also on 'a treaty on general and complete disarmament under strict and effective control'.

In the period since the NPT's entry into force, significant developments have taken place with regard to all of the assumptions underlying the text of the NPT. The desire of nuclear weapon states to safeguard their own nuclear weapons has led to no documented case of the transfer of complete nuclear devices. Moreover, this behavioural rule provided the legal framework within which all nuclear weapons deployed by the USSR were transferred to its recognised successor state, the Russian Federation, following the former's collapse and fragmentation in 1991.

Since 1970, there has been a steady stream of ratifications or accessions to the NPT by non-nuclear weapon states. The result is that only five UN members - Brazil, Cuba, India, Israel and Pakistan - remain outside.[6] However, demands still persist for enhanced security assurances for non-nuclear weapon states, either in the form of unqualified negative commitments by the nuclear-weapon states not to attack them or positive assurances of assistance in the event of a threatened or actual attack.[7]

The IAEA safeguards system proved insufficiently comprehensive to detect Iraq's clandestine nuclear-weapon programme prior to 1991, and as a consequence it has been the subject of significant adaption to

5   The relevant article of the NPT, VI, states that:
    'Each of the Parties to the Treaty undertakes to pursue negotiations in good faith on effective measures relating to cessation of the nuclear arms race at an early date and to nuclear disarmament, and on a treaty on general and complete disarmament under strict and effective international control'.

6   Of these five, Brazil set in train the procedures for its Congress to accede to the NPT on 20 June 1997 when its President requested them to do this. *Vox do Brasil*, Brasilia, 22000 gmt 20 June 1997 as reported by *BBC Monitoring Service, Latin America*, 23 June 1997.

7   For a discussion on the differing forms of security assurance see George Bunn and Roland Timerbaev, 'Security Assurances to Non-Nuclear-Weapon States: Possible Options for Change', *PPNN Issues Review No.7*, (Mountbatten Centre for International Studies: Southampton, for Programme for Promoting Nuclear Non-Proliferation (PPNN), September 1996).

enhance its ability to identify such activities in the future. In addition, it demonstrated in the case of the DPRK an ability to detect false information about past unsafeguarded activities. However, doubts remain about the ability of the international community, and particularly the United Nations, to handle effectively cases of non-compliance by non-nuclear weapon states.

The increased orders for nuclear power plants that followed the Middle-East oil crisis in 1973, followed by the Indian explosion of a nuclear device in 1974, served to crystallise the misgivings held by many Western industrialised states concerning the commitment in the Treaty to allow states parties to develop all aspects of nuclear energy, providing they accepted IAEA safeguards. One consequence was the creation of the Nuclear Suppliers Group (NSG), which progressively laid down guidelines for the national export controls of its members, starting with complete nuclear plants and their components and then, after the Iraq experience, dual-use technologies. It also gained progressive acceptance of the rule that exports could only be made to non-parties as long as they accepted safeguards over all materials within their jurisdiction.[8] The Treaty basis for these supplier activities was the nuclear-weapon states' commitments not to assist other states to acquire nuclear weapons, and the unstated, but logical, assumption that non-nuclear weapon states were subject to similar commitments.[9] Although INFCIRC/153 permits fissile material to be removed temporarily from IAEA safeguards for nuclear propulsion purposes, this provision has never been implemented, although in the late 1980s the issue was discussed at length in the context of Canadian aspirations to acquire nuclear submarines.[10]

8   For a discussion on this subject, see Harald Müller, 'National and International Export Control Systems and Supplier States' Commitments under the NPT', *PPNN Issue Review No.8,* (Mountbatten Centre for International Studies: Southampton, for Programme for Promoting Nuclear Non-Proliferation (PPNN), September 1996).

9   The relevant element of the NPT, Article II, states:
'Each non-nuclear-weapon State Party to the Treaty undertakes not to receive the transfer from any transferor whatsoever of nuclear weapons or other nuclear explosive devices directly, or indirectly', but it contains no direct commitment to refrain from assisting other non-nuclear weapon States Parties from acquiring nuclear weapons. By contrast, nuclear-weapon states are subject to such a direct commitment through Article I of the Treaty.

10 For a full discussion of this issue see Ben Sanders and John Simpson, 'Nuclear Submarines & Non-Proliferation: Cause for Concern', *PPNN Occasional Paper Two,* (Centre for International Policy Studies:

Provisions relating to the use of nuclear explosives for civil engineering purposes have never been activated, but the 1990s have seen a sudden expansion in attempts to create regional nuclear-weapon free zones (NWFZ). The overall effect of this has been to bring the Latin American zone close to being in force fully,[11] move the nuclear-weapon states to ratify the Protocols to the South Pacific zone[12] and bring to fruition negotiations on zones covering Africa and Southeast Asia.[13] As a consequence more than 100 NPT parties are also signatories to NWFZ treaties containing protocols providing them with unqualified negative security assurances. Some of them also have provisions for dealing with non-compliance.

Although nuclear arsenals have been reduced by thousands of warheads in the last decade,[14] there has been little indication that the basic friction between the norms of non-possession, non-acquisition and non-use underlying the NPT and allegations of bad faith and lack of progress by the P-5 in forgoing possession of such weapons has been reduced. This was the cause of the lack of agreement on a final declaration at the NPT review conferences in 1980, 1990 and 1995, and was the basis for the attempt by Mexico to prevent the 1997 NPT PrepCom providing detailed guidance on substantive topics to be given special attention in its 1998 meeting.[15] However, in the 1995 conference and the 1997 PrepCom, a new trend could be identified, namely the emergence of a significant central bloc of NPT parties who were prepared to make common cause in pursuing an incremental strategy towards nuclear disarmament. This bloc included members of the Western European and Others caucus group (WEOG) and of the

Southampton, for Programme for Promoting Nuclear Non-Proliferation (PPNN), July 1988).

11   The position in mid-1997 was that all the states within the zone had signed the Treaty of Tlatelolco, and all relevant external states had signed its Protocols. However, one zonal state, Cuba, had yet to ratify the Treaty, and this alone was preventing it being brought fully into force.

12   Although the Treaty of Rarotonga entered into force 11 December 1986, and China and the USSR ratified its Protocols before 1990, it was not until 25 March 1996 that France, the United Kingdom and the United States signed them.

13   The definitive text of the Treaty to create the African zone was agreed in June 1995, and a signing ceremony was held in Cairo on 11 April 1996. The text of the Southeast Asian zone was agreed in Bangkok on 15 December 1995.

14   Frank von Hippel, 'Paring Down the Arsenal', *The Bulletin of the Atomic Scientists* Vol.53, No.3 (May/June 1997), pp. 33-40.

15   *PPNN Newsbrief No.38* (2nd Quarter 1997), p. 4

Non-Aligned Movement (NAM) group, leaving the nuclear-weapon states in isolation on one side of them and the Mexicans on the other.

As the numbers of states that are not parties to the NPT has decreased, some of the states outside of the Treaty, particularly India, have focused upon the inherent conflict between non-proliferation and the continued possession of nuclear weapons by the P-5 built into the Treaty text as their overt justification for rejecting any possibility of acceding to it. In parallel, as the NPT has come closer to universality and, as a consequence, those remaining outside of it seem to have moved into a more exposed position, some of them appear to have strengthened their resolve never to accede to it. Yet without such universality, it is difficult to see how the norm they nominally seek to implement - the elimination of nuclear weapons - can be achieved.

The Nuclear Non-Proliferation regime thus appears to face several major problems as it moves towards the next decade:

i.   As the number of states party to the NPT has increased, it has appeared increasingly unlikely that universality can be achieved.

ii.   Although IAEA safeguards have been made more comprehensive and effective, arrangements for dealing with non-compliant states remain weak.

iii.   An increasing number of states may posses the potential to develop nuclear weapons rapidly in an emergency, thus placing political commitment and reassurances about the actions of others, rather than technology denial policies, at the centre of the regime.

iv.   Article VI of the NPT, and the norm of non-possession of nuclear weapons upon which the Treaty is based, remain out of alignment.

i. Universality

The existence of three de facto nuclear weapons states outside of the NPT has given rise to several suggestions on how to proceed. These include:

*   Sustaining current policies of pressing the 'hold-outs' to accede to the NPT, in the hope that domestic political changes will make this possible or that they may accept a political deal offering positive benefits to them, such as security guarantees[16] or a permanent seat on the UN Security Council. This seems an unpromising strategy, however, in relation to India, Israel and Pakistan.

* Negotiating a Nuclear Weapons Convention,[17] which would supersede the NPT and contain a time-bound framework for the complete elimination of nuclear weapons. This is unlikely to find favour with a majority of the P-5, however, and unless drafted to prevent any possibility of defections by existing NPT non-nuclear-weapon-state parties, could lead to fears that some of them will refuse to transfer to the new treaty (e.g. Libya).

* Amending the NPT to allow India, Israel and Pakistan to enter as nuclear weapon states.[18] This might appear to solve the problem of universalisation of the NPT but would probably lead to the mass defection of the Arab states, as well as running contrary to the Treaty's purpose. Also, the amendment process is such that it is unlikely that the attempt would succeed.[19]

* Amending the NPT to create a third category of states other than nuclear weapon or non-nuclear weapon ones.[20]

16 For text, see Memorandum on Security Assurances in connection with the Republic of Ukraine's accession to the Treaty on the Non-Proliferation of Nuclear Weapons, 5 December 1994, in Darryl Howlett and John Simpson, eds., *PPNN Briefing Book Volume II: Treaties, Agreements and Other Relevant Documents (Fifth Edition))*, (Mountbatten Centre for International Studies: Southampton, for Programme for Promoting Nuclear Non-Proliferation (PPNN), April 1997), K6.

17 An example of such a convention is the *Model Nuclear Weapons Convention* proposed by the Lawyers' Alliance on Nuclear Policy, New York, April 1997.

18 The relevant element of the NPT, Article VIII, states that:
'Any amendment to this Treaty must be approved by a majority of votes of all the Parties to the Treaty, including all votes of all nuclear-weapon States Party to the Treaty and all other Parties which, on the date the amendment is circulated are members of the Board of Governors of the International Atomic Energy Agency'.

19 Harald Müller, 'Smoothing the Path to 1995: amending the Nuclear non-Proliferation Treaty and enhancing the regime' in John Simpson, ed., *Nuclear Non-Proliferation: An Agenda for the 1990s* (Cambridge UP: Cambridge, 1987), pp. 123-136.

20 Details of such an option can be found in M.J. Wilmshurst's 'Reforming the non-Proliferation system in the 1980s' in John Simpson and Andrew G.McGrew, eds., *The International Nuclear Non-Proliferation System:*

Again, this might lead to mass defections, and it would not be certain that the amendment process could be successful.

* Accepting that accession to the NPT is highly unlikely in some cases due to the regional conflicts the hold-outs are involved in, and attempting to ameliorate the dangers arising from their ambiguous status by offering assistance in areas such as physical security of weapons, permissive action links or command and control facilities.[21]

None of these options appears particularly attractive or feasible, and the way forward may be acceptance that only by resolving the regional conflicts in which these states are involved can any progress be made in persuading some of the current hold-outs to accept the norms of the nuclear non-proliferation regime.

ii. Verification and Compliance Mechanisms

Although there will always be limitations on the intrusiveness of IAEA safeguards techniques, if all current parties accept the newly negotiated protocol to their INFCIRC/153 agreements the chances of detection of undeclared activities will increase, while deterrence of such activities should also be enhanced. However, there is no such thing as providing 100% proof of the absence of an activity. Both these improvements, and the demonstrations in the cases of Iraq and the DPRK that non-compliance with the NPT and its IAEA safeguards agreements is a real, rather than a hypothetical, problem have focused attention on the issue of how to act in the event of non-compliance.

Prior to 1991, this issue was not salient, mainly because the two bloc leaders acted as policemen of the regime in their own zones of influence. They did this through the use of a variety of sticks and carrots, ranging from direct intervention to conventional arms transfers.[22] With the collapse of the USSR, the regime was left

Challenges and Choices (London: Macmillan, 1984), pp. 145-149 and pp. 185-191.

21   Arguments in favour of the US changing towards this type of policy in relation to India and Pakistan can be found in Richard N. Haass and Gideon Rose, *A New U.S. Policy Toward India and Pakistan: Report of an Independent Task Force.*, (Council on Foreign Relations: New York, 1997).

22   This is most visibly the case with US Policies towards Israel and Pakistan. Now this same policy has been utilised in the case of the DPRK. See Arvind

heavily dependent upon the sole remaining policeman, the US, to wield such sticks and carrots. However, the carrots used as part of such a policy may run the risk of appearing to reward regime rule-breakers and, from some perspectives, actively encouraging them. The prolonged negotiations with the Ukraine over the transfer of nuclear weapons to the Russian Federation and the crafting of the Agreed Framework with the DPRK are practical examples of this dilemma.

How to deal with non-compliance is not an issue confined to the global nuclear context: it now arises in all cases of non-compliance detected by the various global and regional WMD verification organisation. In some cases, there exists an executive body which could make a recommendation for action: in others their task is solely to confirm that a rule violation exists, and then pass the problem on to the UN Security Council. At present, however, the UN has no permanent mechanisms to handle such situations, or to receive intelligence information and convey it to the relevant verification organisations. In the case of Iraq, UNSCOM had to be created to perform this task. Proposals have been made that a data and analysis cell should be created within the Centre for Disarmament Affairs in New York to perform such activities on a permanent basis. However, even with such a body in existence, one central issue will remain: how to generate confidence that the Security Council and the General Assembly can handle such matters effectively and decisively.

iii. Political Commitment versus Denial Strategies

Since the early 1970s, a twin track strategy has been pursued by both Western and Eastern bloc states towards strengthening nuclear non-proliferation: obtaining political commitments to non-possession through the NPT, but reinforcing this with supplier arrangements to restrict access by 'suspect' states to sensitive nuclear technologies and materials. The NSG has progressively expanded its guidelines to cover dual-use technologies, with the result that little scope appears to exist for further major initiatives in this area. It can update its export control lists and make sure that they correspond to the list of items which would trigger IAEA safeguards if exported to a non-NPT party, but their further expansion appears improbable. Indeed, although the NSG is continuing to incorporate additional suppliers into the Group, the major challenge is to institutionalise its activities in such a way as to make them acceptable to other NPT parties. This may not be an easy task, given that members of the Group are unlikely to wish to change their guidelines or consultative mechanisms.

The creation of additional NWFZs may offer greater scope for movement in the area of political commitments to non-possession norms. Discussions on a Central Asian zone have started, and proposals have been made for others in Central Europe and the Middle East, though rapid progress in these latter areas appears unlikely. Yet it is unclear when the US Senate and Russian Duma will ratify the protocols to the South Pacific and African Treaties, or when these states will sign the Southeast Asian one. In addition, problems exist in persuading African states to ratify their own NWFZ. Despite its limitations, this regional approach appears to be the only avenue currently available to reinforce existing NPT commitments, as well as offering the unconstrained security assurances from the P-5 that developing states, led by South Africa, are seeking.

iv. Aligning the Non-use and Possession Norms underlying the NPT with the Situation in the De-facto and De-jure Nuclear Weapon States

The most contentious issue facing the nuclear non-proliferation regime has been, and remains, the inherent contradiction between the norm of non-possession which is at the basis of the NPT, and the probability that nuclear weapon possession by the nuclear weapon states will continue into the indefinite future. A significant element of this contention revolves around what would constitute an acceptable political commitment on the part of the nuclear weapon states to implement nuclear disarmament, and whether their current actions constitute non-compliance with their NPT commitments. This in turn complicates the creation of strengthened compliance mechanisms to deal with alleged proliferant activities by Treaty parties. To explore this issue further, however, it is necessary to examine the background and nature of the current nuclear disarmament context in more detail.

Nuclear Weapon and Disarmament Realities Past, Present and Future

The numbers of nuclear weapons present in the world and perceptions of their utility have in the past been a product of many factors, including:

* the evolution of military technologies and their associated operational doctrines
* threat perceptions
* the availability of resources to develop, procure and maintain nuclear weapons and their operational infrastructures, and
* the frameworks of arms management, regulation and control surrounding them, including provision of security guarantees and assurances.

From 1947 onwards, the pervading concern influencing the implementation of 'pure [nuclear] deterrence', and thus strategic nuclear weapon policies and doctrines, was to counter the possible disarming consequences of a surprise attack. A dominant requirement was that strategic nuclear forces had to be survivable, both to negate the consequences of pre-emptive attack and to reduce the incentive for it. This requirement was heavily conditioned by the assumptions of implacable ideological hostility inherent in the bi-polar US-USSR relationship. At the same time, increases in strategic warhead numbers appear to have been driven both by the identification of additional 'military targets' in the USSR and perceptions that the increase in their numbers would add to the insurance against a disarming first-strike. In parallel, the numbers of nuclear weapons being acquired to compensate for limitations in conventional capabilities also increased dramatically through to the late 1960s. This was partly a product of the availability of a steady supply of new fissile materials and the perceived inability of existing conventional weapons and forces to perform a range of military roles effectively.

Since 1991, this picture has changed radically. Although the capabilities created during the Cold War by the US and USSR still generate concerns about surprise attack, the core concern now is action resulting from inadvertence and accident, rather than malevolence. The survivable quick reaction alert forces of the Russian Federation are reported to consist of two missile submarines at sea at any one time, plus 18 SS-25 mobile missiles. Other nuclear capabilities are in varying states of readiness and repair. At the same time, the Russian Federation's early warning capabilities are slowly degrading, with key satellites not being replaced and electricity being withheld from early-warning ground radar facilities as no money is available to pay for it.

Although a limited, residual state of mutual threat and deterrence can still be perceived to exist between the US and the Russian Federation, political change has meant that a purposeful surprise disarming strike is no longer the threat driving strategic nuclear weapon procurement and operations. This development seems likely to be strengthened with the imminent entry of officers and officials of the Russian Federation into the corridors of NATO headquarters on a permanent basis.

This same political change has also allowed developments in weapon technologies to impact fully upon thought and action concerning the role of nuclear weapons in 'indirect' deterrence. From the late 1960s onwards, precision guided munitions gradually made it unnecessary to mount nuclear warheads on missiles and aircraft to compensate for delivery inaccuracies in specific roles, but the full impact of these developments was not felt until 1991, when both the Cold and Gulf Wars ended. The consequence was that nuclear warheads were removed from almost all their 'war-fighting' roles by NATO. Yet the concept now seems to have made a reappearance in the Russian Federation to offset its conventional military weakness, and in arguments from India that nuclear weapons may be the only means of combatting the threat or use of advanced conventional capabilities by the US.

But nuclear weapons are not like cannon balls: they do not sustain their capabilities indefinitely, but are subject to a process of ageing through which, even if well maintained and carefully stored, their ability to function as intended becomes increasingly suspect. Reports suggest that such 'technological' disarmament is advancing rapidly in the Russian Federation, and that by 2005 almost all the non-strategic weapons in the Russian Federation will cease to be capable of reliable operation, with no obvious means or money being available to replace them.

These developments can be argued to have had several significant consequences for the future of nuclear weaponry. The first is that global numbers of immediately available operational weapons have declined radically since 1991, with total numbers of warheads in an assured survivable deployment mode in the Russian Federation now probably not exceeding 500. Several sets of questions flow from this:

> *   What are the doctrinal implications of having a much reduced portion of state inventories of nuclear weapons in a survivable deployment mode?

* What will be the impact upon such inventories of the continuing processes of bloc obsolescence; design-life expiry; ageing; and lack of priority for financial and other resources to sustain them?

* How will capital expenditure on new nuclear weapons systems and warheads be justified to domestic and international publics, when no immediate nuclear threat exists?

* What will be the impact upon governments if current political de-targeting policies persist, targets cease to be clear and nuclear systems appear by default to be operating on an 'existential deterrence'[23] basis?

* Will doctrines of 'existential deterrence' be seen to contradict the basis for existing non-proliferation policies in a more provocative manner than mutual deterrence doctrines?

* What will be the consequences, if any, when almost all nuclear-weapon systems are operated in a 'conventional arms' mode, and spend most of their time in storage facilities, garages or tied up to the quay, only moving to a more immediate operational mode for the occasional exercise?

The post-2000 security environment seems likely to be characterised by political and security uncertainties, but a low risk of catastrophic global nuclear conflict. The nuclear-weapon states may need to adjust their policies to the changing realities of a world where:

* nuclear weapons will not be as salient to them as in the past

* resources available for them will be significantly constrained

* a nuclear test moratorium will place the emphasis on maintaining existing physics packages, rather than developing of new ones, and

23 In its purest form, 'Existential Deterrence' is deterrence based upon the existence of a capability alone, rather than technically credible inventories of weapons and plans for their use.

> * articulating the need for nuclear weapons on anything other than a 'come in handy' basis will become increasingly difficult.

It could also be a world where elements in the United States will press for global nuclear disarmament on the basis that it would enhance the potential for their power projection capabilities. On the other hand, the security pressures that drove the US and USSR to use nuclear deterrence as the backbone of their political relationship may still persist in other areas of the world - South Asia; the Middle-East; and East Asia.

One consequence may be that two main issues will dominate the future global nuclear security and arms control agenda:

> * How to translate what is actually happening to the nuclear-weapons and doctrines of the P-5 into binding undertakings to cap numbers and to deploy the majority of weapons in a 'storage', rather than a survival deployment or 'quick reaction alert' posture
>
> * How to constrain the de facto nuclear weapon capabilities of India, Israel and Pakistan, and facilitate their inclusion in a global nuclear disarmament process.

Ultimately, the willingness of the nuclear-weapon states to eliminate their nuclear weapon stockpiles will depend on them changing their current perceptions that they are vital for their security. Yet they will probably be reluctant to make such a judgement so long as the de facto nuclear-weapon states retain their capabilities - or in the unlikely event that they are confident they can deploy a 'leak-proof' nuclear defence system. And given the more acute security situation of the de facto nuclear weapon states, this is unlikely to happen unless the same type of political transition occurs in their regions as has occurred in Europe. In this situation, therefore, what are the prospects for further institutionalising of nuclear non-possession and non-proliferation norms?

Can Nuclear Non-possession and Non-proliferation Norms be Further Institutionalised?

To address this question, it seems necessary to seek answers to four specific questions:

* what further agreements need to be, and can be, negotiated in the nuclear weapons area
* what arrangements need to be made for implementing existing agreements
* what precisely does non-possession involve, and
* how will the conflict between non-possession and non-proliferation evolve, and what will be its impact upon the existing nuclear non-proliferation regime?

i. Negotiating Agreements

The negotiating track to institutionalising non-possession norms seems likely to be stalemated on a global level for the foreseeable future, given that the majority of the nuclear-weapon states and some of their allies reject the incorporation of a time-bound framework within any nuclear weapon convention, while the states of the non-aligned movement (NAM) are opposed to negotiating a FMCT on the basis of the current CD mandate,[24] despite this being designated by them as having second priority to a CTBT in the 1995 NPT Principles and Objectives decision document. This stalemate masks a further issue, however: that there exists no clear vision of how the multilateral nuclear disarmament process might progress in an incremental manner beyond an FMCT. While some may argue that this can be overcome were agreement to be reached to hold a fourth Special Session of the UN General Assembly on Disarmament [UNSSOD IV] before the end of the decade, it is equally likely that without some prior agreement on the future nuclear weapon negotiating agenda, there will be no UNSSOD IV. The outlook for the negotiating path to norm building thus looks decidedly bleak, with the possible exception of the creation of additional NWFZs. A similar outlook can be argued to exist for the START process, though here the problem revolves more around the failure of legislatures to ratify existing agreements, and fear that they will refuse to ratify new ones, rather than any lack of vision concerning the scope of new agreements.

The irony is that despite this stalemate, it seems inevitable that age and lack of resources will drive warhead numbers down in a semi-

---

24   For a discussion of the details of this situation, see 'The CD: Crisis and Opportunity', Rebecca Johnson, *Disarmament Diplomacy*, Issue 8 (September 1996), pp. 2-6.

autonomous manner over the next decade. This in turn leads one to ask several open-ended questions:

* will it be possible and is it desirable to negotiate agreements to cap these lower numbers
* how can progress be made in safeguarding materials and technology released from retired weapons, and in lengthening the time for reconstitution of these weapons
* might it be possible to negotiate agreements to create greater transparency over warhead numbers and fissile material production and stocks in the nuclear-weapon states, and
* how can current and future retirement and dismantling activity be related to the non-possession norm underpinning the NPT?

Despite the negotiating path towards disarmament being increasingly blocked, little effort is being made at the moment to institutionalise this probable decrease in numbers and make it irreversible. Some progress can be made through agreements on the transfer of fissile materials from military stockpiles in the nuclear-weapon states to IAEA safeguards, and the application of such safeguards in future on material emerging from reactors and enrichment plants in these states, but more visible and comprehensive commitments are not on the current disarmament agenda.

ii. The Implementation of Existing Agreements

A web of agreements have been created to combat the production and use of WMD, and some would argue that their implementation has equal priority for resources with negotiating additional ones. This issue highlights the increased budgetary costs for all states of implementing existing arms control agreements, and the difficulties of sustaining the verification systems attached to them. Major problems of co-ordination and information sharing exist between the organisations responsible for implementing these systems, which can only be overcome by a greater UN effort to link their activities together. States which regarded such a shift in priorities as a thinly disguised attempt to reduce the resources available for negotiating new disarmament agreements, and to impose additional constraints on developing states, are likely to oppose such a move, however.

Yet even if the UN secretariat is restructured to give equal significance to both the implementation and negotiation of disarmament agreements, it will not necessarily strengthen compliance procedures where this is most needed: the generation of a greater expectation that the Security Council will act decisively if faced with a case of non-compliance. Although the Iraq case has indicated what the Security Council can do, the case of the DPRK has also demonstrated its limitations.

iii.What does Non-Possession of Nuclear Weapons Imply?

Although the nuclear-weapon states did commit themselves to conclude nuclear disarmament agreements in Article VI of the NPT, or so the Advisory Opinion of the International Court of Justice (ICJ) has determined,[25] there has been little debate on what this implies in practice, or of the collateral measures that might be necessary to achieve this objective. One argument that has been advanced is that nuclear disarmament is a state of virtual proliferation or non-weaponised deterrence,[26] where the key issue determining whether it could be sustained would be the time needed to reconstitute a nuclear force, and in particular how many warheads could be made operational in a limited period of time. In short, a potential crisis nuclear arms race. This issue has already started to emerge as a significant issue in relation to Start II and III. In all probability, reconstitution times would only increase slowly as implementation of any disarmament agreement progressed, and safeguarding and 'denaturing' weapons-usable material would play a central role in this process.

Whether this situation would be more or less stable than a low salience nuclear world is an open question: much would probably depend on political circumstances. Equally, it remains unclear how the transition from an armed to a disarmed world should be handled if instabilities are to avoided, or how the transition to a minimally armed world could be accomplished without encouraging the 'conventionalisation' of nuclear weapons, once the threat of global catastrophe from use of such weapons recedes. Moreover, if low numbers of nuclear weapons lead to reliance upon doctrines of

25   The full text is contained in ICJ Communiqué No.96/23, 8 July 1996.
26   On virtual proliferation, see Michael J Mazarr, 'Virtual Nuclear Arsenals', *Survival*, Vol.37:3, pp. 7-26. On non-weaponised deterrence see George Perkovitch, 'A nuclear Third Way in South Asia', *Foreign Policy*, No.91 (Summer 1993), pp. 85-104.

'existential' deterrence, will this provide a justification for some of the existing non-nuclear weapon states to proliferate? Finally, one suspects that few of the developing states who advocate nuclear disarmament have assessed the consequences for them of a world where US conventional military power might be perceived as more usable and where nuclear disarmament would not undermine and destroy the global power structure, but would rather reinforce it.

These considerations have significant implications for both non-possession and non-proliferation of nuclear weapons. Rather than the NPT constituting a two-stage process towards nuclear disarmament, starting with non-proliferation and using this as a basis for disarmament, the effect of nuclear disarmament might be to divide the world between the virtual proliferators and the rest, with the former being differentiated by reconstitution or constitution times and physical access to fissile materials.

This is not to argue against seeking the elimination of nuclear weapons, merely to point out that although the term may be an effective political slogan, what it implies in reality is uncertain, and that such an end-state might be a more unstable nuclear-weapon world than a low-salience one. In addition, at the same time that advanced weapon technologies and new military concepts appear to be making nuclear weapons less salient for existing nuclear weapon states, they may generate new security incentives for nuclear proliferation among non-nuclear weapon states. The irony is that while many non-nuclear weapon states regard the 'general and complete disarmament' context for nuclear disarmament (contained in Article VI of the NPT) as a device that nuclear-weapon states are using to avoid acting upon their nuclear disarmament pledges, it may become a condition that others will also insist upon, if it leads to constraints on the advanced military capabilities that they regard as most threatening. There is thus a wide range of practical and policy issues related to nuclear disarmament that have yet to be adequately explored, but unfortunately there does not appear to be any obvious way for international institutions to do so. This leaves research organisations and other NGOs as the only groups capable of undertaking this task.

iv. Non-Possession and Non-Proliferation Norms, and their Impact Upon the Existing Nuclear Non-Proliferation Regime

It seems clear that rapid progress is unlikely in the immediate future in negotiating further institutionalisation of non-possession norms. This seems to suggest that the current conflict over the implementation of non-possession and non-proliferation norms will continue indefinitely. One way of viewing this is that it is an inevitable consequence of the way the existing non-proliferation regime has been constructed, but that security self-interest will prevent non-nuclear weapon states seeking to withdraw from the NPT or otherwise weaken the regime. Another is to ask whether there may be ways to argue that Article VI is being fulfilled, despite the lack of progress in negotiations.

Two issues become central at this point. One is the option to consolidate the reductions in weapon numbers that have taken place via a FMCT, greater transparency and placing former military material under IAEA safeguards. A second is agreements, tacit or otherwise, to constrain the ways in which nuclear warheads are deployed and nuclear delivery systems operated. The Canberra Commission on the Elimination of Nuclear Weapons made several proposals in this area, such as demounting warheads from missiles and placing them in central storage areas,[27] in order to increase the time that it would take to activate a nuclear system, and thus decrease the risk of accidental or inadvertent use. The objectives of these proposals might be partially achieved if agreement could be reached on deploying the bulk of a state's nuclear capability in this manner, leaving a small percentage invulnerable to surprise attack. An alternative is to remove guidance packages from delivery systems in a manner which would necessitate several hours of work for their re-insertion.[28]

Disarmament advocates, however, are likely to characterise such proposals as unnecessary distractions to the achievement of their objective, while those advocating retention of weapons are likely to regard them as *de facto* disarmament, and thus movement down a slippery slope. As a consequence, while such measures are being implemented for budgetary and other reasons, they seem unlikely to be institutionalised as they lack an effective political constituency on the inter-state level, and are unlikely to be seen as fulfilling the nuclear-weapon states' Article VI commitment, unless they can be argued to be integral to any 'cessation of the arms race'.

27 Report of the Canberra Commission on the Elimination of Nuclear weapons, (Canberra: August 1996), p. 12.
28 Some of these options are discussed in Frank von Hippel, op.cit.

Some Tentative Conclusions

The practical problem with the NPT has always been that some states viewed it as primarily a nuclear disarmament treaty and others a non-proliferation one. Nuclear disarmament and non-proliferation can be argued to be two distinct objectives, even if they are linked to a common norm, as non-possession and non-proliferation of nuclear weapons are both sought because of the destructive qualities possessed by those weapons. While possession of nuclear weapons by others does not condition the need to prevent additional states acquiring them, it does generate a compelling normative argument for the nuclear disarmament objective, hence the diplomatic battles over Article VI of the NPT.

The disintegration of the USSR in 1991 triggered major changes in both the nuclear non-proliferation regime and in the global nuclear weapon context. New initiatives were taken in many areas of the nuclear non-proliferation regime, to the point where the future options for further institutionalisation of its underlying norm appeared limited to the creation of additional NWFZs and the strengthening of enforcement mechanisms. The changes also left the states within the regime facing stark choices with regard to three of the five states which are non-parties to the NPT, and are usually regarded as *de facto* nuclear weapon states: business as usual seemed unlikely to persuade them to accede to the Treaty, while if they were to become declared nuclear weapon states this would create a class of states incompatible with the provisions of the NPT.

These three non-party states appear to be motivated in their ambiguous nuclear weapon stance, at least in part, by the regional conflicts that they are involved in. By contrast, similar acute security pressures are no longer driving the policies of the five *de jure* nuclear-weapon states, leading to reductions in global warhead numbers and less emphasis on the need to safeguard forces against surprise attack. This in turn is creating a need to ensure that this process of dismantlement does not provide the means for other states to proliferate, and changes in nuclear doctrines a justification for this. Yet in parallel the disarmament negotiating process is largely stalemated, because of the politics surrounding it, both domestic and international, and a lack of authoritative vision. It seems probable that numbers will continue to decline, but not as a direct consequence of negotiations, while conflicts will arise within the UN and elsewhere over the priority and resources to be allocated to the implementation of existing agreements, rather than the negotiation of new ones.

Two routes from the present to the future have been proposed in this context: the nuclear-weapon states implementing nuclear disarmament to comply with the provisions of Article VI of the NPT or a nuclear weapons convention being agreed to supersede it. Both, however, beg the important questions of what will be the end state of that nuclear disarmament process, and how stable will be that world and the intermediate phases that will have to be traversed to achieve it. These are issues that have yet to be analyzed and debated in practical detail, rather than on the basis of normative advocacy. Until they are, and disarmament negotiations catch up with the realities of the existing nuclear weaponry situation, the normative debate at the heart of the NPT regime seems destined to persist, and serve to generate continued uncertainty concerning the long term viability of nuclear non-proliferation and nuclear disarmament as international policy objectives.

The changes in perception concerning the assumptions which underlay thinking about nuclear weapons and their proliferation in the 1950s and 1960s serve to remind us that arms limitation, and the perceptions underpinning it, are part of a dynamic process. By way of conclusion, several open-ended questions can be derived from these changes, and the issues discussed above, which may serve as an agenda for future discussion and research on these matters:

* To what extent is current thinking concerning nuclear weapons driven by the unique circumstances of the Cold War, rather than ahistorical political and technological forces? And if so, what will replace this Cold War 'conceptual overhang' as the basis for discussion and action on these issues?

* To what extent has the fifty-two year taboo against the use of nuclear weapons, and by extension the lack of incentive for their possession, been based upon factors other than the qualitatively different nature of the destructive potential of such weapons?

* If traditional designs of nuclear weapons are no longer the 'most lethal or modern' weapons, what will replace them in this role, and what will be the impact of such changes upon future perspectives on nuclear weapons?

* Are the IAEA and regional nuclear organisations capable of sustaining confidence in their ability to detect diversion of fissile material from peaceful uses or its clandestine production and manufacture into weapons, and is the UN capable of handling politically those cases of non-compliance that such organisations uncover?
* Will the current emphasis upon 'pure', rather than 'indirect' deterrence persist, or will 'conventional' military considerations re-emerge as a powerful motive for nuclear weapon possession?
* Will the existence of states with advanced conventional military capabilities serve as a stimulus for nuclear proliferation, and will those capabilities also offer incentives for some of the P-5 to move towards nuclear weapon elimination?

Chapter 10

Nato Expansion and the Russian Question

Peter Shearman

Introduction

I begin my chapter with an old joke: one bright spring day in the 1970s in the former Soviet Union, General Secretary Leonid Brezhnev and Prime Minister Aleksei Kosygin were taking a quiet stroll through Moscow's Gorky Park. Kosygin, in wistful mood, asked Brezhnev if he foresaw the day when he would draw back the Iron Curtain and open up Soviet borders. 'Well, yes, I have considered this', replied Brezhnev, 'only I'm afraid everybody would rush out and that we would be the only two left'. Kosygin looked at his General Secretary in astonishment: 'You and who else?' he asked! Of course, one of his successors, Mikhail Gorbachev, *did* open up Soviet borders - but the vast majority of Russians have not since been in a position to simply pack up their troubles and leave for rosier places. The point is: capital may be mobile, but people, generally, are not. Despite the intellectual conceit and arrogance among many (mainly) Western academics, as the Philip Swallows and Morris Zapps of academia's *Small World* scoot around the international conference circuit talking of globalisation and post-statal relations, the vast majority of 'global citizens' are trapped, by the lottery of their birth, within the territorial boundaries of nation-states.[1] Whilst the forces of globalisation and interdependencies cannot be ignored in contemporary world politics, what should also be borne in mind is that politics nevertheless still takes place within the boundaries of sovereign states. The more interdependent states become the more it seems that people wish to reassert what it is that makes the nation-state distinct. However, the

---

1 Swallow and Zapp are the two main characters in David Lodge's comic novels, *Changing Places* (1975), and *Small World* (1984), both published originally in London by Martin Secker & Warburg, and later by Penguin Books.

political process *within* states - debates, controversies, elections, the development of policies and programmes - are often influenced by events taking place *outside* the boundaries of the state.

One of the recent buzz words in much contemporary theorising on the state and the nation is 'reimagining', a term stemming from Benedict Anderson's work on 'imagined communities'.[2] National communities may well be imagined - but they are not, therefore, made imaginary: they are indeed very real. If Russia is in the process of 'reimagining' itself - seeking to find a new post-imperial, post-Soviet, post-communist identity - then it is doing so, in what for Brezhnev and Kosygin would surely have been the most unimaginable of circumstances. This chapter will show how the expansion of NATO impacts on the debates, controversies, elections, and the development of policies and programmes in the Russian Federation.

The question of NATO expansion is no longer 'if' or 'when', but who is to be next? At the NATO summit in Madrid in July 1997 Poland, Hungary, and the Czech Republic were formally invited to become the first new members of NATO since Spain's accession to the Washington Treaty in 1982. In Paris, a few weeks prior to the Madrid summit, NATO leaders and Russian President Boris Yeltsin signed the Founding Act on Mutual Relations, Cooperation and Security between the Russian Federation and NATO. The meetings in Paris and Madrid have been hailed as finally putting an end to the Cold War and conflict between Russia and the West, and providing a conclusive and lasting peace in the Euro-Atlantic area in which democracy and security will flourish. U.S. President, Bill Clinton, argued that expanding NATO to Central and Eastern Europe helps to finally realise the goals set for Europe fifty years previously by the Marshall Plan.[3]

In this chapter, I argue that NATO expansion to Central and Eastern Europe, and the Founding Act between Russia and the Alliance, portend dangers to, rather than increased prospects for, European security - and, indeed, dangers to wider security issues outside the Euro-Atlantic area. The rationale and logic of NATO expansion are fatally flawed, and the agreement reached with Russia conceals differences and disagreements rather than resolving them,

2   Benedict Anderson, *Imagined Communities: Reflections on the Origin and Spread of Nationalism* (London: Verso, 1991, revised edn. - first edn. published in 1983).
3   See the remarks by President Clinton from the White House transcript released by Office of the Press Secretary, Paris, 27 May 1997.

leaving the future open to increased tensions between Russia and the Alliance.

Military alliances, in classical theory and common practice, have been generated by a common threat . NATO was no exception, and the common threat to those forming the alliance between the United States and Western Europe in 1949 was perceived, correctly, to be an expansionist ideological adversary represented by the Soviet Union. The primary objective of joining an alliance has typically been the provision of enhanced security that could not be guaranteed through self-reliance or other instruments, such as disarmament or international law. The stimuli for joining alliances have traditionally been motivated by and targeted against perceived adversaries, and not due to any ideological or cultural affinities between alliance members. Alliances are formed not so much to maintain a balance of 'power' as to ensure a balance of *threat*.[4] The Soviet Union certainly had substantial power capabilities, but these were not sufficient to warrant a global alliance network incorporating all of the world's most powerful states. It was the perception of the multifaceted Soviet threat, based upon perceived intentions linked to military might and ideological challenges, that explains the global containment network of the Cold War, with NATO as the central pillar. But when the threat disappears alliances degenerate - they do not expand. Stephen Walt, in an article published as the Cold War was winding down in the early 1990s, argued then that if this process was to continue NATO would eventually dissolve entirely and '...only a dramatic resurgence of the Soviet threat is likely to preserve' it. Walt suggested that 'optimistic rhetoric' about maintaining NATO should be viewed with scepticism.[5] In 1990, with the demise of the Warsaw Pact and communism in Central and Eastern Europe *Time* magazine, breaking with the usual practice of naming 'Person of the Year', named Mikhail Gorbachev 'Man of the *Decade*'. In line with traditional alliance reasoning Strobe Talbott, then a journalist with the magazine, argued in the same issue that 'It is time to think seriously about eventually retiring the North Atlantic Treaty Organisation' which can only be 'at best a stopgap until something

4   See Stephen M. Walt, *The Origins of Alliances* (Ithaca, NY: Cornell University Press, 1987).

5   Stephen M. Walt, 'Alliances in Theory and Practice: What Lies Ahead?', in Charles W. Kegley Jr. and Eugene Wittkopf, eds., *The Global Agenda: Issues and Perspectives* (New York: McGraw Hill, 3rd edn., 1992), pp. 189-196, p. 195.

more up to date can be devised to take its place'.[6] Having played a large role himself in bringing about a peaceful end to the East-West confrontation, Gorbachev expected his dream of a 'Common European Home' to become a reality.

Yet, some seven years on, Talbott, as Clinton's Assistant Secretary of State, had become one of the leading proponents of NATO not only surviving, but expanding, with Gorbachev warning that this would be like putting a time-bomb under the future of Europe.[7] Given Gorbachev's warnings and Talbott's earlier views, what is now the logic behind NATO expansion? A number of issues should be noted. First, the drive for NATO expansion has been principally an American endeavour. And it is interesting to observe the strange bedfellows that can be found on the side of those calling for NATO expansion, for realists such as Henry Kissinger and Zbigniew Brzezinski, along with liberals like Talbott have all been pushing the case to include Central and Eastern Europe in the Alliance. The opponents of NATO expansion also include both academic realists and neo-idealists, political conservatives and liberals.[8] There are, then, deep divisions in the United States (and this is true also of other Alliance members). However, all NATO governments speak with one voice on the general issue favouring enlarged membership, although there have been and are likely to be more differences over the process, financing, and membership of an expanded alliance.

Realist Arguments for Expansion

Kissinger and other realists have been pushing for NATO expansion to Central and Eastern Europe on the basis of traditional balance of power arguments, with Russia as the central issue. It is necessary, in this view, to expand NATO's military scope to incorporate those states left

6   *Time* , 1 January 1990.
7   Interview with Gorbachev, *Interfax* , 14 March 1997.
8   For example an open letter to President Clinton published on the eve of the NATO Madrid summit, calling expansion of the alliance an 'error of historic proportions', was signed by some fifty U.S. foreign policy experts including Robert McNamara (Secretary of Defence, 1961-1968), Paul Nitze (Ronald Reagan's chief arms control negotiator), Admiral Stansfield Turner (Jimmy Carter's Director of the CIA), Jack F. Matlock and Arthur Hartman (two fomer U.S. ambassadors to the former USSR), Sam Nunn (a retired Democrat who was a key defence expert in the Senate) and professors Richard Pipes, Marshall Shulman, Michael Mandelbaum, and Eduard Luttwak. The text of the letter can be found on http://www.nyu.edu/globalbeat.

in a 'security vacuum' after the end of the Cold War. Kissinger sees NATO as the key institutional link between the United States and Europe, one which ensures America a dominant role by providing a vehicle to ensure the defence of U.S. 'vital interests'.[9] Russia, Kissinger maintains, has been an expansionist power for four centuries, and has '...relentlessly pushed its frontiers outward from the area around Moscow to the center of Europe, the shores of the Pacific, the approaches to India and the edge of the Middle East'.[10] Central to Kissinger's thesis is the assumption of continued Russian 'imperialism'. However, now that Russia is temporarily weakened by the multiple problems of adjustment and transition following the collapse of communism, the opportunity should be taken to expand NATO to counter future Russian geopolitical power moves in Central and Eastern Europe. U.S. policy should be determined by 'permanent interests', not by Russian domestic politics.

Although U.S. Secretaries of Defence and State, William Cohen and Madeleine Albright, have sought to ease Russian fears and justify expansion in liberal terms (i.e., to assist democratic development in the former communist bloc) they nevertheless make explicit the *strategic* logic of their goals. In testimony to the U.S. Senate Armed Services Committee, Cohen stated that NATO enlargement flows from a single 'fundamental truth: NATO is first and foremost a military alliance'. At the same committee meeting Albright spoke of her role as America's chief diplomat: 'I know that a diplomat's best friend is effective military force and the credible possibility of its use'.[11] Justifying support for only Poland, Hungary, and the Czech Republic as new members in a first round of expansion U.S. officials refer, if only obliquely so as not to upset Russia, to the 'strategic' importance of these states. The choice of the three seems to be based upon the idea that they somehow have particular 'strategic value' situated in the central European 'strategic corridor' between Eastern and Western Europe. In a report to the U.S. Senate Foreign Relations Committee, Joseph Biden spoke of NATO expansion as a mechanism for maintaining U.S. leadership in organising the security of Europe, and at a Department of State briefing Nicholas Burns argued Washington

9   Henry Kissinger, *Diplomacy* (New York: Simon & Schuster, 1994), pp. 818-820.

10   Henry Kissinger in the *Washington Post*, 30 March 1997. Also see his 'Expand NATO Now', *The Washington Post*, 12 December 1994.

11   *U.S. Information Agency* (5380), 23 April 1997.

was using its leadership to support only three new members at the Madrid summit because those three will 'strengthen' the Alliance and not weaken it.[12] Slovenia, whose application for NATO membership has been vigorously supported by some members of the Alliance, meets the political, social, and economic threshold criteria for joining, but has not been ranked so highly as Poland, Hungary, and the Czech Republic due to its lower strategic importance. The U.S. Administration clearly believes that, at this stage, having Slovenia in NATO would 'weaken' and not 'strengthen' the Alliance. Situated near the Balkans, Slovenia could place an expanded NATO in a potentially insecure environment not warranted by vital U.S. national interests. Russia's potential threat to the Visegrad states is of far more concern, hence the rationale for the new wave of NATO members. Despite public commentary to the contrary it is manifestly evident and, given the history of the region, understandable, that the idea of a potential Russian threat has also motivated the governments in Poland, Hungary and the Czech Republic to seek membership of the Alliance.

It is not difficult to conclude from official statements in Washington (and the capitals of the Visegrad states) that realist thinking has played a strong role in determining policies in the United States (and in Central and Eastern Europe) on NATO expansion. According to this logic, expansion of NATO is seen as serving multiple purposes: it is a means for the United States to enhance its position in the one institution in Europe that allows for it; it strengthens the Alliance's military capabilities; it increases the Alliance's geographical range; it fills a security vacuum; and last, but not least, it checks and deters Russian power.

Problems with Power Politics

Realism for many is an outdated, moribund, and dangerous theoretical framework for offering policy prescriptions for contemporary security issues. Other chapters in this book point to the limitations of realist thinking for security in a globalised world in which traditional notions of state sovereignty are becoming compromised. Here, I will offer a critique of the realists' arguments pertaining to NATO expansion, showing the flaws in their own logic and assumptions pertaining to

---

12   See *Congressional Record*, 12 June 1997, and *Daily Briefing*, Department of State, 12 June 1997.

this specific issue.[13] Of course, we should not ignore history, for to do so is to make policy in an intellectual vacuum. But bad history is a poor guide for prescribing policies for the future. Realists such as Kissinger provide in support of their arguments for NATO expansion selective and distorted accounts of history in which Russia is viewed as an inherently expansionist and imperialist power, and hence it is deemed necessary to extend a military security guarantee to Central and Eastern Europe, a traditional area of Russian geopolitical ambitions. This history is selective for it ignores the fact that, although Russia has been expansionist during the past few centuries, so have most of the other major European states, including England, Germany, and France. For realists, the way to maintain stability in an anarchical struggle for power and influence is to form a balance of power between the major states. Hence, according to realism's own logic it should be recognised that history does indeed show that Russia has perceived interests in Eastern Europe and if any balance of power is to work in the contemporary era then any attempt to incorporate this region into NATO's 'sphere of influence' would be detrimental to a workable balance of power. Shut out and excluded from its traditional sphere of influence, Russia, humiliated and psychologically wounded, could be tempted to upset what is perceived as an unacceptable balance of power.[14]

For realists, a balance of power needs to be based upon credibility. It is not sufficient to merely have military power, it is necessary to demonstrate a willingness to employ it, as Albright hinted in the quote above, in order to deter that which threatens. Extending NATO's Article 5 guarantee to Central and Eastern Europe surely suffers from a huge problem of credibility. Even during the Cold War, there were concerns about the U.S. commitment to sacrifice Los Angeles for Lisbon in the event of a hot war in Europe. Especially, given the more recent fiasco in responding to the Bosnian crisis, what credibility will NATO's security guarantee provide its new members in

13   There are different strands to realist theory on the issue of alliances. See Charles W. Kegley, Jr., and Gergory Raymond, *A Multipolar Peace? Great Power Politics in the Twenty-first Century* (New York: St. Martin's Press, 1994), pp.90-101.

14   For the *destabilising* role alliances can play see Quincy Wright, *A Study of War* (Chicago University Press, 2nd edn. 1965); JohnVasquez, *The War Puzzle* (Cambridge University Press, 1993); and Bruce Bueno de Mesquita, *The War Trap* (New Haven: Yale University Press, 1981).

the event of war? Will American citizens and Congress be willing to sacrifice Washington for Warsaw, Boston for Budapest, or Phoenix for Prague?[15] Extending the Alliance, again based upon realism's own logic, could ultimately push Russia into a much more belligerent stance whilst simultaneously undermining the unity of the Alliance. For in the absence of a real and present danger, without a clearly defined mutual threat (which realists acknowledge is the case at present, for Russia remains weak) extending the Alliance to areas where in the event of conflict unity of purpose would perhaps be impossible to reach, would simply result in internal Alliance divisions.

One lesson we can learn from history is that pertaining to the events leading up to the Second World War. Punishing Germany after World War I and excluding it from meaningful participation in the security architecture that was then constructed led to resentment, hypernationalism, and World War II. Excluding Russia from participating as a full and equal member in the security architecture following the Cold War could have similar results, creating a strong sense of grievance amongst Russian political, and, especially, military elites, leading to hypernationalism, militarism and another Cold War - or even worse. After 1918 Germany was isolated, left to help itself in its attempts to make a transition to democracy. Hyperinflation and national humiliation ultimately led to a transition to fascism. The lesson is that transitions to democracy by defeated imperial nations are very risky enterprises, and the risks can be lessened or exacerbated by external forces. The positive role that external forces can play is evidenced by the inclusion and integration of West Germany (and Japan) into Western institutions after 1945, and the important impact of the Marshall Plan, a political and *economic* programme that had enormous social consequences facilitating domestic (and hence international) stability and security in Western Europe.

The Importance of Domestic Politics

The most serious problem with realist logic is that by definition domestic politics should not be of concern to policy makers, as the significant issues which should guide policy are balances of power,

---

15   Paul Kennedy suggests that the expanded NATO commitment to the security
     of Central Europe would be as likely to be realised in the event of crisis as
     Britain's commitment to uphold the Locarnro Treaty of 1925. See *Boston
     Globe*, 17 May 1997.

defined essentially in military terms, capabilities of others, and possible intentions based upon worse case scenarios. However, history surely tells us that domestic politics and leadership at the domestic level, especially in states undergoing economic crisis, those in transition to democracy, or those recently defeated in war, are key factors explaining insecurity, instability, and the onset of civil violence and wider internationalised wars.[16] Having lost a protracted global contest, the Cold War waged between 1947 and 1990, Russia is attempting, in a time of economic crisis, transitions to political democracy and the capitalist market at the same time. The dangers of fascism and the politics of resentment in Russia should not be underestimated, despite the victory of Yeltsin in his re-election bid for the Russian Presidency in 1996. Western states earlier recognised the potential of NATO expansion to hinder democratic transition in Russia, evidenced by the postponement of the decision until after the Duma elections of 1995 and the Russian Presidential election of 1996. Delaying the actual decision on expansion was due not to Russian objections, but to Russian *elections*.[17]

The Russian Parliament is dominated by communists, to all intents and purposes now representing a brand of Russian national socialism.[18] Gennady Zyuganov, leader of the Communist Party of the Russian Federation (CPRF) who won some 30 million votes in the presidential election in 1996, stated in his report to the Fourth Congress of the CPRF in April 1997 that his party's main task was to

16   See for example Edward D. Mansfield and Jack Snyder, 'Democratisation and the Danger of War', *International Security*, vol. 20 (1995), pp. 5-38.
17   President Bill Clinton first gave a timetable (i.e., new members to be admitted by 1999) in a 'presidential' speech in Detroit. Although this was considered not to be a 'campaign' speech, it was delivered on the eve of the 1996 presidential elections in a city that is home to large numbers of voters of East/Central European origin. See *New Europe*, 27 October-2 November 1997. There are nearly twenty million Americans of Central European descent in the U.S., most heavily concentrated in fourteen states accounting for 194 electoral votes - more than two thirds the amount needed for a majority in the last presidential election. See Jeremy D. Rosner, 'The American Public, Congress and NATO Enlargement', *NATO Review*, vol. 45, no. 1 (January 1997), pp. 12-14. Clinton recognised that what was a potential vote winner for gaining his own second term in the White House would have been a potential vote-loser for Yeltsin in his bid for a second term in the Kremlin.
18   See Peter Shearman and Mick Cox, 'The Russian Far Right', in Paul Hainsworth, ed., *The Extreme Right in Europe and the USA* (London: Pinter, 1998) (forthcoming).

resolve the common problems of 'national and state salvation'.[19] Mortality rates in Russia are higher than in all states in Europe, Asia, and the Americas with the exceptions of Afghanistan and Cambodia. In terms of life expectancy, Russia ranks 135th in the world, whilst some 70% of Russians are living in poverty.[20] Opinion polls demonstrate that Russian citizens have lost hope in the future, with nearly 70% in a March 1997 poll thinking that things would only get worse and were going in the wrong direction.[21] Whilst a few in Russia are getting richer, perceived by most citizens to be a result of corruption, the majority of people are becoming poorer. Whilst the wealthy avoid paying taxes, soldiers, pensioners, and state employees go without their salaries and pensions. There are one hundred thousand homeless people in Moscow. Homicide rates are three times that for U.S. cities. The military in Russia is also in a state of crisis, highlighted in a recent report by Moscow's Council for Foreign and Defence Policy. The report suggests that the possible dangerous consequences of this crisis could involve a disintegration of the armed forces, loss of control over military equipment, including nuclear forces, and the emergence of separate armed groups.[22] Lev Rokhin, Chairman of the Duma Defence Committee, made an appeal to Yeltsin and the Supreme Commander of the Russian armed forces to deal effectively with the crisis in the military. Rokhin argued in his appeal that the West is deliberately ignoring Russian interests in the process of shaping Europe's security, and that the IMF is shaping Russia's military reform by demanding that defence spending not exceed 3.5 % of the annual budget.

In the opening address to the conference from which this volume originates, the New Zealand Foreign Minister referred to the New Zealand armed forces being under-funded and inadequately equipped. But things can be said to be relative: at least New Zealand sailors and soldiers are issued with warm clothing, have sufficient food to eat, and receive their wages on time and at regular intervals. Less than half of Russian conscripts (it is still a conscript army) have been issued with warm winter hats. If a Russian soldier is lucky enough to receive his

19   *Sovietskaya Rossiya*, 22 April 1997.
20   See Bob Reynolds, 'Russia's Population on the Critical List', and *St. Petersburg Times*, 7-13 July 1997, both on *Johnson's Russia List*, 25 July 1997.
21   *RIA Novosti*, 28 March 1997.
22   See *Nezavisimaya gazeta*, 14 February 1997.

pay - average salary in mid-1997 is around 5,000 roubles per day - it is still less than that required to buy the equivalent of the rations given to prisoners in Russia's decaying public prison system. Only 10 per cent of the Russian army is fully-equipped with basic, standard clothes. More than ten soldiers die each day from suicides, abuse, or malnutrition. In 1996, 526 soldiers and officers committed suicide. Martin van Creveld notes in his chapter that in all the wars that Israel has fought since its establishment as a separate state the total number of battle deaths is 18,000. In Russia in 1996 alone, fully 10,000 soldiers died due to non-combat causes.[23] This represents more than half of the total number of Soviet troops killed in the nine long years of the war in Afghanistan. Poverty, hunger, starvation, homelessness and hopelessness are not the sort of features one associates with a strong, well-disciplined and effective defence force.

This represents a classical situation that is ripe for the development of hypernationalism. Extending NATO closer to Russia's borders can readily be used for instrumental purposes by figures on Russia's far right to mobilise mass political support. Whereas there are divisions in the West amongst the security community about the benefits and risks of NATO expansion, there has been (and remains at the time of writing) unanimity in Russia that it is a bad policy. All political, foreign and security policy elites have expressed their opposition to NATO expanding closer to Russia's borders. Whilst most acknowledge that expansion does not represent an immediate security threat to the Russian Federation, they all nevertheless see it in negative terms. Sergei Rogov, Director of the Institute for the Study of the USA and Canada in Moscow points out that there are differences over every issue among Russia's political elites bar one: on the question of NATO expansion there are 'no disputes at all'.[24] Rogov argues that expansion of NATO is detrimental to Russia's 'vital interests' and should not be accepted by Moscow 'lying down'. Russia, he states, is being 'forced out of Europe' and should not sit back passively whilst America increases its hegemony on the

23 On the plight of the Russian armed forces see *Sunday Times*, 18 May 1997, and *Argumenty i fakty*, no. 32 (1997). On the dangers regarding control of nuclear weapons see Bruce W. Nelan, 'Present Danger', in *Time*, 7 April 1997. Lebed also has referred to some 100 'suitcase nuclear bombs' unaccounted for in Russia: interview on *60 Minutes*, NBC, 7 September 1997, although Russian authorities have dismissed this claim, suggesting that Lebed would say anything to get back into the media spotlight.

24 *RIA Novosti,* 2 February 1997.

continent.[25] NATO assurances that expansion is not directed against Russia are not convincing. As Russian officials are fond of pointing out, perhaps with solid realist foundations, no country can base its policy merely on other states' declarations of good intent.

The NATO-Russia Founding Act includes the statement that NATO has no intention, no plan, and no reason to station nuclear weapons on the territory of its new members.[26] However, intentions, plans, and reasons change and, as the Russian Foreign Minister states: 'For any reasonable politician, plans are a variable factor but potential is a constant factor. Having a powerful military bloc being formed on our borders or near our territory irrespective of whether it poses a threat today or not, is unpleasant. It is against our interests'.[27] Alexander Lebed has described the Founding Act as merely a 'piece of paper', an 'empty agreement' that NATO has tossed to the Russian leadership in its attempt to save face in the eyes of Russian citizens.[28] Press commentary in Russia after the signing of the Act generally shows the negative appraisal of Russia's elites. Some see the Act as being the best Russia could get in limiting what was anyway inevitable, and something which at least provides Moscow with a voice (if not a veto) in security debates. But some see it as a sell-out of Russian interests, with Andranik Migranyan comparing it to Versailles, only this time it is Russia's fate as the 'vanquished power' to be 'humiliated'.[29] Migranyan is alluding here to the psychological impact NATO expansion could have in Russia, as humiliation, stemming from the Cold War settlement, could incite anti-Western sentiments, Russian militarism, and a bond between angry, frustrated masses and radical, authoritarian zealots that could reverse democratisation and create an aggressive hypernationalism.

The next elections to the Duma are due to take place in 1999, those for the Presidency in the year 2000. Yeltsin has been the best friend of the West in the Russian leadership since the demise of the Soviet Union, but he will not be contesting the next election and he

25   *RIA Novosti*, 11 February 1997.
26   *Founding Act on Mutual Relations, Cooperation and Security Between the Russian Federation and the North Atlantic Treaty Organisation*, United States Information Agency, 27 May 1997.
27   Interview on Russian television (NTV), 16 February 1997, reproduced in *Johnson's Russia List*, 21 February 1997.
28   *Interfax*, 13 May 1997.
29   *Nezavisimaya gazeta*, 27 May 1997.

leaves behind no political party in his name and image. In 1999, during celebrations of NATO's fiftieth birthday, Poland, Hungary, and the Czech Republic will be welcomed as fully-integrated members, and, possibly, a second group of states will receive invitations to join. It is most likely that parties and presidential candidates will employ the issue of NATO expansion in attempts to mobilise votes. It is most *unlikely* that any candidate or party seriously wishing to get elected will come out in strong support of NATO expansion. Many commentators routinely state that the Russian people simply have no interest in NATO expansion, and do not spend sleepless nights worrying about this issue as they have far more important economic and social concerns which will be most salient in determining voting patterns. Strobe Talbott has argued that the Russian nationalist threat is exaggerated and that the Russian population as a whole is not worried about NATO.[30] This is an unfounded assumption. President Clinton was surely correct in not making expansion a public issue until after the Russian elections of 1995 and 1996. Even without NATO expansion as an issue, the CPRF became the dominant party in the Duma, with a respectable showing still for the ultra-nationalists of Zhirinovsky's LDP, and Zyuganov, as noted above, polled well in 1996. At this distance from the next Presidential election, it is not possible to predict who will run, let alone win, but on the basis of current possible contenders then some brand of nationalism and statism appear to be the strongest forces that will dominate the election.

Although NATO expansion is not of key concern for many Russians as they go about their daily routines, during the elections it could well become a key issue. Opinion polls do indicate that the majority of Russians perceive NATO expansion as a potential threat to Russian security. For example, one poll taken in March 1997 found that 51 percent of Russians considered expansion of NATO to represent a 'serious threat to Russia', with only 14 percent disagreeing with this statement.[31] Two other state-wide Russian polls on Russia's place in the world and external threats found that 75 percent of respondents considered it important that Russia regain its position as a global 'superpower', 65 percent that foreign policy priorities should be to protect the interests of Russians in the 'near abroad', and the West

30 Strobe Talbott, 'Russia has Nothing to Fear', *New York Times*, 18 December 1996.
31 *News and World Report*, 24 March 1997 (quoting a *Moskovskiie novosti* poll).

and the United States topped a list of sources of threats. Asked whether plans for NATO expansion to the East were a source of concern, 30 percent answered 'yes', and 16 percent 'yes rather than no'.[32] These polls identified strong, mass patriotic sentiments and a profound sense of humiliation at Russia's loss of international status. These psychological factors can be readily mobilised by those elites seeking personal political advancement, and the democratic electoral process provides the most powerful and effective force for such mobilisation. NATO expansion will be an instrument that political elites and parties, leading figures in the media, and senior military officials will not be able to resist employing.

The China Card

Excluded from the West, or given only second-rate membership of Western institutions, Russia will be encouraged to look elsewhere for partners to balance the power of the U.S. This was already evident during the time that NATO and Russia were negotiating the Founding Act, as many elites from across the political spectrum were already seriously prescribing or obliquely warning that if NATO did expand Eastwards then Russia too should look to the East. This is linked to questions of pride and identity, and not simply issues of power. From the mid-1980s through to the mid-1990s, the Russian leadership sought to gain acceptance and admission as an equal partner in the 'West'. Against the backdrop of economic crisis and underlying nationalist sentiment, of nostalgia for the past with democratisation itself fuelling these sentiments, it was always going to be a difficult path for Yeltsin to follow. With increasing frustration at what was perceived to be a blind pro-Western policy that took insufficient account of Russia's real national interests, Yeltsin was forced to replace his liberal pro-Western Foreign Minister, Andrei Kozyrev, with the more conservative, pragmatic exponent of realism, Yevgeny Primakov.

Primakov became the only survivor of the hard-nosed conservatives in the higher echelons of the government following the reshuffles that Yeltsin instituted after the 1996 Presidential elections. Primakov has always pushed for a more balanced set of priorities in the conduct of Russian foreign policy rather than relying too much on relations with the United States and the West. Indeed, even during the

32 *Nezavisimoie voiennoie obozrenie*, 7-13 June 1997.

Gulf War in 1990-91, at a time when the Soviet Union was demonstrating its new cooperative credentials by supporting the West's reaction to Saddam Hussein's aggression against Kuwait, Primakov, as Gorbachev's special envoy, was trying, through his own personal diplomacy in Baghdad (as bombs were raining down on the city), to salvage some influence for Moscow in Iraq. At the time, this was perceived as undermining Soviet Foreign Minister, Eduard Shevardnaze's strong stance against Saddam Hussein. During that same period, Gorbachev was given an oral guarantee from President Bush's adminstration that if the Soviet Union accepted the reunification of Germany then NATO would *not* be expanded to the East. The origins of the Cold War were tied to the German question, and the moment the Cold War can perhaps be said to have finally ended was when Gorbachev agreed to the reunification of Germany. Numerous Russian officials have cited this as indicative that the West cannot be trusted - for just a few years following these promises the United States was leading the cause of NATO expansion.[33]

Moving to the East for Russia as a response to the expansion of NATO implies moving towards China. Many policy makers and specialists on International Relations would dismiss the prospect of any partnership between Moscow and Beijing as a most unlikely outcome, but it would be wrong and dangerous to ignore such a possibility. At the least, it is instructive to note that senior Russian officials, including Yeltsin himself, Primakov, more energetically, Zyuganov, Vladimir Lukin (one of the leaders of Yabloko and head of the Duma International Affairs Committee), Sergei Rogov, Pavel Grachev (Defence Minister from 1992 to June 1996), and many more, have all called for some sort of alliance or partnership with China *as a direct response to NATO expansion*.[34] With the path to the West, as one Russian writer put it, being permanently blocked by NATO expansion, China offers comfort for both the Yeltsin administration

33   Gorbachev recalls in his memoirs the assurances that he was given on this issue, stating that he warned his 'American friends' that 'the policy of enlarging NATO will be considered in Russia as an attempt to isolate it. But it is impossible to isolate Russia. It would mean disregarding both history and reality'. See Mikail Gorbachev, *Memoirs* (London: Doubleday, 1996), p. 675.

34   In his report to the 4th CPRF Congress Zyuganov said the objective of NATO was to orchestrate a *cordon sanitaire* around Russia, hence it was necessary to develop diverse ties with China, India, and the Arab World. See *Sovietskaya Rossiya*, 22 April 1997.

and the political opposition. Yeltsin can employ China in any attempt to bargain with the United States, to remind the West that Russia has options if it is to be treated with suspicion and as an outsider, and for many members of the opposition, China's economic modernisation under Communist Party leadership is seen as a possible model for Russia.[35] China also offers a huge market for military equipment - indeed, China has become second to India as a purchaser of Russian arms (China has purchased two *Sovremenny* missile-carrying destroyers, four kilo-class attack submarines, S-300 anti-aircraft missiles, and has a contract for SU-27SK fighter aircraft).[36]

Meeting in Moscow in April 1997, Yeltsin and Chinese President Jiang Zemin signed a 'political declaration' - an 'unprecedented document' aimed at preventing any one country (i.e., the United States) from becoming dominant. The declaration stated bluntly that China and Russia are opposed to attempts at unipolarism, and that both states are intent on ensuring a new international order on the basis of 'multipolarity'. The two leaders referred to their new level of relations as representing a 'strategic partnership'.[37]

It would be inappropriate at present to exaggerate the significance of this term: in future years it is not inconceivable that a more nationalistic and confident China will clash with the United States on a range of issues such as trade, human rights, Taiwan, the Spratly Islands, or some other unforeseen issue. A more nationalistic Russia, as China's main arms supplier, could be drawn in to take sides. Unlike the Gulf War situation in 1990-1991, when Russia sided with the US against Iraq in the hope of joining the West, the subsequent marginalisation by the West could tempt a new post-Yeltsin leadership into identifying with a larger anti-Western alliance. If this all seems far-fetched, one should recall that any idea in the early 1980s of the collapse of communism, the demise of the Soviet Union, and the end of the Cold War, would have seemed just as unbelievable.

35   Andrei Grachev in *Moskovskiie novosti*, no. 31, 3-10 August 1997. He cites here former Defence Minister Pavel Grachev as saying, whilst still in office, 'If NATO goes East, we too will go East'.
36   Fred Weir, *Hindustan Times*, 10 September 1997 - from *Johnson's Russia List*, 10 September 1997.
37   *Interfax*, 23 April 1997.

Perceptions and Misperceptions

It is instructive to note that all senior Western officials, whilst arguing that NATO expansion is not meant as a threat to Russia, nevertheless acknowledge that many Russians perceive that it is, but that this interpretation in Moscow is based upon *misperceptions*.[38] Recognising this, yet proceeding with NATO expansion against the opposition of the entire political class in Russia, is perhaps to court danger given what we know about the role of misperceptions in international relations. For example, John G. Stoessinger's classic study on wars in the twentieth century concluded that 'the most important single precipitating factor in the outbreak of war is misperception'.[39] History has demonstrated time and again the role misperceptions can have on the conduct of international affairs.[40] It is not simply stated intentions of others, nor even an objective appraisal of capabilities, but complex psychological factors that come into play when individuals and groups make decisions in response to external factors. In discussions with a large number of Russian analysts, politicians, and military officials in 1996, Flora Lewis was struck by the fact that regarding their opposition to NATO expansion 'again and again, psychological factors [were] given pre-eminence'.[41] Russians recall the promises made by Bush and Secretary of State James Baker that NATO would not expand. Now they may well recall the words of another former U.S. Secretary of State, Dean Acheson, when giving testimony to the U.S. Congress on proposals to form NATO nearly fifty years ago: 'It is not aimed at any country; it is aimed solely at armed aggression'. Acheson claimed also that NATO was designed to advance 'international cooperation to maintain the peace, to advance human rights, to raise standards of living, and to promote the principle

---

38   This is reflected also in important official documents. For example, in a U.S. State Department *Report to the Congress on the Enlargement of the North Atlantic Treaty Organisation: Rationale, Benefits, Costs and Implications*, U.S. State Department, Washington D.C., 24 February 1997, it is stated that Russian opposition to NATO expansion is 'based upon a misperception that it will be detrimental to Russia's security and position in Europe'.

39   John G. Stoessinger, *Why Nations Go To War* (London: Macmillan, 4th edn., 1987).

40   Generally on this question see Robert Jervis, *Perception and Misperception in International Politics* (Princeton: Princeton University Press, 1976).

41   Flora Lewis, 'Why NATO - Not the United States - Frightens Russia', *Transition*, 23 February 1996, pp. 50 - 51.

of equal rights and self-determination of peoples'.[42] It should not be surprising that NATO expansion - now that the logic of its creation has gone with the end of the Soviet threat - should genuinely be seen as potentially threatening by many Russian officials. To say that this is based upon misunderstandings and misperceptions is both to acknowledge Russian fears but then also to pass them off as unimportant, expecting somehow that Russia will come to accept and cooperate with the new expanded NATO. This could turn out to be wishful thinking, as NATO expansion could result in a self-fulfilling prophecy for those who do see Russia as a potential threat: that is to say, it will become one as a direct result of moving the Alliance up to Russia's borders.

Aleksei Arbatov, Deputy Chairman of the Duma's Defence Committee, and widely considered one of the leading analysts of trends in Russian security and foreign policy, has argued that the Madrid summit in July has already 'revived some traditional misunderstandings and created new misperceptions between Russia and the West'.[43] If, as Clinton and others proclaim, Russia is not a threat, then why leave Russia on the periphery of the evolving post-Cold War security architecture, why dismiss Russia's opinions, and why only give Russia a junior role, a small but non-binding 'voice' in the issues of European security? Many Russian elites believe the answers to these questions are self-evident: the U.S. is using NATO expansion as a military and strategic encirclement of Russia whilst maintaining its own political hegemony in Europe, to isolate Russia from Central and Eastern Europe, to block Russia's foreign trade in high technology and arms, to undermine the Russian economy, to obstruct integration of the former Soviet republics, and even to foster the disintegration of the Russian Federation. In terms of perceptions, if, as Jervis has said, 'it is disastrous to mistake an enemy for a friend but not so costly to take a friend for an enemy, then decision-makers are well-advised to suffer the latter misperception rather than run a high risk of the former'.[44] Even if the United States and the West do have good intentions towards Russia, expanding NATO is likely to be increasingly (mis)perceived by Russians as an unfriendly act.

42   Quoted in Kissinger, *Diplomacy*, p. 459.
43   *New York Times*, 26 August 1997.
44   Jervis, *Perception and Misperception*, p. 424.

Expanding NATO and Expanding Democracy

The above analysis implies that NATO expansion runs a very real danger of undermining democracy in Russia - yet the arguments made by many proponents of expanding the Alliance are that this would be an instrument to *strengthen* the prospects of democracy in East/Central Europe. As with the realist logic for expansion, this neo-liberal argument is also deeply flawed. The theoretical basis for this argument is that democracies do not go to war against each other, hence policies designed to expand the zone of democracy should guide foreign policy behaviour. On the basis of statements made by Clinton, Albright, and Talbott, this idea would appear to be a central component motivating and guiding U.S. foreign and security policies, from the intervention in Haiti to the expansion of NATO. Tracing these ideas back to Kant, recent literature on this topic is vast, and need not concern us here in any detail.[45] However, it should be pointed out that there is a large number of conceptual and empirical problems with the democratic peace thesis. For example, those relating to definitions of democracy (often subjectively produced, linked to interests, with values changing over time - and democracy however defined able to be reversed), those relating to psychological factors (rather than norms and institutions moderating influences towards violent conflict, *individuals* and *groups* count - leaders matter, and in a crisis situation normal institutional constraints are weakened, so what is important is not what type of political system we have, but what personality type, what type of leader we have), and the empirical evidence itself is certainly not conclusive.[46] Even so, if we accept the democratic peace thesis as a

45 See, for example, Michael Doyle, 'Liberalism and World Politics', *American Political Science Review*, vol. 80, no. 4 (1986), pp. 1151-1169 (reprinted in *The New Shape of World Politics*, published by Foreign Affairs: New York, 1997, pp.39-66); Bruce Russett, *Grasping the Democratic Peace: Principles for a Post-Cold War World* (Princeton University Press, 1993). Talbott's own ideas on this subject can be found in Strobe Talbott, 'Democracy and the National Interest', *Foreign Affairs*, vol. 75, no. 6 (November/December 1996), pp. 47-63. For a critique of Talbott's arguments see John L. Harper, 'The Dream of Democratic Peace: Americans Are Not Asleep', *Foreign Affairs*, vol. 76, no. 3 (May/June), 1997, pp. 117-121.

46 For example see Raymond Cohen, 'Pacific Unions: A Reappraisal Of The Theory That 'Democracies Do Not Go To War With Each Other'', *Review of International Studies*, vol. 20, no. 3 (1994), pp. 207-224. For an assessment of how far Russia has come along the path to democracy see Peter Shearman,

principle motivating factor for the Clinton Administration's policy on NATO, then its application is clearly misguided or reflects a misunderstanding of the theory.

In her testimony to the US Senate Committee on Armed Services on April 23, 1997, Albright argued that the 'fundamental' goal of NATO expansion is 'to build, for the first time, a peaceful, democratic and undivided transatlantic community'. Yet in the same breath she stated that the 'fate of Russian democracy is certainly not at stake in NATO's decisions on enlargement'. As with Germany after 1918, so with Russia after the end of the Cold War (and the ensuing collapse of communism and demise of the Soviet/Russian empire), Russia must build democracy and an open society depending only, as Albright put it, 'upon the ability of its [own] leaders and people'.[47] One could reasonably ask why Poland, the Czech Republic, and Hungary are the only three states that are deserving of institutional assistance in their march towards democracy. The argument seems to be that they are already the furthest along this path - but then surely they would require the least assistance? But even this argument is unconvincing: the Baltic states could be said to be as far along the road to democracy as these three states. However, the real problem is that the democratic argument to expand NATO has no grounding in neo-liberal theory.

The idea that a military machine, a defensive alliance structured around war-waging objectives, should act as a key institution for facilitating and spreading democracy, is perverse. Although alliances, originally established to counter a common threat, may take on a life of their own and form part of what has been termed a 'security community' amongst its members, expanding alliances to incorporate new members in order to encourage democratic development has never before (in spite of political rhetoric to the contrary) been tried or even seriously contemplated. Nowhere in democratic political theory do military alliances figure. There are three basic schools of thought relating to democratic development, and not one of them suggests a military alliance could act as a vehicle for furthering the prospects of democracy.[48] From the ancient Greeks through to the present day,

'Russia and Democracy', *Russian and Euro-Asian Bulletin*, vol. 5, no. 11 (1996), pp. 1-9.

47 'Testimony to the U.S. Armed Services Committee', U.S. Information Agency, 23 April 1997.

48 See Robert D. Putnam, *Making Democracy Work* (Princeton University Press, 1993), pp. 9-11.

theorists of democracy have focused upon domestic institutions, socio-economic and political factors, political culture, and the role of elites. It is not 'war-making' machines that spread democracy. But even assuming that NATO is somehow different, and we are in 'new times', in expanding its membership to transitional states that have as their stated project the development of democracy, why not invite Slovenia, Romania, the Baltic states, Ukraine, and Russia itself to join?[49] The answer must be that democracy is not the real reason for expanding the alliance, and that, like Dean Acheson in earlier times, Secretary of State Albright in contemporary times feels it necessary to articulate U.S. policy in a neo-liberal, idealist framework, both to gain domestic support and not to upset the Russians.

What we do know about states in transition is that during the process of democratisation, democratising states are much more likely to become aggressive, militaristic, and war-prone, than even authoritarian states. Given what we also know about the power of misperceptions in the onset of conflict, then the expansion of NATO to include East/Central European states is almost certain to run the risk of reversing the remarkable progress - remarkable, given centuries of authoritarianism - that Russia has made along the path towards democracy since 1992. The group most likely to consider NATO expansion as a potential threat, and to structure its operating procedures, strategy, and procurement policies accordingly, is the Russian military. We have already noted the plight of the armed forces, but it also worth pointing out that most studies find that the military is the most conservative, least democratic of all institutions, whilst at the same time opinion polls show that it is also the one institution that Russians trust above all others.[50] In psychological

49   Many leading Russian officials have suggested the resolution of the problem is indeed to invite Russia to join the alliance as a full and equal member. Aleksei Arbatov has made this argument: see *RIA novosti*, 11 March 1997, and so too Boris Fyodorov (former Presidential candidate and a leading eye surgeon): see *Rossiiskiie vesti*, 26 March 1997.

50   On the weak democratic credentials of the military see Yuri Kirshin, 'Ensuring Military Security in A Democratic Society', *NATO Review*, vol. 45, no. 1 (January 1997), pp. 22-15. A recent nationwide poll was conducted in July 1997 where it was found that the armed forces topped the list of those institutions that Russians trusted. The question was simply 'Whom do you trust?' and the results were: The Armed Forces: 48%, the Orthodox Church: 44%, the Security Services: 29%, the Government: 12%, the President: 12%, and Members of Parliament: 11%. In this same poll only 5% of respondents

terms too, being effectively placed on the margins of the West, Russia's search for a national identity could well result in a non-Western, neo-Slavophile (and possibly non-democratic) form of belligerent Russian nationalism guiding future policy. Surveys of Russian opinion taken in the years since 1992 indicate that a 'Western democratic path' has decreased in popularity as a preferred model of development. Whereas in 1992 56% of respondents favoured this path for Russia, by 1995 this had decreased to 10%. In contrast those preferring a 'specific Russian' path of development had increased from 18% in 1992 to 52% by 1995, and those favouring a 'Soviet socialist path' had increased during this period from 16% to 21%.[51]

The institution that can perhaps best serve as an instrument to facilitate inclusion of the former communist states into a broader democratic 'security community' is the European Union. It is also perverse that a military alliance without a threat should seek to expand at a time when existing members are making cuts on defence expenditure, and new members are engaged in market transitions and surely cannot afford the burden of the increased expenditure that will be necessary to integrate their militaries into the alliance. Again the lessons of the post-1945 period are instructive. West Germany's integration into the European Community, a political and economic organisation, was a key factor in stimulating and facilitating democratic development. And the Marshall Plan, recognising that US security was tied to democracy in Western Europe, formulated an assistance package that was explicitly based upon the assumption that socio-economic factors were paramount for preventing Europe experiencing a return to hypernationalism, the spread of communism, and crises and conflict. In his Harvard address in June 1947, George G. Marshall argued that US assistance was required to fight 'hunger, poverty, desperation, and chaos', stating that the purpose of American aid 'should be the revival of a working economy ... so as to permit the emergence of political and social conditions in which free institutions

considered that NATO was 'friendly to Russia', only 5% considered the inclusion of Poland, Hungary, and the Czech Republic would 'improve' Russian security, only 9% agreed that the Russian defence budget should be cut, and 64% agreed that Russia would be under military threat until the end of the century. For details see *The Economist*, 2 August 1997.

51   *Rossiiskiie vesti*, 15 April 1997.

can exist'.[52] Central to the plan was integrating the vanquished power, Germany, into the Western community of nations. If the Marshall Plan is to be completed following the end of the Cold War it is not by expanding a military alliance, but by helping, as far it is possible, to ensure that the requisite political and social conditions exist in which free institutions can flourish right across Europe, and not just selected parts. The most important part, given its size, its history, its geography, natural resources, and its nuclear weapons, is the Russian Federation.

Conclusion

Membership of NATO is likely to have little if any impact on democratic development in those states that have been invited to join, but could have a negative impact on the prospects for democracy for those that are left out, especially in the Russian Federation. Nothing in the theory and past practices of alliances and nothing in democratic political theory would suggest that military organisations are in any way useful vehicles for fostering domestic democratic development. On the contrary, the relevant literature demonstrates the important role of perceptions and misperceptions in international relations relating to the formation of military alliances, and how these can pose dangers for domestic politics in the form of stimulating hypernationalism. NATO expansion could ultimately threaten democracy in Russia.

With regard to security, deterrence and maintaining a balance of threats - the primary goals of alliances - it has been shown that expanding NATO in the absence of a real and present threat could ultimately serve as a self-fulfilling prophecy. Leaving a crisis-ridden Russia on the margins of Europe could easily play into the hands of anti-Western forces, which with the old geopolitical thinking taking hold in Moscow could culminate in a new Cold War between Russia and the West. According to this scenario, other potential anti-Western forces such as China as well as Iran, Iraq and India could, depending upon the nature of any future international crisis, tacitly ally with Moscow. Existing security agreements like START and CFE could be put in jeopardy while other increasingly more salient aspects of security encompassing environmental issues, nuclear proliferation,

52 George G. Marshall's Harvard Address of June 1947: 'Against Hunger, Poverty, Desperation and Chaos', reprinted in *Foreign Affairs*, vol. 76, no. 3 (May/June 1997), pp. 160-161.

drug trafficking and terrorism might be left in a state of limbo. It is not a military bloc from Vancouver to Warsaw that is required, but a proper inclusive security community from Vancouver to Vladivostok. The Marshall Plan fifty years ago recognised that there was a 'social bomb' waiting to go off in Europe, as both victors and vanquished were left cold and hungry and on the verge of socio-economic crisis. In Russia today, there is a similar 'social bomb' waiting to explode, and it is not the expansion of a Cold War Alliance that is needed, one that effectively excludes Russia whilst offering what is perceived as a sop in the form of the Founding Act, but some far-sighted thinking to prevent the bomb from detonating. Any inclusion of the Baltic states in a second round of NATO expansion will clearly be unacceptable to Russia, and this could be the catalyst to transform Russia back into an aggressor and antagonist of the West. Alliances, as they mature, develop other functions than those relating strictly to military affairs - for example, they provide networks for elite communications, enable access to other policy makers, and can provide a forum for discussing other issues of mutual concern. They can facilitate a sense of belonging, a sense of group identity, and provide for a dialogue of cooperation. However, those left outside the alliance, outside the group, will, especially in the event of disagreements over specific issues, feel isolated and different, fostering a sense of the 'other'. The Russia-NATO Founding Act could, in the event of serious disagreements, simply turn into a forum for a dialogue of confrontation. Outdated realist notions concerning balances of power should not determine the shape of international security policies into the next millennium. If democracy is a chief objective, then it is necessary to engage Russia in an equal dialogue, a more inclusive cooperative framework in which positive networks are created which could both stimulate democratic development in Russia and enhance European security. Selective expansion of NATO is not creating an inclusive security community, but rather, by definition, establishing new divisions in Europe, a new system of insiders and outsiders - no matter how many 'partnerships' and 'acts' might be founded. This chapter has examined some of the potential problems relating to Russia of NATO expansion (there are many others that do not relate directly to Russia). The decision to expand NATO was taken without any serious debate on this subject. Before any decisions are made about the future of NATO beyond its fiftieth birthday in 1999 more serious consideration of these issues will need to be conducted.

Chapter 11

Defence by Other Means:
Australia's Arms Control and Disarmament Diplomacy

Ramesh Thakur

Australia's national security is more centrally dependent on the actions of, and relations between, other powers than on its own military preparedness. During the Cold War, the determining axis ran from Washington to Moscow. After the Cold War, it is the China-Japan-US triangle that fundamentally impacts on Australia's security. Australia spends around A \$10 billion each year on its military. What can Australia, a self-conscious middle power, do to enhance its security through arms control and disarmament diplomacy - defence by other means?

In this chapter, I shall:

1. Outline the historical, political and bureaucratic contexts of Australia's arms control diplomacy;
2. Examine the disarmament agenda with respect to weapons of mass destruction (WMD), namely nuclear, biological and chemical weapons;
3. Discuss the arms control agenda for conventional weapons;
4. Describe the Track Two Seminar held in Jakarta in 1996; and
5. Look at Australia's disarmament credentials.[1]

---

1 This is a revised and updated version of Ramesh Thakur, 'Arms Control', in F. A. Mediansky, ed., *Australian Foreign Policy: Into the Next Millennium* (Sydney: Macmillan, 1997).

Historical Background

Trevor Findlay has noted that interest in arms control and disarmament by Australian governments is of relatively recent origin.[2] Unlike most colonies which became independent on one date, Australia's process of independence was evolutionary. Control over foreign and defence policies was acquired gradually. Interest in the problematique of international security followed the progressive assertion and exercise of independence in world affairs and the pursuit of national security by national means and through alliances. Another reason for Australia's historical detachment from disarmament causes is that until the Second World War, international relations were centred mainly on Europe. After the war, Australia's main priority was securing, and then preserving, a military alliance with the United States as the centrepiece of national security. Until the 1970s, Australia was content to be a passive spectator in efforts to control the number, spread and use of arms either globally or in other regions.

At the end of the 20th century, however, Australia's train of interests are far-flung and diverse. The historical origins and cultural roots of most of its people lie in Europe, its primary strategic alliance is with the United States, its primary security focus is on Southeast Asia, and its major trading partners are in Northeast Asia. Consequently, Australia today has a general, and sometimes more specific, interest in preserving international and regional order in many parts of the world. The gathering winds of globalisation mean as well that Australia has been influenced by peace movements and anti-war debates elsewhere. The peace movement acquired strength in particular with the passions unleashed by the Vietnam War in the late 1960s and early 1970s, and then again with the second Cold War in the following decade.

Since the 1970s, therefore, Australian foreign policy has had to reconcile competing demands and interests from an active, vocal and determined peace constituency with a deep-seated belief in 'peace through arms control and disarmament', on the one hand, and the 'peace through arms' bureaucratic and political constituency on the other. Liberal-National Coalition Governments have generally been more sympathetic to the latter. During the Hawke and Keating

2   Trevor Findlay, 'Disarmament and Arms Control', in F. A. Mediansky, ed., *Australia in a Changing World: New Foreign Policy Directions* (Sydney: Maxwell Macmillan, 1992), pp. 162-78.

Governments (1983-96), the left and centre-left factions of the Labor Party favoured the opposite argument, as do the Democrats and the Greens; but the right factions of Labor were relatively more mindful of 'realpolitik' and alliance calculations. In most cases, but not always, the competing policy determinants are sufficiently reconciled to produce a coherent policy.

Foreign policy under Labor was directed by two people with a personal commitment to the disarmament agenda, Bill Hayden and Gareth Evans. The establishment of the Peace Research Centre at the Australian National University by Hayden in 1984 was one indicator of the new government's commitment to a broader security agenda; the emphasis on cooperative security by Evans was a significant departure after the end of the Cold War from the realist pursuit of security *against* potential adversaries in favour of seeking security *with* others.[3] Both ministers achieved a surprisingly high profile in regional and global security diplomacy and contributed to the perception that, to use a peculiarly ill-fitting metaphor, Australia punches above its weight. The South Pacific Nuclear Free Zone (SPNFZ, 1985) was yet another initiative of the Hawke Government, as was the National Consultative Committee on Peace and Disarmament. The NCCPD, which meets once a year in Canberra, brings together representatives of peace groups and other bodies, including the Returned Services League (RSL).[4] It is addressed by the Minister for Foreign Affairs and briefed comprehensively over a full day by various officials from the Department of Foreign Affairs and Trade as well as defence officers and officials. The 23-member committee provides a vehicle for the exchange of views and information on peace and disarmament issues between the government and the wider community.

Australia's bureaucratic capacity for addressing arms control and disarmament issues was greatly strengthened in the 1990s. The Hawke Government was instrumental in the appointment of a full-time Ambassador for Disarmament. Arms control and disarmament is handled by several branches in the International Security Division of the Department of Foreign Affairs and Trade (DFAT). The Peace, Arms Control and Disarmament Branch, comprising 12 officials, includes a chemical and biological disarmament section and a conventional and nuclear disarmament section. The Nuclear Policy

3   Gareth Evans, *Cooperating for Peace: The Global Agenda for the 1990s and Beyond* (Sydney: Allen & Unwin, 1993).
4   I have been a member of the NCCPD since 1995.

Branch has two sections dealing with nuclear safeguards and non-proliferation. Their work is generally complemented with support from the appropriate regional branches and divisions, as well as the United Nations section. Australia's delegation to the Conference on Disarmament (CD) comprises four officials and its work is backed up by chemical weapons and seismic monitoring advisers. Australia's ambassador to Vienna is cross-accredited to the International Atomic Energy Agency (IAEA). Finally, the Australian mission to the UN plays a full and active part in arms control and disarmament deliberations in the UN system.

The opportunities and incentives for progress on arms control have expanded in the 1990s, for positive and negative reasons. In the first category are the bilateral agreements between Russia and the United States and the increased cooperation between the major powers in addressing the threat of proliferation. The negative impetus has come from the appreciation of how close to the edge of Weapons of Mass Destruction (WMD) proliferation the world came with Iraq, and from the fear of the leakage of skills and material from the former Soviet Union.

Australia is a member of a number of key international bodies for controlling proliferation and negotiating arms control and disarmament: the IAEA, the Nuclear Suppliers Group (NSG), the CD and the Coordinating Committee for Multilateral Export Controls (COCOM). It is a participant in the negotiations for a convention on the safety of radioactive waste management which began in July 1995 under the auspices of the IAEA.

Prime Ministers Bob Hawke and Paul Keating guided Australia through a fundamental and long-term reorientation to Asia-Pacific. Efforts to pursue policies of arms control and disarmament simultaneously with a policy of engagement with Asia-Pacific were affected by the regional consequences of the end of the Cold War. Asia-Pacific is one of the few regions in the world where military spending is still rising.[5] Many Asian-Pacific countries are characterised by socio-economic fragility and regime brittleness, and some by enduring insurgencies. The kaleidoscope of cultures, cleavages and conflicts in Asia-Pacific does not permit a simple

5   See Desmond Ball, 'Arms and Affluence: Military Acquisitions in the Asia-Pacific Region', *International Security* 18:3 (Winter 1993-94), pp. 78-112; and Gerald Segal, 'Managing New Arms Races in the Asia-Pacific', *Washington Quarterly* 15:3 (Summer 1992), pp. 83-101.

intercontinental transposition of the Euro-Atlantic security architecture. To the extent that Asia-Pacific is Australia's main security preoccupation, therefore, regional engagement for Australia - reaffirmed by the Coalition Government as its highest foreign policy priority - must include arms control diplomacy.

The bureaucratic and political commitment, and the quality of political leadership, especially that of the Prime Minister and Foreign Minister, have been important explanations for Australia's disarmament profile being higher than would be warranted by its size and resources. Nevertheless, the latter weaknesses, compounded by geographical and strategic isolation, are permanent constraints on Australian influence. Membership of the Western alliance is both an asset and a constraint. It is an asset to the extent that Australia gains access to the most influential US policymakers and is able to communicate to them its own views and be an interlocutor between the US and other governments. It is a liability to the extent that Australia's public pronouncements must always be tempered by alliance-induced caution. Asian diplomats, for example, argue that Australia's disarmament diplomacy is characterised by preemptive appeasement of US concerns. Critics within the country and in the region made the same charge against SPNFZ, that it was carefully crafted by Australia in order to avoid antagonising Washington on a single sensitive item.

Nuclear Weapons

The nuclear arms control agenda has two interlinked components: disarmament and non-proliferation. Five different categories of proliferation-sensitive actors can be identified. First are the irresponsible nuclear-weapons states (NWS) themselves. The existence of weapons-proliferating NWS within the Non-Proliferation Treaty (NPT) undermined the non-proliferation norm and seemingly institutionalised international nuclear 'apartheid'.[6] The second category of concern is NPT splinters, or fragmenting NWS. When the old Soviet Union broke up, suddenly we faced the prospect of an additional three NWS (Ukraine, Belarus and Kazakhstan). Fortunately, all three were amenable to persuasion and renounced their

6   The use of the word 'apartheid' by critics of the NPT is unfortunate. The emotive word entails entirely negative connotations. But in fact apartheid referred to a system where a minority imposed its order on a majority by coercion. The NPT has been signed by the majority of the world's countries exercising their free choice.

nuclear-weapons status by destroying or transferring their nuclear weapons to Russia. Third are the NPT cheats, those who, like Iraq and North Korea, have signed the treaty but are engaged in clandestine programmes in violation of its obligations. The fourth category of proliferation-sensitive countries is the threshold NWS (Israel, India, Pakistan) who do not claim possession of nuclear weapons; have not forsworn the nuclear-weapons option; produce significant amounts of their own nuclear material and equipment; and refuse to accept international control over their material and equipment. The final worry is about the acquisition of nuclear weapons, skills and delivery systems by terrorist groups.

The NPT, the centrepiece of the global non-proliferation regime, has the widest membership of any arms control agreement in history. The past decade has seen astonishing progress in nuclear disarmament. The INF (intermediate-range nuclear forces, 1987) and START (strategic arms reduction, 1991, 1993) treaties eliminated intermediate and short-range nuclear missiles from Europe and have greatly reduced the number of long-range strategic weapons. Nuclear weapons were eliminated from battlefield stockpiles and surface ships in 1991. Nuclear testing was ended in 1996. The world has also made progress in putting in place other planks of the disarmament structure, especially with the addition of the Chemical Weapons Convention (CWC), developments in the control of conventional arms and other measures, and regional nuclear-weapons-free zones (NWFZs).

Even so, the US continues to deploy over 8000 nuclear weapons, Russia over 11,000. The two erstwhile Cold War enemies have reduced nuclear delivery vehicles, but have not yet agreed to dismantle nuclear warheads. France, China, Britain, Israel, India and Pakistan too have active nuclear-weapons programmes.

Australia was initially interested in keeping open all nuclear options, including the acquisition of weapons, civilian nuclear energy and peaceful nuclear explosions. The NPT was signed by Australia two years after its negotiation, and ratified by the Whitlam Government in 1973. Bill Hayden revealed in his autobiography that the nuclear-weapons option was canvassed as late as 1983-84.[7] This account has been confirmed by other members of the Hawke Government at the time. Worried about the acquisition of nuclear-weapons capability by Indonesia or other regional countries, the

---

7   Bill Hayden, *Hayden: An Autobiography* (Pymble, NSW: Angus & Robertson, 1996), pp. 422-23.

defence establishment canvassed the option of maintaining a latent Australian capability to produce nuclear weapons within six months.[8]

The public record shows the NPT to be the core element in Australia's non-proliferation policy. Australia has been active in the five-yearly NPT review conferences. Canberra has invested much diplomatic effort in bilateral and multilateral lobbying to widen adherence to the NPT by an increasing number of states. DFAT also supported second-track activities, for example a series of workshops organised by the Peace Research Centre in conjunction with a counterpart institute in Canada just before the preparatory committee meetings leading up to the 1995 NPT conference.

The NPT was indefinitely extended after being reviewed at a major conference in New York in April-May 1995. The Western countries were in favour of indefinite and unconditional extension. Some governments and many non-government organisations (NGOs) wanted to extend it for a limited period and make further renewal conditional on NWS disarmament. Many Australians supported this stance because the NPT is discriminatory and unfair.[9] The alternative view is that the 1995 conference gave a window of opportunity to make the admittedly imperfect NPT permanent.[10] The indefinite extension locked in the security benefits of the non-proliferation regime in perpetuity, removed the uncertainty and risk in long-term planning for national security, and created a stable strategic environment for further reductions of weapons. Australia, among the most active proponents of indefinite extension, hailed the outcome as a major security and foreign policy triumph. Gareth Evans argued that a failure to extend the NPT, or its conditional extension, would have had three deleterious consequences. It would have undermined the normative effect of the treaty, lessened the likelihood of the NPT rejectionists looking some day for security in the renunciation of nuclear weapons, and delayed the eventual elimination of nuclear weapons by the NWS, since only strong assurances against

8   Mike Steketee, 'Hawke advisers drew N-arms plan', *Weekend Australian,* 6-7 April 1996.
9   See Senator Dee Margetts, 'Limit Nuclear Treaty Extensions', *Pacific Research* 8:2 (May 1995), pp. 14-15.
10 See Ramesh Thakur, 'It might not be perfect, but so far it's the best we've got', *Australian Financial Review,* 12 April 1995.

proliferation can provide the security environment most conducive to this goal.[11]

Safeguards and Export Controls

From the dawn of the nuclear age, the world faced the difficulty of distinguishing the application of nuclear energy to peaceful purposes (for example propulsion, electricity production, and civil engineering and mining) from its potential for military use. Safeguards, comprising technical measures such as inspections and nuclear accounting, are of fundamental importance in non-proliferation regimes. The NPT requires non-NWS to declare the quantities, composition and location of all nuclear materials to the IAEA, which is the fulcrum of the international safeguards system.

Australia played a part in the establishment of the IAEA. In turn, partly because of its uranium export potential and partly as the most industrialised state in Asia-Pacific, Australia gained a permanent seat on the IAEA Board of Governors at its inception in 1957. As part of its support for the NPT regime, Australia has campaigned vigorously for the IAEA safeguards system including the application of fullscope safeguards to any transfer of nuclear material. The IAEA has an annual budget of A $90 million. This meagre amount is not sufficient for the global mandate for research and development in safeguards technology, and has to be supplemented by national efforts. The Australian Safeguards Office, set up in Canberra in 1974 after Australia's ratification of the NPT, is a vital component in the global chain. It contributes to the development of safeguards approaches and methods. (The CWC Office has been co-located with the Safeguards Office.)

Export restraints regimes are the technical means of preventing dissemination of proliferation-sensitive materials. They add to the technical difficulty, raise the costs of the nuclear-weapons option, compel proliferators to take a more circuitous path, and introduce a longer lead-time and so buy time for offending governments to change their mind and the international community to organise a suitable riposte. The Nuclear Exporters Committee, formed in 1971, agreed in 1974 on a 'trigger list' of equipment or material which would activate

---

11   'Statement by Senator Evans on 18 April 1995 to the 1995 Review and Extension Conference of States Parties to the Treaty on Non-Proliferation of Nuclear Weapons', *Peace and Disarmament News* (September 1995), pp. 10-14.

IAEA safeguards if exported to non-nuclear countries not party to the NPT. The Nuclear Suppliers Group, set up in London in 1975 to bring France into the export controls regime (but also including Argentina and New Zealand), promulgated guidelines in 1977 which sought to deny access to potential proliferators of material, facilities and dual-use technology; and to ban the export of reprocessing and enrichment technology.

The spread of long-range missile technology has been a focus of Western concern for some years. Missiles are an acutely destabilising form of weaponry because little defence is available against them. Armed with chemical or nuclear warheads, they are lethal means of mass destruction and military intimidation. While some problem states can produce missile components domestically, most require critical high-technology components from the developed countries. The G7 industrialised countries established the Missile Technology Control Regime (MTCR) in April 1987 in order to stem the tide of missile proliferation. Other states have also become involved, including Australia in 1990. While the rules were designed in 1987 to control the spread of missiles capable of delivering nuclear weapons, they were amended in 1992 to cover biological and chemical weapons. This was consistent with Australia's concern from the beginning about the proliferation of missile technology regardless of the type of warhead.

Nuclear Testing

Altogether there have been about 2000 nuclear tests conducted in the world since 1945. Australia's original ambivalence about nuclear testing arose from the inconsistencies between a global disarmament posture and the requirement to support the strategies of its allies. The Australian Government welcomed British nuclear tests on Australian territory in the 1950s. Of the five NWS, China and France were the NPT holdouts until the 1990s. They were also the two testing recalcitrants. France tested nuclear systems in French Polynesia - a dramatic example of the seizure of the global commons - until January 1996.[12] China conducted its last test on 29 July 1996. Talks on the Comprehensive Test Ban Treaty (CTBT) resumed later the same day in Geneva.

12   See Ramesh Thakur, 'The Last bang before a total ban: French nuclear testing in the Pacific', *International Journal* 51:3 (Summer 1996), pp. 466-86.

The depth, breadth and resilience of the opposition to French nuclear testing in 1995 caught the Australian government off guard. The global re-mobilisation of anti-nuclear feelings brought home the realisation that many people had simply assumed that the nuclear arms race too had become a casualty of the end of the Cold War. Australia was perceived as a reluctant follower of public protests and as having been upstaged by the more robust reaction of the New Zealand Government. Evans' initial reaction - 'it could have been worse' - although intellectually defensible, fuelled public anger. His measured assessment gave priority to broader arms control objectives. Evans was conscious that strident opposition to the testing decision would be interpreted as attacks on the credibility of France's presence in the Pacific; on the credibility and authority of a newly-elected president who would be in office for at least another seven years; and on the credibility of France's national security policy based on the independent deterrent. On a wide range of international trade, economic, environment and security issues in which Australian interests are engaged, Paris exercises considerable influence. Moreover, France had made three important concessions. Testing would cease after the new series, France would sign a CTBT, and no new weapons systems would be developed.

In addition to such bilateral manoeuvres as recall of ambassadors, Canberra tried to build regional and global coalitions. The campaign culminated on 12 December 1995 with the adoption of a resolution by the UN General Assembly (UNGA) deploring nuclear testing and calling for its immediate halt. Australia also supported the unsuccessful New Zealand challenge in the World Court seeking to revive the 1974 case against French testing.

Ironically, the political fallout from the French testing accelerated the international drive towards the CTBT. There was an upward trajectory of support mobilised by Australia and New Zealand since the mid-1980s for their annual UNGA resolution on the CTBT. Between 1991 and 1993 Moscow, Paris, Washington and London imposed and extended voluntary moratoria on nuclear testing. In December 1995, UNGA50 adopted a resolution calling for the conclusion of a CTBT in 1996 in time for signature by UNGA51.

Australia played a critical role in the CTBT negotiations at the CD in Geneva. Consensus was formed around the March 1995 Australian definition of the scope of the treaty, prohibiting 'any nuclear weapons test explosion or any other nuclear explosion'. On 29 February 1996,

Australia presented a detailed 'model' text of the treaty, which formed an important part of the final draft produced by the chair of the negotiating team, Jaap Ramaker of the Netherlands. Australia also presented a large number of working papers and drafting proposals. On balance, the draft treaty met Australia's basic requirements, although Australia would have preferred a different formula.

On 20 August, India vetoed the adoption of the CTBT by the CD in Geneva because it was allegedly discriminatory in permitting the modernisation of nuclear stockpiles through computer simulations and laboratory experiments; it failed to link the end to testing to a nuclear disarmament timeframe; and it would degrade India's national security. All three arguments are specious, but underpinned by an overwhelming national consensus in India.[13] Because the treaty required the signature of all 44 countries that have nuclear research reactors, including India, to become operational, India also vetoed its transmission to the UN.

Many countries were not prepared to let nearly three years of intensive negotiations be frustrated by one country. Australia took the lead in sidestepping India's veto by forwarding it directly to the UN General Assembly. Canberra argued that the world could not afford to miss, because of one recalcitrant, the unique opportunity to end nuclear testing definitively. Disarmament ideals have to be tempered by what is achievable and practical. The treaty's commitments and compromises reflect the best attainable balance of different countries' interests. It will stop testing, end the arms race, prevent proliferation and mark a milestone on the road to disarmament. Failure to close on this treaty in 1996 would have meant the loss of a CTBT for the foreseeable future. The Australian procedural tactic could be criticised on grounds of principle, logic and politics.[14] Nevertheless, the CTBT was approved by the UN General Assembly on 10 September 1996 by a vote of 158-3.

Australia has also been prepared to provide technical expertise. The CTBT includes an effective verification regime based on four detection technologies: seismic, hydroacoustic, infrasound and radio

13   See Ramesh Thakur, 'India's Intransigence on a Test Ban Is Dangerous', *Asian Wall Street Journal,* 27 June 1996, and 'India in the World: Neither Rich, Powerful, nor Principled', *Foreign Affairs* 76:4 (July/August 1997), pp. 15-22.
14   Ramesh Thakur, 'Get Test Ban Treaty Operational and Let India Join Later', *International Herald Tribune,* 9 September 1996.

nuclides. Australia made a significant contribution through provision of technical experts to the development of a global network of monitoring stations. It has played a major role in the Group of Scientific Experts established by the CD to examine the feasibility of seismic verification of a CTBT. The Australian Seismological Centre was set up in Canberra to engage in test detection and eventually to form one of the four International Data Centres to be set up as part of the CTBT verification regime.

Nuclear-Weapons-Free Zones

Nuclear-weapons-free zones (NWFZs) are regional confidence-building measures undertaken by non-NWS which fear being ensnared in outsiders' nuclear webs. In the 1970s, the New Zealand Labour Government's proposal for the establishment of a NWFZ in the South Pacific did not find favour with the Whitlam Government in Canberra. In 1983, the Hawke Government revived the idea and obtained the support of the South Pacific Forum meeting in 1984. An Australian official chaired the working group which drafted the treaty adopted at the Forum meeting in Rarotonga on 6 August 1985. Its core obligations are not to manufacture or otherwise acquire, possess or have control over any nuclear device; not to assist or encourage others to make or acquire nuclear weapons; to prevent the stationing or testing of nuclear weapons on its territory; and not to dump radioactive wastes at sea anywhere in the zone, and to prevent such dumping by others in its territorial sea.[15] Tonga became the last regional country to sign SPNFZ on 7 May 1996. The NWS were integrated into SPNFZ by means of three protocols. While China and the Soviet Union endorsed them in the 1980s, Britain, France and the United States did not sign the protocols until March 1996, after the cessation of French testing.

Peace activists were not impressed with SPNFZ, for it failed to address any of the items of concern to them: uranium mining, port visits by nuclear-propelled and nuclear-armed ships, transit through the zone by such ships, missile tests, and the firing of nuclear weapons from within the zone. The Australian Government's response was that SPNFZ represented the largest circle of consensus that was achievable in the region. SPNFZ was a worthwhile achievement from

---

15   See Ramesh Thakur, 'The Treaty of Rarotonga: The South Pacific Nuclear-Free Zone', in D. Pitt and G. Thompson, eds, *Nuclear-Free Zones* (London: Croom Helm, 1987), pp. 23-45.

a number of angles. It put an extra element of pressure on French nuclear testing in the Pacific, consolidated the non-proliferation norm in the region and offered an example to other regions of the world for disengaging from the nuclear madness. It was also a testament to successful regional non-proliferation diplomacy by Australia .

The Elimination of Nuclear Weapons

The Canberra Commission on the Elimination of Nuclear Weapons, set up by the Keating Government in November 1995, submitted its report to the Howard Government on 14 August 1996.[16] Its analysis of the nuclear cross-roads is lucid, the logic of its recommendations compelling. Its report is especially effective in rebutting the case for nuclear weapons. Nuclear weapons cannot be kept indefinitely yet never be used. They have no military utility against other NWS. The political cost of using them against non-NWS is so great that humiliating military setbacks have been accepted instead. Their possession by some is a constant stimulus to proliferation by others. They could be used by terrorists. The recommended steps to a nuclear-free world are taking nuclear forces off alert; removing warheads from delivery vehicles; ending the deployment of non-strategic nuclear weapons; ending nuclear testing; negotiating further reductions in US and Russian nuclear arsenals; and reciprocal no-first-use agreements. These must be reinforced by a ban on weapons-grade fissile material and verification arrangements.

The authority of the Canberra Commission was three-pronged. The commissioners were internationally eminent people, a solid mix of generals, cabinet ministers, ambassadors, scientists and a Nobel Peace prize winner. The report was the product of a government initiative, not just a think-tank enterprise. And the Commission recruited an impressive body of analysts from around the world to write background papers for the project.

Yet the authority of the Commission was diminished by flawed composition. Only one of 17 commissioners was a woman. Considering the prominence of women in the peace movements around the world, this was unfortunate. It had an industrial country bias, with only five being from developing countries. Most crucially, eight - almost half the total - came from the five NWS; not one from the three

16   *Report of the Canberra Commission on the Elimination of Nuclear Weapons* (Canberra: Department of Foreign Affairs and Trade, 1996).

threshold NWS. As a result, the report did not get the balance right between proliferation and disarmament, between the sensitivities of the NWS and the concerns of the threshold NWS. Determined to be realistic, the Commission eschewed exhortative and aspirational sentiments. Yet for its report to have any chance of implementation, the anti-nuclear rage will have to be maintained through arguments, political representations and public mobilisation. For this the advisory opinion delivered by the World Court on 8 July 1996 may prove more important.

The Court found, by a split opinion, that nuclear weapons are generally contrary to international humanitarian law. The Canberra Commission's call for the NWS' commitment to complete elimination is less forceful than the World Court's unanimous opinion that they have 'an obligation to pursue in good faith *and bring to a conclusion* negotiations leading to nuclear disarmament in all its aspects under strict and effective international control'.[17] The long-term effect of the opinion will be to strengthen the normative structure of restraints on the possession, threat or use of nuclear weapons. In time, legal principle will prevail over state practice.

Australia was among the 22 countries to make oral submissions to the World Court in 1995. The Australian delegation was led by Foreign Minister Evans, himself a lawyer. Procedurally, Evans argued that the Court should decline to give an opinion, because the issue under consideration was fundamentally a political and security concern, not a legal matter. Australia was also concerned that the consequences would be deleterious regardless of which side the Court came down on. If the Court ruled that nuclear weapons were illegal, and the NWS simply ignored the opinion, then the authority of the Court and the majesty of international law would be undermined. Alternatively, if the Court opined that nuclear weapons were legal under some circumstances, then the cause of nuclear disarmament and non-proliferation would be set back. If, however, the Court did decide to take up the substance of the case, then Evans urged it to find that nuclear weapons are illegal under international law. However, even then Australia urged the Court to recognise the need for transitional arrangements to give time to the NWS to fulfil their legal obligation to

---

17   International Court of Justice, 'Legality of the Threat or Use of Nuclear Weapons: Advisory Opinion', *Communiqué* 96/23 (8 July 1996), p. 2; emphasis added.

negotiate disarmament and to ensure the maintenance of stable deterrence.

Chemical and Biological Weapons

Australia has been less reticent on other WMD. Compared to conventional weapons, biological weapons are quite cheap; yet their lethal effect is comparable to nuclear weapons. The Biological Weapons Convention (BWC), concluded in 1972 and in force since 1975, was the first to ban an entire class of weapons. It prohibits the development, production, stockpiling, acquisition and retention of toxic and biological weapons; and provides for cooperation in the peaceful uses of biological agents and toxins. The verification weaknesses of the BWC reflect the scientific state of the world in 1972. Because of these weaknesses, the BWC has not prevented the proliferation of biological weapons. Australia has been an active participant in the multilateral efforts to strengthen the convention, including export controls.

Chemical agents have been used as weapons of war on a number of occasions during this century. The use of about 100 million kg of chemicals killed around 100 000 people in the First World War and injured another million. Millions of Jews were gassed to death by Hitler. Iraq used chemical weapons against Iran, and also against its own Kurdish population, as recently as the 1980s. On 20 March 1995 a secretive Japanese religious sect, without access to large scientific resources, carried out a terrorist attack on the Tokyo subway using the nerve gas sarin that killed ten people, injured thousands and terrified millions.

The CWC (1993) is notable for the comprehensiveness of its provisions and its ground-breaking verification and inspection regime. It covers the development, production and stockpiling of chemical weapons, and their destruction within ten years. In force since 29 April 1997, the CWC will make an important contribution to best international practice in arms control because of its scope and also in the area of verification. This is important because the compliance and verification measures need to be more rigorous for chemical than for nuclear weapons. Russia and the United States can keep track of each other's nuclear-weapons programmes through satellite technology and high-altitude reconnaissance planes. Such techniques are less useful in detecting nerve gas plants, which cannot be distinguished easily from plants making weedkillers and ink for ballpoint pens. The CWC verification and monitoring regime calls for visits to chemical works by trained inspectors.

Australia was involved in the UN investigation of the use of chemical weapons in the Iran-Iraq war (1980-88). Australian diplomats and scientists were involved in the verification and destruction of Iraq's chemical weapons capability after the Gulf War. Australia was an active participant in the negotiations in the CD that produced the CWC. The Australian Government hosted a series of seminars and workshops to raise the awareness of regional countries about the complex issues involved in finalising the CWC and in implementing it thereafter. The goal was to develop a consensus in Asia-Pacific about the value of the CWC and facilitate the speedy and wide regional adherence to it.

Since 1985 the Australia Group, an informal arrangement between the European Commission and 29 countries, has sought to define lists of problem substances and technologies, exchange intelligence on problem countries and coordinate export controls. The Australia Group meets biannually at the Australian Embassy in Paris with no set rules of procedure. It is inherently difficult to establish the effectiveness of the Group in preventing the proliferation of chemical weapons. At the very least it helped to delay the acquisition of chemical-weapons capability by forcing problem countries into alternative, less efficient and more costly supply and delivery routes. The Australia Group has also helped to raise industry awareness about the risks associated with chemical agents.

Conventional Weapons

Because of the gravity of the threat posed by WMD, the attention of most people and governments tends to focus on them. In reality, however, the overwhelming bulk of the world's military expenditure and manpower is devoted to conventional arms and forces. The nuclear threat is grave, but also distant and abstract. The threat from light arms is concrete and seemingly ubiquitous.

In conventional disarmament diplomacy, Australia faces the same contradiction that bedevils the major powers, albeit on a lesser scale. On the one hand, the latter preach to all developing countries to eschew the use of force as a means of settling international disputes. On the other hand, they wish to retain their military advantage. Their arms manufacturers meanwhile sell as many weapons platforms and weapons to as many countries as they can. Hence the absurdity of the five permanent members of the UN Security Council being the six biggest arms traffickers. (The sixth is Germany, which wants to become a permanent member.)

Australia is prepared to advocate bold and far-reaching measures which do not impose any alliance and economic costs. It is represented on the UN Expert Group on Conventional Arms Transfers which has been examining the transparency of conventional arms transfers. Australia is a strong supporter of the principle of transparency in armaments and openness in dealing with arms transfers. It already declares its military expenditure to the UN and is ready to provide information to the UN Conventional Arms Register set up by the General Assembly in 1991.

Where there are economic costs to domestic sector groups, Australia's arms control policy becomes ambivalent, for example with respect to the mining and export of uranium. A similar inconsistency is evident with respect to the export of conventional weaponry. Australia favours a policy of defence self-reliance. To be credible, this requires the development and maintenance of an indigenous defence industrial base. Given Australia's market size, a national defence industrial base can be viable only through economies of scale achieved by exporting Australian defence wares.

The Labor Government substituted the visionary idealism of nuclear disarmament diplomacy with a pragmatic and minimalist view of conventional arms control. The threat of WMD has been constrained by a network of legislative, normative and supplier-groups restraints. By contrast, the risks of conventional arms build-ups have been downplayed to avoid impediments to the sale of Australian-sourced materiel. In 1989-90, Australia explored prospects for arms sales to Burma, Somalia, Iraq and Pakistan. In 1993-94, it was keen to sell locally manufactured Steyr rifles to Thailand, despite suspicions voiced by Evans himself on the closeness of the links between elements of the Thai military and the Khmer Rouge.[18] The justifications advanced for the continuance of the policy tend to be self-serving: the right to self-defence is legitimate, therefore the right to sell arms to enhance self-defence capability is equally legitimate; defence sales contribute to Australia's overall defence self-reliance and its industrial, technological, economic and employment base; refusal to

18   Graeme Cheeseman, 'Australia, Disarmament and Arms Control', in James Cotton and John Ravenhill, eds, *Seeking Asian Engagement: Australia in World Affairs, 1991-1995* (Melbourne: Oxford University Pres, 1997), p. 91.

sell would damage Australia's larger commercial credibility, have adverse implications for strategic partnerships with neighbouring countries and diminish Australia's ability to influence recipient countries; the ready availability of alternative defence suppliers and so forth.

Nevertheless, by world standards, Australia is a 'good international citizen' even with respect to the international trafficking in conventional arms. COCOM was set up by NATO in 1949 to control the export of military equipment and dual-use technologies to Eastern bloc countries. The regime was terminated in March 1994 and has been succeeded by the Wassenaar Arrangement which was agreed to by 33 countries in July 1996. Unlike the mandatory COCOM controls, the Wassenaar Arrangement is a voluntary regime based on information exchanges on transfers, denial of listed goods and the application of national export controls. Its goal is to prevent the acquisition of conventional arms and dual-use technologies by states or groups whose behaviour is a cause for serious international concern. Australia is a co-founder of the Wassenaar Arrangement. The reporting obligations of the regime will be based on the UN Arms Register which focuses on weapons platforms. Australia wanted the regime to cover weapons systems as well.

Australia is no longer ahead of the world norm on anti-personnel (AP) landmines. These are the real weapons of mass and indiscriminate destruction today. They kill many more civilians than soldiers, often long after conflicts have ended. There are an estimated 85-110 million landmines deployed in 68 countries.[19] Afghanistan, Angola and Cambodia are among the worst affected. The annual global death toll from AP mines is estimated to be over 10,000, with another 15,000 injured; 90 percent of the casualties are civilians. They are cheap ($3 each) and easy to make and use, but far more difficult, dangerous and costly ($100-1000 each) to detect and remove. Between 0.5 and two million new mines are deployed each year,[20] twenty-fifty times their rate of removal. In many countries the maimed survivors of

19 Zdzislaw Lachowski, 'Conventional Arms Control', *SIPRI Yearbook 1997: Armaments, Disarmament and International Security* (Oxford: Oxford University Press for the Stockholm International Peace Research Institute, 1997), p. 495.
20 Ibid.; Judy Aita, 'U.N. session spotlights need to ban landmines worldwide', *USIS Washington File* EPF406, 15 August 1996, p. 10. The figure of 2-5 million, sourced to the United Nations, may be out of date. It seems hard to think of where mines might be being laid in such numbers today.

mine blasts have no further useful roles. Rejected by society, they end up as outcasts, sometimes forming marauding gangs of 'mutilados'. Other 'cost multipliers' include the loss of arable land for food production. Landmines are also one of the most significant dangers to the deployment of peacekeeping missions: 42 peacekeepers were killed and 315 injured by landmines during the operation of the UN Protection Force in former Yugoslavia (UNPROFOR).[21]

The International Committee of the Red Cross (ICRC) published a report that cast doubts on the military case for the continued use of AP landmines in light of their employment in 26 actual conflicts since 1940. In only a few instances did APL use conform to international law (requiring proportionality of response and discrimination between combatants and civilians) or military doctrine. The claim that AP mines are indispensable weapons of high military value could not be substantiated.[22]

Australia's defence and foreign policy establishments have been at odds over the utility of landmines and the international campaign to ban them. The preference of the defence forces prevailed during the Labor Government. Three considerations were said to lie behind this.[23] The Australian military wished to retain the option of using AP landmines for the defence of Australia and the safety of Australian soldiers. In their view, landmines are legitimate weapons of self-defence when used properly. Second, the government did not wish to offend its friends and allies, including the UK and the US, who are major manufacturers of landmines. Third, Australia had a commercial interest itself in producing and selling AP landmines.

The Labor Government voiced concerns over the *indiscriminate* use of AP landmines, and provided $20 million worth of assistance in de-mining and rehabilitation programmes from 1989 to 1995. At the first review conference of the Inhumane Weapons Convention (IWC, 1980) held in Vienna from 25 September to 13 October 1995, Australia argued for a ban on AP mines which did not self-destruct, did not deactivate, and were undetectable; a ban on the supply of AP landmines to non-government entities; and extensions of the coverage of the Convention to internal conflicts. One of the earliest decisions of

21   Aita, 'U.N. session spotlights need to ban landmines worldwide', p. 10.
22   *Anti-personnel Landmines: Friend or Foe? A study of the military use and effectiveness of anti-personnel mines* (Geneva: ICRC, 1996).
23   Ian Buckley, 'Landmines - The Hidden Killers', *Pacific Research* 8:3 (August 1995), pp. 10-11.

the Coalition Government, announced by Alexander Downer on 15 April 1996, was to support the negotiation of a total ban on the production, stockpiling, use and transfer of AP landmines and to impose an immediate unilateral suspension on their operational use by the Australian military.

A substantive problem with arms control negotiations is the difficulty of translating a generalised will for an agreement into the devotion of sufficient time, attention and resources to produce a particular text. A familiar procedural obstacle is the requirement for decisions to be made by consensus. Despite the efforts of some countries, the UN conference reviewing the IWC in Geneva (22 April-3 May 1996) failed to agree on a total ban on the production of AP landmines. In particular, China and Russia, two key landmine stockpile holders, were opposed to any radical limitations.

The next IWC review conference will be held in 2001. In the meantime, when the new Labour Government of Britain announced that it would be destroying its stock of landmines by 2005,[24] Australia declined to follow suit.[25] Currently, the most serious diplomatic effort is being vested in the 'Ottawa Process'. The conference 'Towards a Global Ban on Anti-personnel Mines', held in Ottawa in October 1996, brought together 50 participating and 24 observer states as well as international organisations, UN agencies and NGOs for three days of intensive discussions. The resolution on AP mines developed from the conference was adopted by the UN General Assembly in December by a vote of 156-0, with ten abstentions. The Canadian government then launched a 'fast-track' diplomatic effort to achieve an AP mine ban treaty by the end of 1997. Work on a draft treaty began in Vienna in February 1997. The next significant meeting in the process was held in Brussels on 24-27 June. A month later, around 100 countries had signed the Brussels Declaration, including New Zealand and the UK but not Australia and the US.

Australia supports the Ottawa process, but only as a complementary measure to the CD in Geneva which remains Canberra's (and Washington's) forum of first choice. An Ottawa Treaty, if and when one emerges, will not have been an internationally negotiated text. Some key players, including China and Russia, will

24   Michael Evans, 'Blair vows to destroy landmines', *Australian,* 23 May 1997.
25   George Lombard, 'Dragging chains on mine ban', *Canberra Times,* 24 May 1997; Stephen Lunn, 'Brits alone on mine ban', *Weekend Australian,* 24-25 May 1997.

not have been part of the process. Symbolism for its own sake is not part of the Australian tradition. Canberra prefers to emphasise 'efficacy' over symbolism. There is also the danger that the pursuit of symbolism through the Ottawa process could undercut the efficacy of the CD as the world's only standing negotiating body for multilateral disarmament.

The ARF Track Two Seminar on Non-Proliferation

A striking feature of contemporary Asia-Pacific activity is the quasi-diplomatic second track channel of dialogue and discussion. The formula of allowing officials to participate in a private/personal capacity gives them the latitude to deal with pressing issues a little more creatively than would be possible solely within the constraints of official positions. While officials try to shed some inhibitions on free dialogue, academics try to address problems with a greater sense of awareness of the real world of policy choices facing decision-makers. Track Two is the medium for the dialectic between cutting edge thought and diplomatic best practice.

Asia-Pacific has only one region-wide Track One security framework, namely the Association of South-east Asian Nations (ASEAN) Regional Forum (ARF). The Forum is unusual in that those in charge of its establishment, agenda and management are not the major powers. ASEAN Foreign Ministers chair the ARF summits in rotation, and ASEAN officials chair the meetings of the ARF senior officials and the inter-sessional support groups. The ARF is unusual also in that while the driving seat is occupied by ASEAN, the primary focus of security concerns is Northeast Asia. Because Southeast Asia could not be insulated from a breakdown of peace and order to its northeast, nesting Northeast Asia security discussions in ARF provides detached concern without vested interests. This in combination with the Council for Security Cooperation in Asia-Pacific (CSCAP) and the regional network of Institutes of Strategic and International Studies, places ASEAN at the hub of Asia-Pacific's government and second track security dialogue, confidence building and preventive diplomacy activities.

The ARF is also trying to integrate Track One and Two. In 1996, it gave formal blessing to a Track Two Seminar on Non-Proliferation under the combined sponsorship of Australia, Germany and the European Union (EU). The initiative for the Seminar came from Germany and it received significant German and EU, as well as

Australian, financial support. Germany accepted the Australian suggestion that it would be good to hold the Seminar in the region with regional co-chairs. The three organising institutions were the Centre for Strategic and International Studies (CSIS), Jakarta, the Stiftung Wissenschaft und Politik (SWP), Munich and the Peace Research Centre, Canberra. The three chairmen were Jusuf Wanandi of the CSIS, Winrich Kuehne of the SWP, and the present author.[26]

The Seminar, held in Jakarta on 6-7 December 1996, was attended by more than fifty academics and officials in their personal capacities, including representation from every ARF member as well as the EU troika. It provided an opportunity to introduce WMD proliferation as a significant new element into the ARF's consideration of regional security issues. Ensuring that Asia-Pacific remains WMD-free is a primary objective of Australian foreign policy. Injecting this discussion into the ARF process thus has a direct bearing on relevant Australian interests. In fact, the Jakarta Seminar demonstrated, more clearly than ever, how ARF and regional approaches on non-proliferation and disarmament issues can reinforce global regimes that Australia (and New Zealand, which will host the next seminar later in 1997) believe to be important and deserving of broad adherence. Most participants acknowledged that the prosperity of the region would have remained a more distant goal without security to underpin it, and that the absence of WMD has contributed to the maintenance of regional security. Conversely, the introduction of WMD into the region would undermine its stability, and therefore its prosperity and wellbeing. From this, it is a logical step to argue that the goal and regimes of WMD non-proliferation require regional political and financial support, including, as appropriate, signature-cum-ratification of global regimes.

Among the ARF members, the most substantial holdout from nuclear non-proliferation regimes is India. An idea that received general, although not universal, support in the Seminar was that ARF membership could expose India to the reality of non-proliferation being a deeply-held conviction in the Asia-Pacific region. Accordingly, one of the recommendations was that a Track Two seminar could be convened in India to discuss the CTBT. Other ARF members would get the opportunity to listen to India's security perspectives which underpin its nuclear options. In turn, India's security elite would

---

26 The organisational input from the SWP up to the holding of the Seminar came from Dr Matthias Dembinski.

understand that the regional fervour for non-proliferation has little to do with US pressure.

At the same time, there is considerable sympathy throughout Asia-Pacific for the Indian argument that non-proliferation cannot be viewed in total isolation from disarmament. Ambassador Izhar Ibrahim of Indonesia's Ministry of Foreign Affairs criticised the key global non-proliferation instruments as being deficient, not supported universally and subject to the uncertain political will of the major powers. The Chairs' Statement made clear that Seminar participants were guided by the vision of a world eventually free of all weapons of mass destruction, and that the agendas for the non-proliferation and disarmament of WMD and their means of delivery remain incomplete. As well as an educational campaign for India and endorsement of existing global regimes by regional countries, therefore, the Seminar recommended immediate ratification of START II, the early commencement of negotiations on START III, implementation of Decision 2 on Principles and Objectives of the 1995 NPT Review and Extension Conference, and the establishment of an ARF study group to assure non-NWS against the threat or use of nuclear weapons.

Australia's Disarmament Credentials

I have already mentioned the liabilities of Australia's size, resources and geographic location. Notwithstanding these constraints, Australia, a non-nuclear, industrialised Western country, has three great advantages in pressing for nuclear disarmament after the collapse of the Soviet threat and the resulting dominance of Western ideals and institutions. After decades of faithful alliance credentials, its political loyalty is not suspect. Its capacity to produce nuclear weapons quickly is also beyond question: if Australia does not need nuclear weapons, it can argue more persuasively that neither do the existing NWS. Australia's human and material capabilities give it the scientific expertise to engage in a critical evaluation of the NWS' technical arguments for maintaining the status quo, and for providing detailed, practical and scientifically credible maps to a nuclear-weapons-free world. The Canberra Commission is an excellent example of this.

Greg Sheridan, foreign editor of the *Australian,* warned that the Canberra Commission could endanger the US alliance and take

Australia down the New Zealand road.[27] Ironically, David Lange, Prime Minister of New Zealand during the turbulent years of the ANZUS rupture, made a number of derisory observations about Australia's anti-nuclear credentials while casting 'considerable doubts. .. on the value of the Canberra commission as a catalyst for nuclear disarmament'. Gareth Evans was attacked for being 'wedded, still, to nuclear deterrence, while claiming engagement to disarmament'.[28]

Lange's criticisms have since been levelled at the Coalition Government. Laurie Brereton, the opposition spokesman on Foreign Affairs, claims that after the 1996 election, defeated Prime Minister Paul Keating urged his successor John Howard to deliver the report of the Canberra Commission to the United Nations himself rather than leaving it to the powers of persuasion of the Foreign Minister.[29] The advice was not heeded. In opposition, Alexander Downer described the Commission as a pre-election stunt. As Foreign Minister, he was at first sceptical about the exercise. He was persuaded of the merits of the Commission's report. Nevertheless, one of the Commissioners, Dr Ronald McCoy, believes that the Howard Government's 'lukewarm' support for the Report is responsible for the failure to promote it more vigorously.[30] His judgement was supported by the *Australian's* New York correspondent.[31] Downer rejects such criticism, arguing that the government has promoted the Report to the maximum realistic extent.[32] In November 1996, the government's commitment to nuclear disarmament was questioned afresh when Australia abstained on the Malaysian resolution at the UN General Assembly, approved by a vote of 94-22 (26 abstentions) calling for multilateral negotiations to begin in 1997.[33]

---

27 Greg Sheridan, 'Disarmament talk endangers US alliance', *Australian,* 24 January 1996.
28 David Lange, 'Evans's nuclear initiative reeks of hypocrisy', *Age* (Melbourne), 29 January 1996.
29 In an address to the Medical Association for Prevention of War (Australia) conference on 'Visions and Actions for Peace', Canberra, 24 April 1997.
30 Quoted in George Lombard, 'Nuclear push lacks conviction', *Canberra Times,* 26 April 1997.
31 Cameron Stewart, 'Ambitious plan dies in silence', *Australian,* 23 May 1997.
32 Alexander Downer, 'Dialogue best route to disarmament', letter to the editor, *Weekend Australian,* 19-20 April 1997.
33 *Canberra Times,* 17 November 1996.

Australia has also been accused of inconsistency between its nuclear disarmament efforts and the sale of uranium to France. Although formal agreements precluded France using Australian-sourced uranium in its nuclear weapons programme, it freed uranium obtained from other sources for the weapons programme. The export of uranium is thus an unusually clear example of economic imperatives of foreign policy colliding with and overriding disarmament goals. The three-mines policy of the Labor Government was a compromise that satisfied neither side. Anti-nuclear activists were not appeased and pro-mining interests not pleased by the restrictions placed on additional uranium export. The Howard Government announced in March 1996 that the three-mine restrictions on the mining and export of uranium would be lifted.

Another question mark over Australia's nuclear disarmament credentials is posed by the manner in which it is integrated into the global US nuclear infrastructure. The United States maintains several installations in Australia concerned with military communications, navigation, and satellite tracking and control. During the Cold War the 'joint' US-Australian facilities collected vital military intelligence, spied on Soviet missile sites, detected nuclear explosions, helped verify arms limitation agreements, and were meant to provide the Americans with early warning of any Soviet attack.

The Pine Gap and Nurrungar stations excited controversy in part because of the secrecy when they were established.[34] In the 1980s, as many people in Western countries became alarmed at the bellicose rhetoric emanating from the Reagan Administration, peace activists condemned the joint facilities both for Australia's complicity in the US nuclear strategy and for making Australia a nuclear target of US enemies. Successive Australian governments argued that no country, allied or neutral, could escape the consequences of a nuclear war between Moscow and Washington. Verification, early warning and the ability to control and communicate with nuclear forces were said to be critical both to stable deterrence and arms control. The joint facilities were more important for the stability they provided than either the instability caused by their potential for nuclear war-fighting, or the danger they posed to Australia becoming a nuclear target. From this, it was but a short step to arguing that Australia has 'a moral obligation . .

---

34 Gareth Evans and Bruce Grant, *Australia's Foreign Relations in the World of the 1990s* (Melbourne: Melbourne University Press, 1991), p. 77.

. to discharge its responsibilities to prevent nuclear war' by hosting the joint facilities.[35]

As part of its intention to upgrade the security alliance with the United States, the new Coalition Government held ministerial talks in Sydney on 26 July 1996. It decided to renew the Pine Gap station for another ten years, but to close the Nurrungar station by 2000. New satellite dishes to be sited at Pine Gap, and more satellites, will expand its facility and give the United States greater intelligence gathering capability in East Asia and the Middle East.

The main purpose of the joint facilities has been thus to contribute to the strengthening of the nuclear infrastructure of the Western alliance and so enhance the stability of nuclear deterrence. As a secondary purpose, they have also formed part of the verification regime of arms control agreements. In a matching set of calculations, Australia has rarely proposed major arms control initiatives, but has generally welcomed such agreements negotiated by Moscow and Washington directly. Its reticence stemmed firstly from the wish not to undermine the Western alliance, and secondly the belief that prospects for genuine progress would be impeded rather than enhanced by outsiders putting pressure on the superpowers.

Conclusion

Anomalies and inconsistencies notwithstanding, over the past decade Australia has contributed to the global delegitimisation of WMD. Like every other country, Australia has the right, indeed the duty, to make its voice heard on arms control and disarmament issues. Given its size, location and freedom from specific threats, Australia places great importance on international legal instruments for its national security. It has worked to ensure that the historic and favourable changes in the world strategic situation are reflected in decisions that consolidate, deepen and reinforce the NPT in its normative, technical-denial and compliance-cum-enforcement attributes. The post-NPT agenda is expected to be less focused, concentrating on institution building rather than new regime creation.

Australia's arms control and disarmament policy can still be said to be driven by the 'soft' options.[36] It is most active on issues, such as non-proliferation of WMD, for which there is bipartisan and public

35   Ibid., p. 78.
36   Findlay, 'Disarmament and Arms Control', p. 176.

support and no pain is inflicted on identifiable economic sectors. It is more prudent and tentative as the bipartisan consensus breaks down or alliance and economic costs come into play, such as the exports of uranium and Australian military hardware. Australia's disarmament diplomacy is most substantial where it has particular assets, such as seismic monitoring expertise. Conversely, Australia's arms control diplomacy is at its most ornamental and rhetorical where public demand for action comes into conflict with economic or military interests. Costs are minimised and support maximised if Australian efforts are channelled through multilateral bodies like the United Nations. In international forums such as the CD, Australia devotes energy, commitment and intellect. As a result of its persistence, Australia enjoys a credibility with all sides. Countries like Sweden and New Zealand might have greater credibility with the disarmament crusaders. Australian ministers and officials have tended to argue that Canberra's efforts are the more efficacious in achieving practical progress.

The most appropriate global forum for the pursuit of arms control and disarmament is the United Nations. The only body which can legitimately employ sanctions to address specific proliferation threats to international peace and security, the UN has generally been dismissed by the 'realists'. The election of the Coalition Government in March 1996 produced a relative upgrading of 'realism' in Australian foreign policy. The world has been transformed fundamentally since the Coalition was last in power. The changes in the world in the intervening years have been nothing short of revolutionary. One of the challenges facing the Coalition Government is to readjust its worldview from 1983 to the realities of the world at the cusp of the century. Nowhere is this more urgent than in arms control and disarmament. Success in this task of philosophical reorientation will ensure that Australia enters the 21st century well prepared to tackle the real threats to national, regional and international security. Failure to refocus the worldview will add avoidable dangers to national security, and betray the principles of 'realism' which underpin the Coalition's philosophy of international relations.

Chapter 12

Korea and East Asian Security into the 21st Century

Byung-joon Ahn

East Asia is a region where the interests of four powers - China, Japan, Russia and the United States - intersect and where the Korean peninsula is still divided between North and South. Prospects for a security order in this strategically important region in the 21st century are not certain. What is the state of economic, geopolitical, historical, and political trends emerging in East Asia? What is the prospect for unification in the peninsula? What are the patterns of major power relations and their implications for regional security? What should be the roles of China, the United States and Korea for security, interdependence and democracy in this region? These are some of the questions that this chapter addresses.

East Asia in Flux: Economic or Political Imperatives?

East Asia is emerging as the centre of the world's strategic and economic gravity. Geopolitically, it is the region where three nuclear powers, China, Russia and the United States are located; economically, it is the most dynamic and fastest growing region of all, encompassing about 40 percent of the world's trade and product. East Asia is currently in flux and in transition because political and economic imperatives are competing in and among the countries that are undergoing rapid change both in their domestic politics and in their international relations.

A good way of explaining the security situation in Northeast Asia is to compare it with that in Europe in terms of geopolitics, history, economics and politics. Geopolitically, Europe is relatively united but East Asia is divided. In fact, Europe opened a new chapter in the post-Cold World War order by signing a 'Founding Act' of mutual cooperation and security between NATO and Russia on May 27, 1997 after the former decided to expand into Central Europe. Not only are most territorial disputes settled in this region but more importantly, NATO members are working toward a United States of Europe through the EU. President Bill Clinton declared at the 50th anniversary of the Marshall Plan: 'We must summon the spirit of the Marshall Plan for the next 50 years and beyond, to build a Europe that is democratic, at peace, and undivided for the first time in history'.[1]

By contrast, East Asia is characterised by diverging countries, ideologies and cultures. There are still territorial disputes such as the Korean division, the Taiwan Straits, the Northern Territories, and the Spratly Islands. The Taiwan issue, in particular, is fuelling Sino-American and Sino-Japanese rivalry. Yet, there are few multilateral institutions like NATO and the EU in Asia and the Pacific. Even though the ASEAN Regional Forum (ARF) was launched in 1994 as an embryonic organization for a security dialogue, it remains a talk shop for 'cooperative security' and preventive diplomacy rather than collective defence and dispute settlement. Most of the important alliances and inter-state relations are primarily bilateral as demonstrated by the US-Japanese and the US-South Korean alliances and by the importance of Sino-American relations.

Historically, the legacies of World War II and the Cold War are fading in Europe after communism collapsed in East Europe in 1989, Germany unified in 1990 and the Soviet Union disbanded in 1991. But historical legacies and memories in East Asia remain as potent as before since communism is alive in China, North Korea and Vietnam while memories of and resentments against Japan's past record are being renewed not only in Northeast Asia but also in Southeast Asia mainly because Japan has thus far failed to make a clean break with her past history.

Economically, Europe is being integrated into one market and is trying to accomplish a common currency by 1999. Trade, investment and technology are market-driven within the EU. But in East Asia some of the leading economic powers have mercantilist policies, although most of the countries are committed to deepening interdependence and 'open regionalism' at the APEC forum. China, the world's largest market, is yet to join the WTO and the United States is yet to grant Most Favoured Nation status permanently to

1   *Washington Times*, 29 May 1997.

China. As a result, there are mounting trade frictions between the United States and other Asian countries.

Politically, democracy and civil society have been firmly institutionalized in much of Europe. In East Asia, however, these principles are still being experimented with in various forms. Authoritarian rule has yielded to functioning democracy in South Korea, Taiwan and most Southeast Asian countries. But authoritarianism is strongly defended by the communist parties in China, North Korea and Vietnam. Generally, European countries share such values as democracy and human rights but Asian countries certainly do not and many go so far as to assert their own 'Asian' values that are different from Western ones.

Because of these differences, one cannot envisage an East Asian security order in the 21st century in simple terms. As of 1997, however, there seem to be two diverging trends at work: political and economic imperatives. Political imperatives are developing toward nationalism, sovereignty, and balance of power especially in China. But economic imperatives are working toward interdependence, 'open regionalism' and globalization. To use the academic jargon of international relations, the former subscribes to realism and the latter, liberalism. It is most desirable that economic imperatives prevail over political imperatives, as they seem to do in Europe, to ensure security, prosperity and democracy in East Asia. Whether this can be achieved, however, will depend on the transformation of domestic politics evolving in North Korea, China and other countries.[2] For some time to come, though, security in Asia is more likely to result from a balance of power rather than from democracy and market forces in domestic politics as in Europe.

It is a central theme of this chapter that East Asian security depends on the future of North Korea and Korean unification in the short run, and on the future of China and Sino-American relations along with a four-power balance in the long term, and that the United States must perform a stabilizing role in the region until either collective security or a 'concert of powers' takes root.

Three observations are in order to elaborate on this theme. First, the Korean peninsula will be unified in the 21st century on South

2   For this line of reasoning, see Byung-joon Ahn, 'The U.S. in Asia: Searching for a New Role', in James Shinn, ed., *Weaving the Net, Conditional Engagement with China* (New York: Council on Foreign Relations, 1996), pp.191-219.

Korea's terms because the process of North Korea's collapse has already begun. It is incumbent upon South Korea and the United States and other concerned parties to ensure that this process is peaceful and not harmful to the interests of the surrounding powers and regional security.

Second, it will be a major challenge to engage and integrate China as a rising power into the regional system of security and interdependence given that Sino-American and Sino-Japanese rivalry is bound to intensify from now on. Whether this can be accomplished depends on the condition of Sino-American relations and on the outcome of political transformation in China and its impact on major power relations. Possible scenarios include: hard authoritarianism and confrontation, democracy and multilateral security, and soft authoritarianism and a loose balance of power. Given the major trends emerging in East Asia, the last option is the one most likely to emerge, at least, by the second decade of the 21st century.

Third, assuming that this scenario is right, it is incumbent upon the United States to continue its engagement in East Asia to prevent a regional hegemon from emerging, to uphold freedom of navigation and deter the proliferation of nuclear and other weapons of mass destruction. A united Korea should become a bridge between the major powers and assume confidence-building roles, along with ASEAN and other Pacific countries like Australia, New Zealand and Canada promoting transparency and interdependence.

Towards Korean Unification

The Korean peninsula is the world's most heavily armed flashpoint where 1.1 million North Korean troops are deployed along the DMZ with 11,000 artillery pieces that can hit Seoul which is within 30 miles from the front line. Some 37,000 American troops are stationed on the southern side. Maintaining stability and accomplishing a peaceful unification in Korea is crucial not only to the security of the peninsula but also throughout the Asia-Pacific region as a whole. In all probability, Korean unification will be achieved in some form in the 21st century. But the specific prospect for this depends on the future of North Korea.

If we see a North Korean collapse not as one 'big bang', but as a protracted process involving the slow disintegration of the economy, regime, system and state, then this has already started. On this view,

Korean unification will be accomplished by default, if not by design,[3] in the early decades of the 21st century. A reunited Korea with a population of about 65 million and GNP of over $700 billion will emerge as a candidate fifth power in East Asia.

Prospects for Korean unification depend on the nature of political change in North Korea and the opportunities it can offer. There are three possible scenarios: (1) the status quo and confrontation; (2) 'soft landing' and unification by mutual consent; and (3) collapse and unification by absorption. In all probability, the third possibility is the most likely if cooperation and reintegration are to take place between the North and South. Seoul has to play the leading role; the United States, China, Japan and Russia the supporting and facilitating roles to ensure that the process remains non-violent and orderly.

1. North Korea's Future: the Status Quo, 'Soft Landing', and Collapse.

The North Korean leadership under Kim Jong Il is committed to guarding the status quo by all means and wants the United States to ensure its survival and viability by lifting economic sanctions and by normalizing relations. Should things continue on the present course, however, the North Korean leadership may launch a last-ditch offensive as Hwang Jang Yob, Jong Il's ideological teacher, predicted. In that case, the South would prevail albeit at great cost, but the North would be pulverized. Nothing is more important for the US-South Korean alliance than to deter another war from breaking out in a most dangerous spot in East Asia.

It is in the interests of South Korea, the United States, China, Japan and Russia that the North evolves towards a 'soft landing', meaning an orderly and peaceful change through reform and an open-door policy. In fact, these countries are trying to maintain the North on 'life support' by offering food and other humanitarian aids and economic assistance. So long as Kim Jong Il is in charge of the regime, however, it would be extremely difficult for him to undertake structural transformations that negate the very ideology and policy lines advocated by his father, Kim Il Sung, without compromising the legitimacy of his leadership claim. If, indeed, such a happy ending is realized, it follows that both sides can actually accomplish unification

---

3   Byung-joon Ahn, 'The Man Who Would Be Kim', *Foreign Affairs*, vol. 73, no.6 (November/December 1994), pp. 94-108.

by mutual consent. But since the North Korean regime is finding it impossible to resolve the food, energy, and foreign exchange crises in the country, the chances for such a soft landing are diminishing with every passing day.

Judging from these trends, it appears that both a North Korean collapse and unification by default will be inevitable. This being the case, a number of specialists argue that the United States should cease propping up the regime in Pyongyang and let its collapse come sooner because any delay would cost more in terms of risks, resources and sacrifices. It is better to hasten unification by default when a relatively favourable international environment exists. Hence, South Korea and her allies must prepare for all contingencies that can break out in unanticipated ways. Whatever form of unification may occur, one thing is certain: the South has no option but to reintegrate the North by all means at her disposal.

2. Unification as a Process of Non-proliferation, Peace, Cooperation and Reintegration

It is important to see Korean unification as a process that keeps the peninsula nuclear-free. This objective requires the United States and South Korea to entrench the Agreed Framework on the nuclear freeze concluded between the United States and North Korea in 1994 and the KEDO process in a comprehensive strategy to reduce the military threats from the North and to foster a North-South dialogue by sustaining a common agenda. Without this, neither the nuclear accord or a soft landing as such can be implemented. That was clearly shown by the aftermath of the submarine infiltration in 1996 and the food crisis in 1997.

The first Clinton administration focused its Korea policy almost solely on nuclear non-proliferation as part of its global strategy as it was busy preparing for a renewal of the NPT in 1995. By skilfully taking advantage of this opportunity, North Korea has implemented only the nuclear portions of the Agreed Framework. Without addressing conventional security threats and political reconciliation in the peninsula from now on, however, the second Clinton administration can hardly restore trust in its relations with the Seoul government and ensure peace and security on the peninsula. Therefore, Seoul and Washington have little choice but to seek a conditional engagement with Pyongyang through a broad trade-off in food (or money) in exchange for North Korea reducing its military threat, advancing reconciliation with Seoul and carrying out reforms oriented towards an open-door policy.

South Korea, the United States, Japan and other concerned parties must be actually prepared for the endgame that seems to be nearing in North Korea. They also need to cooperate with a clear sense of strategic direction in relation to the process of Korean unification and its implications for regional security.

3. South Korea as the Leader and Other Powers as the Facilitator

Four-party talks involving the two Koreas, the United States and China are the only means for accomplishing these ends. If the North cannot survive without dealing with and even depending on the South, it is natural that South Korea should play the leading role in these negotiations. The United States, China and other powers should help to facilitate the North-South talks and provide international guarantees concerning their implementation.

South Korea is in a good position to render the necessary aid to North Korea, provided that the latter is ready to negotiate peace and cooperation directly with the former. Moreover, in order to deter Chinese or Russian intervention into the North Korean endgame, it would be advisable for South Korea to take the initiative in managing the North Korean transformation. Beyond the role of deterring war and of ensuring peace, as Secretary of State, Madeline K. Albright aptly said: 'The future of the peninsula is for Koreans to decide. Our role is to support the South in its efforts to assure peace. We are doing that, and we will maintain that commitment for as long as our help is required'.[4] When this approach is fully implemented, Korea will be unified as one nation state.

Once North Korea has opted for peace and reform, it is incumbent upon South Korea to initiate a mini-Marshall plan to keep North Korea afloat and to pave the way for a gradual process of peace, cooperation, and unification. It is imperative to keep China engaged in this process so that she can continue to play a constructive role.

Sino-American Rivalry and Loose Balance of Power

As far as major power relations are concerned, the United States can be expected to maintain both its international leadership and military

---

4   '1997 Forrestal Lecture: American Principle and Purpose in East Asia', U.S. Naval Academy, Annapolis, Maryland, 15 April 1997.

superiority into the 21st century, as the recent Quadrennial Defense Review (QDR) envisioned.[5] When the United States redefined its security relationship with Japan toward a regional division of roles, it stimulated growing Sino-American and Sino-Japanese rivalry as China interpreted this development as being anti-Chinese. Depending on the future political shape of China, major power relations may evolve into three patterns: confrontation, multilateral cooperation and a balance of power. Given China's strategic propensity for classical realism, a loose balance of power is the most feasible likelihood.

1. The United States as the Leader

As the 1995 East Asian Strategy Report clearly spelled out, the United States will remain a leader of last resort over the next two decades by deploying military forces forward in Japan, Korea and the West Pacific as long as they are welcome. Besides, East Asia has become the United States' largest market for export, investment and technology; its volume of trade with this region has far exceeded that with Europe. Perhaps with this in mind, Secretary of Defense, William S. Cohen stated in explaining the results of the QDR: 'And while we do not expect a regional great power or a near competitor' to emerge in the next 10-15 years, we must prepare for the possibility in the years beyond and hedge against its earlier arrival'.[6] Until 2020, therefore, the United States will seek to continue a leadership role in maintaining a balance of power and freedom of navigation in East Asia with the help of its allies and friends.

In exercising this role, the US-Japanese Security Treaty, in anchoring the American military and political presence, is equivalent to NATO's role in Europe. To renew the importance of this bilateral relationship, President Bill Clinton and Prime Minister Ryutaro Hashimoto issued the Joint Security Declaration in April 1996 at their summit meeting. This reaffirmed the alliance as 'the cornerstone for achieving a common security objective, and for maintaining a stable and prosperous environment for the Asia-Pacific region as we enter the 21st century'.[7] It is for this purpose that the two allies decided to

5   'Secretary of Defense Issues Quadrennial Defense Review', News Release, 19 May 1997.
6   'Remarks Prepared for Delivery by Secretary of Defense William S. Cohen', Ibid., 22 May 1997.
7   Paragraph 4 of the Japan-U.S. Joint Declaration on Security Alliance for the 21st Century.

review the 1978 Defense Cooperation Guidelines to accommodate the changing nature of the international environment.

2. Sino-American and Sino-Japanese Rivalry

China has begun to see the renewed U.S.-Japan security relationship as being aimed at herself. Chinese military analysts view the United States as the sole superpower and one which is potentially unfavourable to Chinese strategic interests: it can keep China from becoming a regional power by encouraging Taiwan to be independent and block China's entry into the WTO. Beijing favours a more multi-polar world where China can have greater manoeuverability. After Deng Xioping passed away from the scene, the weakened leadership under Jiang Zemin, and the military in particular, resort to nationalism as a legitimising device.

The more Chinese leaders appeal to nationalism, the more they come to share a traditional strategic culture of balancing one power against another in the name of 'using barbarian to control barbarian'. They are embracing a 'hard realpolitik' paradigm which generally places offensive strategies before static defence; they do not rule out use of force for Taiwan; they prefer ambiguous principles to precise commitments.[8]

Allied to this traditional culture is China's sense of grievance stemming from mistreatment by the Western powers and Japan in the 19th century. As an old country recovering its power, China, like Germany and Japan at the beginning of this century, reveals both arrogance and insecurity in dealing with foreign powers.

The challenge of integrating China into regional and global norms and rules will be a daunting task for the United States, especially in Asia and the Pacific. Currently, China's military power is no match for the United States but it could grow to challenge Washington in the first half of the 21st century. Her ICBM capability will threaten the United States and other Pacific countries by 2000.[9] Beijing has been providing ballistic missiles and other technology of mass destruction to Pakistan and Iran. Washington recently imposed economic sanctions

---

8   Alastair Iain Johnston, 'Cultural Realism and Strategy in Maoist China', in Peter J. Katzenstein, ed., *The Culture of National Security: Norms and Identity in World Politics* (New York: Columbia University Press, 1996), pp. 216-270.

9   *Washington Times*, 22 May 1997.

on two Chinese companies and five citizens for selling chemicals and chemical production equipment to Iran.[10]

China's trade surplus with the United States exceeded Japan's in 1997. In the second decade of the 21st century, China's economy is expected to surpass the United States', at least, in absolute terms. Her human rights behaviour has become a most contentious issue in American domestic politics even after the Clinton administration delinked the MFN status from China's human rights performance. Beijing's alleged involvement in the 1996 American Presidential campaign has further complicated the debate on China in the United States. As a result, the China factor has become increasingly politicized in American domestic life.

Of all issues, Hong Kong, Taiwan and the WTO are perhaps the toughest ones to tackle in managing Sino-American relations. Any restriction on the freedom of the press and rule of law in Hong Kong after the British departure will make it difficult for Washington to allow China's accession to the WTO on terms favourable to Beijing as many European countries want. Sino-American relations have been strained since the visit of Taiwan's President, Lee Teng-hui, to Cornell University in June 1995 and especially since Beijing's use of intimidation tactics, including ballistic missile tests and military exercises before the Presidential election in March 1996. The strong United States response consisted of sending two aircraft carrier battle formations to the Taiwan area.

At present, Washington is applying a policy of 'strategic ambiguity' to both sides by professing a one-China policy. There is no guarantee that Beijing's policy of 'one country and two systems' will work in relation to Taiwan. In the event that Washington would not take any military action if Taiwan was either invaded or blockaded by China, the United States' leadership in Asia will suffer irreparably. Hence there is potential for long term rivalry between the United States as a status quo power and China as a rising power.

The advent of Sino-Japanese rivalry is a function of Sino-American rivalry in the sense that the more the United States wants Japan to share regional security roles, the more China fears the rise of Japanese militarism. China only recognizes the role of the U.S.-Japanese Security Treaty in as much as it constrains a unilateral Japanese arms buildup, but opposes its extension beyond the defence of Japanese territories. When Tokyo dispatched SDF vessels to the

10 *Washington Post*, 24 May 1997.

vicinity of the Taiwan Straits in March 1996, for example, Beijing suspected that Japan was trying to expand its military activities. That is why Beijing has become more vocal in challenging Tokyo's assertion of sovereignty over the Senkaku (or Diaoyutai) Islands in the East China Sea. Beijing has recently become increasingly worried about possibilities for Tokyo to develop the TMD system that may make its 'minimum deterrence' capabilities redundant.

Future of China and East Asia: Three Scenarios.

To a large extent, the future of Sino-American relations and East Asia depends on the political future of China. There is little doubt that China will become the world's superstate sometime in the 21st century. More importantly, there is the task of assessing what kind of state, society and culture will shape China in the years ahead. There is good reason to believe that the future of the Chinese political system will exert more influence on East Asian international relations than vice versa. This is not to say that there is a causal relationship between the two; it is only to highlight the importance of the former for understanding the latter.

From this perspective, we can conceive of three possible scenarios: (1) hard authoritarianism and confrontation ; (2) democracy and multilateral security; and (3) soft authoritarianism and a loose balance of power. Of these, the third scenario is most likely to emerge in the 21st century.

1 Hard Authoritarianism and Confrontation

If China's progress toward political and economic reforms is halted or even reversed because of the Taiwan confrontation or domestic political crises, her political system could slide into 'hard authoritarianism', if not totalitarianism, a development which would be conducive to Sino-American confrontation. Such authoritarianism, repressing popular sovereignty and an autonomous society, will resemble fascism in its structure as it will be directed by the Communist Party or a hard line coalition of party and military officials using a coercive system of ideological control. If this system relies primarily on exclusive nationalism as a means of securing legitimacy, Chinese foreign policy would be uncooperative and often hegemonic, especially when it is backed up by military power.

It is important to note that this scenario may result not only from domestic and external difficulties but also from economic successes.

Economic liberalization without political democratization, for example, would destabilize China by encouraging the trend toward authoritarianism at home and hegemonism abroad.[11] As historians of the Cold War point out, the rise of top leaders like Stalin and an ideology like Marxism-Leninism can change the entire course of history.[12] By the same token, the return to power of Deng Xiaoping and his brand of pragmatism made it possible for China to undertake reform and pursue an open-door national policy.

According to this scenario, China would seek to push America's presence back to the centre of the Pacific and support a termination of the U.S.-Japanese alliance. If China attempts to use force to advance its territorial claims on Taiwan and elsewhere, such acts would prompt the United States to seek to contain the Chinese threats by forming a coalition with Japan, South Korea and other willing partners. The United States would move toward another confrontation with China and from it will emerge another Cold War.

2. Democracy and Multilateral Security Cooperation

If China succeeds in instituting democracy, as the West expects, it should be possible for her to share not merely common interests but also common values with other democracies. In this way, Beijing might accommodate such norms, rules and procedures of multilateral security cooperation as transparency and confidence-building measures which ARF and its Track II, CSCAP, are currently attempting to realize. On this view, East Asia will resemble in many ways contemporary West Europe. Trends toward political democracy and economic interdependence would deepen.

There is much hope that China will follow the footsteps of other East Asian 'tigers' such as South Korea, Taiwan and Singapore by adopting democracy in the wake of impressive economic development. With the rapid growth of a middle class in China's cities, it is believed this group will obtain greater freedom to form a vigorous civil society, including civilian control over the military. Once the Chinese accept the rule of law at home, it would be easy for them to do so in the international community as well. This theory assumes in effect that

11   Richard K. Betts, 'Wealth, Power, Instability: East Asia and the U.S. after the Cold War', in Michael E. Brown, Sean M. Lynn-Jones and Steven E. Miller, eds., *East Asian Security* (Cambridge: MIT Press, 1996), pp. 32-75.

12   John Lewis Gaddis, *We Now Know: Rethinking Cold War History* (New York: Oxford University Press, 1997), pp. 192-194.

democracy can survive in Hong Kong after July 1 1997 and spread throughout China after that date.

The key to this scenario is that a new generation of Chinese leaders will continue political and economic reforms toward democracy and the market. Even if this assumption is true, its realization will take a long period of time. Until that time comes, China's position in relation to multilateral security dialogue is that she does not want to be sidelined but prefers bilateral to multilateral negotiations. Beijing does find ARF, CSCAP and the Northeast Asian Cooperation Dialogue useful, for it can assert its views at these forums and counter American and Japanese views as long as these institutions are run on a consensus basis. Beijing has tried to evade any attempts to introduce dispute settlement mechanisms that could constrain its autonomy and vital interests.

In the absence of prior understanding in Beijing's bilateral negotiations with Washington and Tokyo, there are many obstacles to overcome before multilateral efforts at cooperative security go beyond the current level of 'preventive diplomacy' based on consensual agreement. Similarly, it is difficult to expect that Beijing can accommodate rules of collective security and liberal institutions without profound change in its domestic political life. As a revisionist power, China is more interested in changing, rather than accepting, the existing international order and norms.

3. Soft Authoritarianism and a Loose Balance of Power

The most likely scenario for Chinese political development is the emergence of 'soft authoritarianism' at home and a loose balance of power approach abroad. As the Chinese leadership continues its progress toward an outwardly oriented market economy, some pluralism, mainly in the social sphere and economy, could be permitted but it would be limited in the political realm in order to maintain the unity and stability so essential to economic growth and one party rule as Taiwan and South Korea demonstrated up until the 1980s.

Such a regime will seek a rough balance of power in its foreign policy by cooperating with the United States in areas of common interest, but by confronting it when interests diverge especially on issues of national sovereignty like Taiwan and Hong Kong, human rights and other perceived internal matters. Since the United States and other powers will also seek to engage China but counter bellicose actions or unreasonable demands by her, bilateral interaction among the four powers will produce a loose balance of power system until Chinese power becomes powerful enough to challenge America's pre-eminence in the 21st century.

By trying to engage and to integrate China into the international community through regular summit meetings between top leaders, military contacts and economic interdependence, the United States is interested in fostering cooperative relations with China for its regional and national security interests. But a soft authoritarian regime in China would make it difficult for the US Congress to form a political consensus on such issues as human rights, market access, MFN, intellectual property rights, transparency of trade regime, corruption, population control and labour standards. The more Congress raises these issues, however, the more the Chinese authorities and the military, in particular, perceive them as interference in Chinese domestic affairs.

As the Chinese leadership tends to interpret all foreign relations through a domestic political prism, they are suspicious of Washington's engagement policy and will probably resist US calls for the establishment of the rule of law and transparency. There is little guarantee, therefore, that engagement policy will work as intended.[13]

Meanwhile, Beijing is busy forging what it calls 'a strategic partnership' with Moscow against Washington. For example, Presidents Jiang Zemin and President Boris Yeltsin pledged in April 1997 to work together to limit American power in the world by stating: 'No country should seek hegemony, practice power politics or monopolize international affairs'.[14] China has sought to encourage disputes between Japan and South Korea with Jiang openly suggesting to South Korean President Kim Young Sam in November 1995 that 'Japanese militarists' were still posing a threat to both China and Korea.[15] So long as China subscribes to multi-polarity through this type of balance of power policy, the United States has no option but to counter it.

---

13   David Shabaugh, 'Containment or Engagement of China? Calculating Beijing's Responses', *International Security*, vol. 21, no. 2 (Fall 1996), pp.180-209.

14   *New York Times*, 24 April 1997.

15   Richard Bernstein and Rosss H. Munro, *The Coming Conflict with China* (New York: Alfred A. Knopf, 1997), p. 181.

Thus, China's domestic and international politics will almost certainly contribute to making East Asia 'ripe for rivalry' in the 21st century.[16] Indeed, today's East Asia does resemble Europe of the 19th century. What distinguishes contemporary East Asia, however, is the varying degree to which its actors share common interests, values and culture. There are considerable differences in terms of size, political system, and culture amongst the likes of China, Japan, Russia, the United States and Korea. At the same time, unlike Europe, there are few formal treaties or multilateral institutions that link these countries and regulate their relations. Another important difference concerns the role of the US. Unlike Europe during the 19th century, the United States is now deeply involved in East Asia.

Yet a balance of power works in the sense that no one actor can exercise hegemony. If there is an East Asian security order, it results from this rather loose configuration. In the current transitional period of rapid change, which is full of uncertainty and instability, there is much potential for great power rivalry between China and the United States, China and Japan, and Russia and Japan, let alone between North and South Korea, and between China and Taiwan.

4. The Importance of Sino-American Cooperation and United States Engagement

In conclusion, the importance of Sino-American cooperation and United States engagement for East Asian security must be stressed. No less important is it to note that a reunited Korea can build bridges between big powers. In order to prevent a power vacuum from taking place in East Asia, the United States must be firmly engaged in this region to mitigate the revival of Sino-Japanese rivalry in Korea. There is also a critical need for a token American military presence in a unified Korea as an insurance policy against hegemonism either by China or Japan, and the pursuit of a nuclear weapons option.

1. Sino-American Cooperation as the Key to East Asian Security

Accomplishing Sino-American cooperation is the key to maintaining peace and security in East Asia because no major issues like North Korea, Taiwan, and nuclear non-proliferation can be resolved without Chinese cooperation. Developing a peaceful, stable and cooperative

16   Aaron L. Friedberg, 'Ripe for Rivalry: Prospects for Peace in a Multipolar Asia', in Brown et al., eds. *East Asian Security*, pp. 3-31.

relationship with China is a priority for American foreign policy. But since this relationship is subject to increasing domestic political pressures in both countries, that is by no means an easy task.

It is imperative that the United States and China establish effective working relations both to establish a strategic dialogue for exploring common interests and for minimizing conflicting interests. By pledging to have a summit with President Jiang in 1997, President Clinton resumed regular high-level talks. To develop a coherent and long-term strategic relationship with China, the Clinton administration needs to form a consensus with Congress and the public so that US foreign policy can be based on broad popular support instead of the influence of special interest groups.

There is an urgent need for Washington and Beijing to conduct a dialogue on the Korean question and to transform the issue into one of strategic understanding and cooperation to maintain peace and stability, and to facilitate unification in a manner that does not undermine regional stability. This is an area where the US and China can find some common ground. Both have an interest in persuading North Korea to come back to the NPT, keeping to the armistice and calling upon North Korea to exercise restraint in the wake of the 1996 submarine incident.

By the same logic, China also must deal realistically with the issues that trouble her relationship with the United States. There are a number of things that Beijing can do. For example, it can begin serious political negotiations with Taipei, increase the degree of transparency in its military budgeting, grant greater foreign access to its legal and prison systems, and demonstrate its willingness to abide by international agreements and norms.

United States Engagement as a Stabilizing Force

For some time until the 21st century, there is no alternative to the engagement of the United States in Asia as a stabilizing force because no other power is in a position to provide security and maintain free navigation as public goods. It is imperative that the United States stays involved in East Asia also to prevent a regional hegemon from emerging. There is little doubt that if the United States completely disengages from this region, it will result in a power vacuum that can be filled by either China or Japan, and lead to an arms race that could destabilize peace and stability.

At a time when there is no longer a direct threat to world peace, it will be difficult for the United States alone to deal with all cases of potential instability and to bear the costs. This is especially true when the American people are less interested, if not isolationist, in foreign affairs. Such a mood has been reflected in Washington's obvious concern with casualties and costs in its conduct of foreign policy. It is inevitable that allies and friends must share the burden of maintaining security. It is for this reason that Washington and Tokyo began to redefine their security relationship toward a division of regional roles. By anchoring the United States presence in Northeast Asia, the U.S.-Japanese and the U.S.-South Korean alliances are reinforcing each other, for Japan must help the United States in dealing with emergency situations that may arise in the areas surrounding that country.

Korea as a Bridge-builder

Lastly, a united Korea can build bridges between the big powers in the region. It can help promote confidence in a security situation where these other actors have a vital stake. It is a major test of American engagement whether the U.S.-Korea alliance can survive the unification process and continue even after the North Korean threat is gone. If the United States pulls out troops completely from the peninsula, Korea will be left without an ally on whom she can rely. Yet her power alone will be insufficient for playing off one power against the other. In this new situation, there will arise mounting pressures in Korea for developing nuclear weapons as an insurance policy.[17]

Traditionally, both China and Japan have competed in Korea to draw it into their respective spheres of influence. Chinese leaders used to regard Korea as one of the tributaries inhabited by 'Eastern barbarians'. Japanese leaders characterized Korea as 'a dagger pointed at their throat'. The Sino-Japanese War in 1894 was fought precisely over Korea. To deter such rivalry and to keep Korea nuclear-free, it would be better to preserve some American presence as an honest broker and stabilizer.

17   Byung-joon Ahn, 'Toward a Regional Alliance for Unification and Stability: A Test of Engagement' in Fred Bergsten and Il Sakong, eds., *The Korea-United States Economic Relationship* (Washington, DC: Institute for International Economics and Institute for Global Economics, 1997), pp. 11-26.

The challenge for this idea is to convince Beijing that it is not aimed against China and to build popular support for it in Korea, the United States, Japan and China. If the Chinese do not want to confront Japanese power or Korean nuclear weapons on their border, they would tolerate such an American presence. But this is only possible if Sino-American cooperation is sufficiently stable to permit a strategic understanding.

This is why we should develop a strategic vision for Korean and East Asian security in terms of a regional perspective. Located between two giants - China and Japan - and between the Asian continent and the Pacific, Korea can serve as a bridge for building peace, prosperity and stability in East Asia. In this way, Korea could become a regional player that has friendly relations with all neighbouring countries.

The Asia Pacific Region

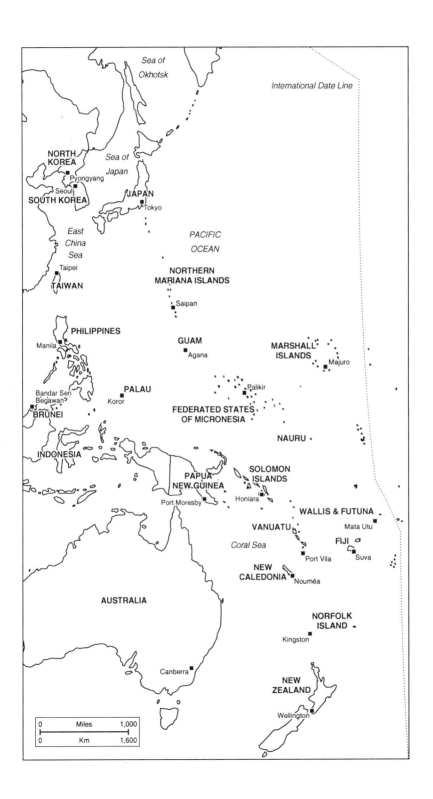

Sea of
Okhotsk

International Date Line

NORTH
KOREA

Sea of
Japan

Pyongyang

Seoul
SOUTH KOREA

JAPAN

Tokyo

East
China
Sea

PACIFIC

OCEAN

Taipei

TAIWAN

NORTHERN
MARIANA ISLANDS

Saipan

PHILIPPINES

Manila

GUAM

Agana

MARSHALL
ISLANDS

Majuro

Bandar Seri
Begawan

BRUNEI

PALAU

Koror

Palikir

FEDERATED STATES
OF MICRONESIA

INDONESIA

NAURU

SOLOMON
ISLANDS

PAPUA
NEW GUINEA

Port Moresby

Honiara

WALLIS & FUTUNA

VANUATU

Mata Utu

FIJI

Coral Sea

Port Vila

Suva

NEW
CALEDONIA

Nouméa

AUSTRALIA

NORFOLK
ISLAND

Kingston

Canberra

NEW
ZEALAND

Wellington

| 0 | Miles | 1,000 |
| 0 | Km | 1,600 |

Chapter 13

Moving Toward a More Secure Asia-Pacific: A Chinese View

Jiemian Yang

The Asia-Pacific region intersects all the major power centres of the world, except for Europe, and for decades has enjoyed sustained economic growth. Since the end of the Cold War, the Asia-Pacific countries have been striving to improve or enhance security cooperation in the new era. According to some scholars, 'economic development and security have been policy priorities among at least the major powers'.[1]

China is an important component of the Asia-Pacific region. The overall regional environment and China's security policy are mutually inter-related and reinforced. As long as China continues its current foreign policy of independence and peace, it is a positive force in building up a safer, more stable and prosperous Asia-Pacific region.

However, in terms of regional security matters, there are also worrying undercurrents, namely, the explosive situation on the Korean Peninsula, territorial disputes, a spiralling arms race and a conspicuous lack of trust among states. As for China, it must squarely address the difficult challenge of dispelling misleading or misplaced concerns about its emergence.

1. Security in Post-Cold War Asia-Pacific Region

The End of the Cold War has brought New Opportunities for Security Cooperation in the Asia-Pacific Region

In order to understand fully China's perspectives and positions on Asia-Pacific security, it is necessary to have a general picture of China's world view. Since the end of the Cold War, China has been working hard to adjust to the changing world situation. The single

---

1   Ming Zhang, 'US Needs Asian Credibility - Success Requires Clear Policy, Multilateral Tactics', *Defense News* (USA) (2-8 December 1996), p. 24.

most important aspect of the Chinese approach is that the world is moving from a bi-polar to a multi-polar system. This aspect featured prominently in the most recent Sino-Russian and Sino-French summits.[2]

Generally speaking, the international political context during this transitional period is fluid. While Europe and Africa suffered great turmoil during the process of change from the Cold War to the post-Cold War era, the Asia-Pacific region enjoyed continued economic growth and relative tranquillity, thus creating new opportunities for security cooperation. As one leading Chinese scholar on international affairs pointed out: the Asia-Pacific is enjoying a relative stability. The reasons for this include swift progress towards multi-polarity, a relatively smooth adjustment to the post-Cold War period, rapid economic development, internal stability in many countries of the region, stronger regional ties and the fact that most conflicts in the region have never got out of hand.[3]

Since the end of the Cold War, the Asia-Pacific region has become more stable, prosperous, predictable, cohesive and forward-looking. The post-World War II experience, both positive and negative, has indicated to the region that economic growth and security are interdependent and mutually reinforcing. Naturally, as the region becomes wealthier, concerns about security have grown. However, the Asia-Pacific lacks collective security arrangements. Unlike Europe, collective security does not have deep roots in the Asia-Pacific region. Most of the key defence relationships have been bilateral in nature with a strong hue of the Cold War legacy. The three multilateral arrangements in place have experienced malfunctioning (the South East Asia Treaty Organisation or SEATO,1954-1977), partial withdrawal(the Security Treaty between Australia, New Zealand and the United States of America or ANZUS, 1951 to the present[4]) or reduced influence (the Five Power Defence Arrangement or FPDA, 1971 to the present).

2   Jiang Zemin's speech at Russia's State Duma, April 23 (1997); full text in *China Daily*, April 24 1997, p. 4; 'Joint Sino-French Declaration on the establishment of a Comprehensive Partnership', *China Daily,* 17 May 1997, p. 4.
3   He Fang, 'The Asia-Pacific and China in the 21st Century', *CCIS International Review* (China Centre for International Studies), No. 2 (May 1995), pp. 8-17, quoted at p. 13.
4   New Zealand's membership was suspended in 1986 because it banned visits by US naval vessels under the US neither 'confirm nor deny' policy.

The Asia-Pacific Security System is Gradually Taking Shape

With the end of the Cold War and the disappearance of the two opposed camps, there is a new opportunity to arrange a security system for the Asia-Pacific region. In past years, major and middle-range powers such as China, Japan, South Korea and the ASEAN countries have been working hard at security cooperation.

But bilateral security cooperation still dominates the region. The United States maintains and strengthens its security arrangements in different forms with Japan, South Korea, Thailand, the Philippines, Singapore, Australia and others.

In April 1996, US President Bill Clinton, and the Japanese Prime Minister, Ryutoro Hashimoto, issued the US-Japanese Joint Declaration on Security. Some scholars pointed out that the statement is essentially a redefinition with the key theme being a shift in the emphasis of the US-Japan Security Treaty from the defence of Japan to Japanese support for the American military presence and mission in the Asia-Pacific region.[5] According to Dr. Douglas Paul, President of the Asia Pacific Policy Centre in Washington and senior advisor on Asian affairs to former US President, George Bush, these new guidelines reflect a concern with China.[6] The US and Australia also issued a joint declaration to strengthen their military cooperation. In May 1997, Japan and Australia strengthened their security cooperation.

On 25 April 1996, the visiting Russian President Boris Yeltsin and the Chinese President, Jiang Zemin, signed the third Sino-Russian joint statement in Beijing. It declared that the two countries had resolved to develop a strategic partnership of equality, mutual confidence and mutual coordination toward the 21st century.[7] In May 1997, China and Russia further strengthened their security ties by issuing another joint summit statement.

We will later examine these bilateral arrangements. However, the multilateral security arrangements command our immediate attention here. The founding of the Council on Security Cooperation in the

---

5   Yoshihide Soeya, 'The Japan-US Alliance in a Changing Asia', *Japan Review of International Affairs* (The Japan Institute of International Affairs), Vol.10, No. 4 (Fall 1996), pp. 265-275.

6   'In New Japan-US Crisis Guidelines, One Eye is on China', *International Herald Tribune*, 7-8 June 1997, p. 4.

7   *Remin Ribao,* 26 April 1996.

Asia-Pacific (CSCAP) in 1993 and the ASEAN Regional Forum (ARF) in the following year marked the beginnings of security cooperation on a regionwide basis. Since then, security cooperation in the Asia-Pacific has forged ahead at an accelerated speed, demonstrating the region's aspiration for a lasting environment of peace. For a long time to come, security will be a top priority for nations in the region.[8]

Multilateral security consultations and arrangements are being given more attention in the post-Cold War era. The most significant forums in the Asia-Pacific region are ASEAN and the ARF. The former, although organised in 1967 to promote economic cooperation, has gained prominence for helping to play a useful role in dealing with the Cambodian conflict. More recently, ASEAN expanded its post-ministerial regional security discussions and this led to a new, 18-member ARF, which includes the seven ASEAN countries, plus Canada, US, China, Japan, South Korea, Russia, Australia, New Zealand, Laos, Papua New Guinea and a representative from the European Union. The first annual meeting was held in Bangkok in July 1994. In 1996, Myanmar was also invited to attend the ARF. The inclusion of all the five permanent members of the UN Security Council in the ARF elevated the organisation's international standing. The forum offers a unique venue for discussing measures for enhancing collective security.[9]

However, in the Asia-Pacific region, there are other multilateral security and sub-regional mechanisms. In North-east Asia, the Northeast Asia Security Dialogue (NEASD) has become a regular channel for unofficial exchanges of views and opinions. The Korea Energy Development Organisation (KEDO) was created in 1995 to facilitate the dismantling of existing North Korean nuclear reactors and the provision of new ones. Although it owes little to the regional mechanism and was not shaped by any regional process, it contributes positively to peace and stability in the region. The South Pacific Forum is also playing an increasingly important role on the sub-regional level.

In Central Asia China, Russia, Kazakhstan, Kyrgyzstan and Tajikistan signed an agreement on confidence-building in military

8   Guo Zhenyuan, 'Asian-Pacific Region Remains Peaceful', *Beijing Review*, 5-11 February 1996, pp. 8-11, quoted at p. 8.
9   Hou Yingli, 'ASEAN Enhances Multilateral Security in Asia-Pacific', *Beijing Review*, 3-9 February 1997, pp. 8-9.

affairs in Shanghai on 26 April 1996.[10] Again, in April 1997, the five heads of states signed another agreement in Moscow on mutual reductions of military forces in the border areas. Together, these two documents, the only such agreements in the Asia-Pacific region, will play a positive role in enhancing friendship, building confidence and maintaining peace in the region and the world at large. They stand for a new concept of security in the post-Cold War era.[11]

But not all aspects of security in the region are rosy. The logic and prejudice of the Cold War did not completely disappear. While some old problems subdued by the East-West confrontation are re-emerging, new worrisome and troublesome challenges are becoming evident: territoral and ethnic disputes, cultural and racial clashes, religious disagreements, mutual suspicions, drug-trafficking, environmental conflicts and so forth. No wonder some scholars like Dr. Jonathan D. Pollack at the US Rand Corporation, hold a pessimistic opinion that beneath a veneer of shared interests (especially related to economic development) loom deeper differences and potential incompatibilities that defy ready resolution.[12]

2. China and the Asia-Pacific Region: Economic and Security Interests

Increasing Interdependence Between China and the Asia-Pacific Region

The Chinese government attaches great importance to the Asia-Pacific region. It is concentrating on its modernisation programme and striving for an international environment that is conducive to such an objective. By re-emphasising its good-neighbour policy, China has succeeded in solving border issues with Russia, normalised relations

10   The agreement stipulates that all parties concerned promise not to attack each other, not to hold military exercises targeting each other, to prevent any dangerous military activities in the region, and to notify all parties concerned of any military activities within the area 100 km from the borders. The agreement also sets limitations on the number, scope, and size of military exercises the parties can conduct within each year. *Remin Ribao*, 27 April 1996.

11   Liu Jiang, 'Another Milestone in Sino-Russian Ties', *Beijing Review*, 5-11 May 1997, p. 4.

12   Jonathan D. Pollack, 'Pacific Insecurity: Emerging Threats to Stability in East Asia', *Harvard International Review* (Harvard Internal Relations Council), Vol. XVIII, No.2 (Spring 1996), pp. 8-11, quoted at p. 8.

with Vietnam, contributed to a solution of the Cambodian issue, and facilitated a relaxation of tensions on the Korean Peninsula. China has also become more positive and active towards regional, sub-regional and multilateral security cooperation.

With the increasing role of economics in the domestic and foreign policies of most countries in the post-Cold War era, China's economic interdependence with the Asia-Pacific region has also increased. The bulk of China's foreign trade and investment is within East Asia. The East Asian economy is growing at 6.2 percent annually, compared with a world annual growth average of 1.2 percent. The amount of intra-regional trade has increased from 33 percent in 1980 to 39 percent in 1988, and to 67 percent in 1993.[13] Five of China's top ten trading partners are in East Asia (Japan, Hong Kong, Taiwan, South Korea and Singapore). More than 65 percent of the $25.7 billion foreign investment in China in 1993 came from East Asia. Hong Kong, Taiwan, Japan, Singapore and Thailand are among the top ten foreign investors.[14]

The Evolution of China's Concepts of and Attitudes toward Asia-Pacific Security

Traditionally, national security is understood as a safeguard from external threats, a bulwark against external pressure, the ability to counter such attempts and neutralise emerging threats. Naturally, the task of ensuring national security is to be solved by each state in its specific historical context.

Since the founding of the People's Republic of China, its conceptions of security have gone through several phases. For a quite long period of time, China was most concerned for its very physical survival in the face of US-imposed encirclement, the Soviet threat and the attempt to stage a comeback by the defeated Kuomintang forces in Taiwan. Since the mid-1970s, with the high tide of the Cultural Revolution receding and its international standing greatly enhanced, China has started to conceptualise security in a broader way.

Today its concept of security is more comprehensive. China increasingly sees the country's economic, scientific and technological competence and international competitiveness as the basis of its

13   *Shijie Zhishi* (World Affairs), No.1142 (1 January 1994), p. 1.
14   *Remin Ribao*, 2 March and 18 May 1994.

growing national strength and security.[15] Other issues such as health, crime, the massive movement of people, the environment and terrorism, and resource supplies[16] are also entering security discussions.

Meanwhile, China has changed its attitude towards multilateral and collective security. In the Cold War era, China strongly opposed such security arrangements. At that time, the United States dominated the scene. Most of the multilateral and collective security arrangements were controlled by the United States. Even in the initial years after the end of the Cold War, China was only lukewarm to proposed multilateral or collective security arrangements. Recently, however, China has become more positive and active. It accepted the invitation to take part in the inaugural meeting of the ARF in 1994. In December 1996, China decided to join the CSCAP after successfully negotiating a settlement of Taiwan's non-participation. This was seen by the Chinese as a virtue of regional multilateralism.[17] On 23 April 1997 China set up its CSCAP National Committee.[18] This represented a further Chinese commitment towards the multilateral security dialogue.

A good example of this changing attitude are the China-ASEAN annual high-level official meetings. In the first two such meetings in 1995 and 1996 respectively, China avoided discussion on security concerns in the South China Sea, where its territorial claims overlap with those of Malaysia, Vietnam, Brunei and the Philippines. But, in mid-April 1997, when China and ASEAN held their third annual high-ranking official meeting in Huangshan, Anhui Province of China, there was a sea-change: Beijing agreed for the first time to talk about ASEAN members' claims in the South China Sea, and offered to frame a code of conduct governing ties with ASEAN.[19]

15 You Ji, 'Interdependence and China's Economic Security,' in Stuart Harris and Andrew Mack, eds., *The Political Economy of Security in the Asia-Pacific* (Sydney: Allen and Unwin), forthcoming.

16 For instance, see Ji Guoxing, 'Energy Security Cooperation in the Asia-Pacific', in *The Korean Journal of Defense Analysis* (Korean Institute for Defense Analysis), Vol. VIII., No.2 (Winter 1996), pp. 269-295.

17 Gerald Segal, 'How insecure is Pacific Asia?', *International Affairs* (Royal Institute of Internal Affairs, UK), Vol. 73, No.2 (April 1997), pp. 235-249, quoted at p. 247.

18 *Remin Ribao*, 24 April 1997, p. 4.

19 Michael Vatikiotis, 'Friends and Fears', *Far Eastern Economic Review*, 8 May 1997, pp. 14-15, quoted at p. 15.

The major reasons for this and other changes can be summed up as follows:

* First, China is modifying its relevant attitudes and policies in light of the changed international environment. Nowadays, the world has become increasingly interrelated. Inter-state interests and contradictions are closely interwoven with each other. Therefore, promotion of interests and solutions to problems can only be managed on a multilateral basis. Besides, many Asia-Pacific countries also strongly advocate involving China with a view to bringing Beijing more into line with the norms of the international community.

* Second, China has become much more active in world multilateral diplomacy in general, and in the Asia-Pacific region in particular. The Chinese President, Jiang Zemin, has participated in all the APEC informal summits. The Chinese premier, Li Peng, took part in the Asia-Europe meeting. China took an active part in the negotiations on the Comprehensive Test Ban Treaty (CTBT), Non-Proliferation Treaty (NPT), Chemical Weapons Convention (CWC) and so forth. It also pledged to stand by the Missile Technology Control Regime (MTCR) although it is still not a part of the Regime. China became a full dialogue partner in ASEAN in 1996, raising to a new level its relations with the region.

* Third, China wants to play a constructive role in establishing a new regional order. Contrary to some peoples' concern that China might challenge the exisiting world order, China is willing to work within this framework. China also wants to be treated properly and contribute to the shaping of the post-Cold War order in the Asia-Pacific region.

China's Immediate Security Concerns

In modern history, China has been repeatedly subject to numerous humiliations such as the loss of territory, the payment of indemnities and even foreign occupation. And again because of US interference, China still faces the unfinished task of unifying the country. Therefore, China is the only major power in the world which has to deal with so many territorial issues with its neighbours as well as a distracting and time-consuming tug-of-war with Taiwan over diplomatic recognition.

On territorial matters, China is confronting three groups of issues. The first group is related to those territories clearly under China's jurisdiction which have separatist movements, like Tibet and Xinjiang. A combination of factors is behind these separatist movements: personal ambitions, race, religion, distorted interpretation of history, mishandling by local Chinese officials, and foreign instigation and encouragement. As to the foreign interference aspect, the Chinese government seeks assurances from bordering and relevant countries, such as those in Central and South Asia, neither to support nor to provide sanctuaries to separatists. On the other hand, the Chinese government has a resolute policy and measures to maintain the country's integrity. So far China has only partially succeeded.

The second group concerns those territories which are not disputed, but lie outside China's jurisdiction. Such places include Macao and Taiwan. To accommodate the special character of these places, Deng Xiaoping developed the One Country-Two Systems formula. Under this creative formula, China recovered sovereignty over Hong Kong on July 1, 1997 and will do the same in Macao in 1999. However, the Taiwan issue is more problematic. Some people on the island of Taiwan are inclined to go independent. The leadership of Lee Teng-hui in Taiwan has been using whatever means available in its quest for international recognition and living space. Such adventurism in diplomacy is dangerous. China has repeatedly made it clear that, while it will continue to work hard to realise its objective to unify the country through peaceful means, it will never make the commitment not to use force.

The third group are those territories which are the subject of dispute with other countries. On these issues, China has been firm on principles but flexible enough to reach compromises. For a series of complicated reasons, China has territorial disputes with a number of countries from Russia to Japan through to Southeast Asian countries. With the spirit of give and take, China has succeeded in negotiating solutions with Russia (to date, 99% of the problems are solved),[20] Mongolia and others. But some of the disputes such as Diaoyu

20   Cf. Shi Ze, 'Chinese and Russian Friendship Growing', *Beijing Review*, 29 April - 5 May 1996, pp. 8-13.

(Senkaku) Islands, Xisha and Nansha (Spratly) Islands remain to be solved.

China's Boader Security Concern

China's broader concern is to ensure global as well as regional peace and stability. China considers the establishment of a new international political and economic order as a long-term goal. As one of the five permanent members of the UN Security Council, China actively and positively participates in solving global issues like NPT, CTBT, CWC, peacekeeping and peacemaking, environmental protection, drug trafficking, terrorism and organised crime. Regrettably, sometimes the international community led by the US does not respond positively. In this vein, the Japanese Deputy Minister for Foreign Affairs, Mr Kazuo Ogura, pointed out: 'Most important and often [overlooked] is the fact that increased interdependence means not just reform in China but continual adjustments by other countries to accommodate change'.[21]

3. China Does Not Pose Threats to Other Countries

In a short span of several years since the end of the Cold War, the West has shifted from its prophecy of the collapse of Chinese Communist rule to a position where China has replaced Japan as a 'threat'.[22] The so-called China threat argument can hardly hold water in terms of China's historical experience, economic development, national defence policies, and domestic preoccupation.

Historically, China has been one of the strongest powers in the world for thousands of years. If China wished, it could easily conquer foreign lands or colonise its Asian neighbours. But China rarely pursued an expansionist policy. Quite a number of prominent Western figures have pointed this out.[23] To the contrary, China has historically

21   Kazuo Ogura, 'The Shadow of China', *Time* (USA), 28 April 1997, p. 61.
22   Stuart Harris, 'The China-Japan Relationship and Asia Pacific Regional Security', *The Journal of East Asian Affairs* (The Research Institute for International Affairs, South Korea), Vol. XI, No.1 (Winter/Spring 1997), p. 121.
23   Professor David Shambaugh at the George Washington University holds that 'History does not suggest that China seeks to conquer or absorb other countries in the region.' David Shambaugh, 'Containment or Engagement of China? - Calculating Beijing's Responses,' *International Security* (Harvard University), Vol.21, No.2 (Fall 1996), pp. 180-209, quoted at p. 187; US Ambassador to China James Sasser described, during an interview with

and repeatedly been subjected to invasion and oppression by outside forces. The Chinese people treasure the hard-won peace they are enjoying today. As the great Chinese sage Confucius said more than 2000 years ago, 'Do not do to others what you would not have them do to you'. This explains the pacific tradition inherent in Chinese foreign policy.

Economically, China's national strength has grown thanks to its policy of reform and opening up, and this has immensely benefited its neighbours rather than posed any threat. According to Mr. Lee Kuan Yew, the former Singaporean Prime Minister, a number of Asian countries enjoy an annual one percent increase in gross national product thanks to their economic and trade ties with China.[24] Also, China's development offers enormous investment opportuniiities for Western business. Therefore, a developed China offers no threat but only stability to the world. Further, as some Chinese scholars correctly point out, the aforementioned threat would in fact have centred on poverty, as well as famine, and the movement of refugees and the chaos which accompany such destitution. Imagine even a conservative estimate of 30 million refugees crossing the sea by boat, or otherwise flocking into neighbouring countries and regions. The number could quite easily have mushroomed to 120 million, or 10 per cent of the total population, had the Chinese nation languished in the grip of poverty.[25]

Militarily, China pursues a defensive policy aimed at resisting outside invasion, safeguarding the country's territorial, air and sea integrity and maintaining national unity. While China's military expenditure is consistent with these security needs, it remains at a very low level. However, it is true that the actual amount China spends on defence has increased. Taking inflation into account, such an increase is minute. Between 1979 and 1994, the annual growth rate of military expenditure was 6.22 percent, but the retail price index increased by 7.7 percent. [26]

Xinhua News Agency, the so-called 'China threat' as groundless if examined from the standpoint of Chinese history. He noted that China has exhibited no expansionist tendencies over the past 500 years. *Beijing Review*, 17 February -3 March 1997, p. 4.

24   Quoted in Ren Xin, '"China Threat" Theory Untenable', *Beijing Review*, 5-11 February 1996, p. 10.
25   Li Haibo, 'Imaginary Threat', *Beijing Review,* 24-30 March 1997, p. 4.
26   Quoted in Ren Xin: '"China Threat" Theory Untenable', *Beijing Review*, 5-11 February 1996, p. 11.

Domestically, China is preoccupied with many problems. According to Chinese official statistics, by late 1996 there were still about 65 million Chinese living below the poverty line, accounting for 5.4 percent of the whole population.[27] Professor Stuart Harris has pointed out that for the Chinese leadership 'Domestic stability and economic development are... top priorities, they legitimise the government and the Party, and increase the international status China regards as critical. This means that China's statements that it seeks a peaceful security environment are likely to be genuine in the next decade or two at least and that great efforts will be made to maintain domestic stability'.[28] Many other Western scholars have expressed the same view.[29] As Japanese Deputy Minister for Foreign Affairs, Mr Kazua Ogura pointed out, 'analysts tend to overlook an important point: China, having lived with the burden of invasion and occupation in recent history, perceives a 'threat' from the outside and feels anxious over its own security'.[30]

Of course, no one could guarantee that China will definitely not seek hegemony when it becomes really strong and prosperous. But according to the mainstream view of Chinese academics, it will take about 50 to 100 years for China to achieve this goal. It hardly makes sense therefore for the West to assume the worst in China rather than seek the historical opportunity to develop cooperation with Beijing. This is what Dr Henry Kissinger meant when he said, 'Before turning

27   *Beijing Review*, 27 January-2 February 1997, p. 4.
28   Stuart Harris, 'The China-Japan Relationship and Asia Pacific Regional Security', *The Journal of East Asian Affairs* (The Research Institute for International Affairs, South Korea), Vol. XI, No.1 (Winter/Spring 1997), p. 143.
29   For instance, Professor David Shambaugh pointed out: 'The Chinese leadership will be preoccupied with complex domestic issues for some time to come'. David Shambaugh, 'Containment or Engagement of China?- Calculating Beijing's Responses,' *International Security* (Harvard University), Vol. 21, No. 2 (Fall 1996), pp. 180-209, quoted at p. 206. Dr Alfred D. Wilhelm Jr. pointed out: 'Under the most likely scenarios, China will continue to give highest priority to economic development, probably throughout the period (to the year of 2010)'. Alfred D. Wilhelm, Jr., 'China and Security in the Asia-Pacific region through 2010', Center for Naval Analysis (USA), *CRM* 95-226 (March 1996), p. 3.
30   Kazuo Ogura, 'The Shadow of China', *Time* (USA), 28 April 1997, p. 61.

to confrontation [between China and the United States], a cooperative relationship must be given a chance'.[31]

4. Some Security Issues

Mutual distrust

Great distrust exists among the Asia-Pacific countries. According to a new report prepared for the ARF's 21 members, virtually every Asian country has land or maritime boundaries that are subject to dispute. The report went on to say that East Asia's maritime disputes were difficult to settle because they covered areas that contain valuable marine and seabed resources and are symbols of national integrity and influence. 'Few governments have the courage to resolve such claims if resolution means potentially having to concede ownership, even though leaving such disputes unsettled could provide tinder for future conflict'.[32]

Against this background, China is still suspicious about the different proposed multilateral security arrangements for the following reasons. First, China is concerned about the intentions of the United States. So far, the United States is still undecided whether to treat China as a friend or an enemy. Even during his recent trip to Beijing, General John Shalikashvili, Chairman of the US Joint Chiefs of Staff, listed four specific threats that US sees in the Asia-Pacific region: the unpredictable regime in Pyongyang, proliferation, territorial disputes and Hong Kong, three of which are related to China.[33] Western countries have tried to engage and integrate China into international security arrangements. But the West tries to use the rules and procedures of such arrangements to confine China. Second, China is concerned about some other countries, especially the members of ASEAN, which seek to use multilateral bargaining to exert collective pressure on Beijing in the South China Sea islands disputes. Third, China is concerned about Taiwan. The Taiwan authorities have made it clear that it wants to use collective security arrangements for protection.

31   Henry A. Kissinger, 'A World We Have Not Known', *Newsweek* (USA), 27 January 1997, pp. 23-25, quoted at p. 24.
32   *International Herald Tribune*, 14 April 1997, p. 4.
33   John M. Shalikashvili, 'U.S.-China Engagement: Military-to-Military Contacts', speech at the Chinese People's Liberation Army Defense University, 14 May 1997; *USIA Wireless File*, 15 May 1997.

Innovative Thinking is Needed for the New Era

Currently, there are still some people advocating 'balance of power' strategies to deal with the security issue in the Asia-Pacific region.[34] The China 'threat' argument is conceived within the balance of power theory. At present, China is the main communist power after the collapse of the Soviet Union. After a geostrategic redistribution of power in the international system and, as an emerging power in the multi-polar system, China is seen as trying to fill a power vacuum in Asia. In addition, many detect a historical analogy between China's rise and that of Germany and Japan in the 19th century. The intense industrialisation and economic development in China, it is believed, will be followed by expansion.[35] Old thinking does not go away easily. In the Asia-Pacific, geopolitics and military alliances have assumed a growing role in international relations.

The recent consolidation of the US security alliances with Japan and Australia respectively has aroused great concern among the Chinese. Professor Zhao Jieqi, a research fellow, and former Deputy Director of the Japanese Studies Institute of the Chinese Academy of Social Sciences pointed out: 'The short-term goal of the [US-Japan and US-Australia] alliances is to deal with the "instability" in the Taiwan Straits, the South China Sea and on the Korean Peninsula. The long-term goal is to deal with the imaginary 'troubles' made by an economically and militarily stronger China'.[36]

Building up Viable Security Cooperation Mechanisms

The Asia-Pacific region has greatly diversified. Regional awareness and identity are still being developed. Moreover, as security issues are closely linked with the core of nation-state interests, any agreements on security cooperation need high levels of mutual trust and understanding. Countries in the region need to work hard to build and maintain confidence among themselves and coordinate their efforts to produce some mechanisms that fit the reality of local conditions.

34 For instance, Gerald Segal holds this view in his 'How insecure is Pacific Asia', *International Affairs* (Royal Institute of International Affairs, UK), Vol.73, No.2 (April 1997), pp. 235-249, especially on pp. 245-248.

35 For instance, see Samuel P. Huntington, 'America's Changing Strategic Interests,' *Survival,* Vol. 33, No.1 (January/February 1991), p. 12.

36 Chen Yali, 'US-Japan alliance not conducive to peace', *China Daily,* 26 May 1997, p. 4.

The existing ARF is obviously not enough to deal with regionwide security issues. And the major powers, such as the United States, China, Japan and Russia have not seen eye to eye on future regional security cooperative mechanisms.

Some Existing and Potential Security Problems

Security cooperation in the Asia-Pacific region has not been and will not be plain sailing. Some of the prominent problems include the Korean Peninsula, South China Sea dispute and arms competition.

The Korean Peninsula is the most explosive place in the region. The greatest uncertainty is that no one knows clearly what is happening in North Korea, how North and South Korea will interact with each other and what shall happen if the present nuclear framework does not function. The most immediate problem concerns the grave consequences of the present food shortage in the North.

Territorial disputes over the South China Sea islands present another challenge to the Asia-Pacific region. Until the mid-1970s, no country challenged China's sovereignty of the Nansha and Xisha islands in the South China Sea. However, at present, there are six claimants for the islets and reefs in the South China Sea. These territorial disputes not only impose great limitations on the manoeuvrability of the governments involved, but also have the potential to arouse nationalist emotions and sentiments. Therefore, any mishandling of these matters could result in serious consequences.

An intensifying arms buildup and the proliferation of nuclear, biological and chemical weapons in the region also warrants serious attention. Several factors contribute to this new development: long-term confrontations such as on the Korean Peninsula have made it imperative for the affected parties to continue to match the military capability of rivals; economic prosperity has enabled countries to start modernising their national defence sectors; and foreign arms dealers are looking to the Asia-Pacific region to replace markets lost elsewhere.[37]

37 Cf. Pan Zhenqiang et al., *Guoji caijun yu junbei kongzhi* [International Disarmament and Arms Control] (Beijing: National Defense University Press, 1996), especially Chapters 12 and 19.

5. Towards a Gloomier or Brighter Future?

Convergence and Divergence

With the approach of the next century, almost all countries, big or small, are slowly but definitely moving toward some sort of consensus: they are looking forward to a time of peace, economic growth and social stability. While concentrating on domestic affairs, they are also trying to shape a favourable external environment. Therefore, they are working hard to alleviate tensions over hot spots, prevent the eruption of potential troubles, and searching for new mechanisms to ensure peace, stability and security in the region.

The Asia-Pacific countries are experiencing a growing sense of interdependence. The regional economic miracle has reinforced the fact that economic prosperity is dependent on mutual co-operation. Similarly, on security matters, they must work together for a safer and better future.

In parallel fashion, the divergence among the Asia-Pacific countries is also evident. Their differences in political, economic and social systems, long-term suspicions of each other, the existence of inter- and intra-national conflicts, mutually exclusive national goals and values of some countries, the lack of coherent regional awareness and identity have all served to constrain the development of a more mature and institutionalised security cooperation framework within which they can work together.

The countries concerned should also find effective ways to prevent domestic factors from excessively affecting their foreign and security policies. As mentioned above, all governments are now paying greater attention to their own domestic affairs. However, domestic factors vary from time to time and from country to country. Understandably, they are not always overlapping. Sometimes they even conflict. For instance, US domestic policies and economics used to lead to 'Japan bashing'. But 'China bashing' has now become a favoured method to score points with domestic constituencies.

The United States Holds an Extensively Pivotal Position in Shaping the Future Security of the Region

First of all, the United States should review its regional strategy. As Professor Shi Yinhong pointed out, 'The United States has been accustomed to and taken for granted Western dominance for so long and is therefore not prepared yet for the rise of non-Western power.'[38] The United States should consult on an equal footing with all the Asia-Pacific countries, rich or poor, big or small, on how to work out a regional new order in the post-Cold War era.

Second, the United States should reconsider its military presence in the region. This is a legacy of World War II and the Cold War. Objectively speaking, such a presence did play, to some extent, a positive role in maintaining regional stability in the past. However, with the end of the Cold War, the United States should reconsider the validity of its military presence. In particular, it should not invent new reasons for a prolonged stay in the region.

The regional reaction towards the US military presence is mixed. Some show their opposition at the governmental level and call for its phasing out. Some show their resentment at the non-governmental level. Okinawa is a case in point. In a referendum held in Okinawa in the summer of 1996, nine out of ten voters opposed the presence of US forces. And according to numerous opinion surveys, some two-thirds of the Japanese want to rethink the old security treaty.[39] In May 1997, 3,000 landowners refused to renew leases on territory used by the US as bases. Consequently, Tokyo had to introduce a law that effectively denied the property rights of such opponents

Third, the US should fulfil its own commitment to multilateral efforts on security matters. Upon entering the White House, President Clinton apparantly changed the established US policy of bilateral security arrangements in the Asia-Pacific region. He began to talk about a 'New Pacific Community'.[40] However, the deeds of President Clinton did not live up to his words. The United States has continued along its well-trodden path. It has strengthened its bilateral alliances with Japan and Australia while remaining somewhat inactive in the multilateral security sphere.

Looking Creatively Into the Future

The Asia-Pacific region is unique in and of itself. It should learn from any useful experience of other regions, such as Europe. But it should

---

38 Shi Yinhong, 'US to Deal with Rise of Non-Western Powers', *Beijing Review,* 28 April-4 May 1997, p. 7.

39 *Time* (USA), 28 April 1997, p. 52.

40 President Clinton's speech at Waseda University, Tokyo, 7 July 1993.

not copy Europe blindly. Diversity, pluralism and inclusiveness are among the characteristics of the Asia-Pacific region.

Security is a very sensitive issue. It requires creative thinking. In the post-Cold War era, we should not be confined to old ways of thinking, such as 'balance of power' notions, zero-sum thinking and alliance systems. As is well-known, foreign and security policy is, to a certain extent, a matter of perception. If you perceive someone as an enemy, then they are likely to become so in what becomes a self-fulfilling prophecy. Therefore, we should all use our imagination to work for common security and move towards a win-win future.

The Asia-Pacific countries should take concrete confidence building measures and gradually work out feasible agendas for regional security cooperation. Some Asia-Pacific countries have long adopted peaceful means to settle their differences, including the use of the International Court of Justice to help resolve territorial disputes. China has also proposed the formula of joint development while shelving differences concerning the South China Sea. A senior Chinese Foreign Ministry official said, 'With much at stake, no one in the region wants to raise a "rumpus". With our overriding common interest and given the political will, those challenges are not impossible to meet.'[41]

'Second Track' mechanisms are an effective supplement to official efforts to deal with regional security. Through the 'Second Track' approach, government officials can attend seminars in a private capacity to exchange views and enhance mutual trust. Sometimes, tensions are eased through such channels. In these forums, academics have considerable scope to show their creativity, imagination and talents in contributing to regional and global security.

Moreover, the scientific and technological revolution has contributed new factors to the regional security situation. The internet is integrating mankind in the four corners of the world. The internationalisation of production and distribution has blurred national identity. The movement of capital and technology has virtually removed national physical boundaries. Easier and faster transportation has made the earth a smaller place. What have not yet happened are changes in our conceptions of security and behaviour in relation to it.

41 Speech of Mr Chen Jian, assistant foreign minister of China, at the first general meeting of the CSCAP, Singapore, 4 June 1997; *China Daily*, 5 June 1997.

Indeed, we need a more comprehensive view of security rather than the traditional military-based conception.

China is an important member of the world community. It takes very seriously its responsibility for regional and global security. Therefore, China has two positions of principle on the establishment of a security dialogue: Beijing is prepared to consult with other Asia-Pacific countries on questions of common concern, and to conduct dialogues in various forms, at different levels and through multi-channels.[42] Together with its neighbours, China will make its due contribution to security in the Asia-Pacific region.

Postscript

Since the above text was written, the financial crisis in Southeast and Northeast Asia has erupted. This recent development has once again vindicated a broader notion of security and security co-operation.

---

42   President Jiang Zemin's interview with the president of Asashi Shinbum, August 1993.

Chapter 14

Asia-Pacific Security: A New Zealand Viewpoint

Terence O'Brien

The last thirty years of the 20th century have witnessed remarkable economic success in countries of East Asia which, while the growth and prosperity is not uniformly distributed, is unequalled in modern history in both the speed and extent of its impact. The result is that on the doorstep of a new century, the Asia-Pacific region as a whole constitutes a vital engine force for the global economy, and, at the same time, is itself deeply affected by the impacts of globalisation - in particular the factors of trade, information and technology - that are transforming the global economy everywhere. Trade, in particular, has been growing faster than output and is projected to continue to grow at a rapid rate. Driven in part by technological change, economic integration has been deepening in ways that signal fundamental change in the global community.[1] In Asia, the emergence of trans-border growth triangles that interlock regional economies is one manifestation of this trend.

Within the next fifty years, the world population will probably surpass nine billion and global economic output will grow five times. Scarcities of non-renewable resources will increase sharply.[2] Asia is projected to become an energy deficient region over the next three decades making it more dependent on OPEC supplies. Dependency in East Asia doubles every twelve years (globally it doubles every twenty eight years). Asian demand for food will likewise increase dramatically as a function of rising affluence; and the rate of urbanisation will accelerate, so that it is estimated 55% of Asia's people will reside in

1   J. Sewell, 'Economic Security of Asia-Pacific Nations', Discussion Paper, 11th Asia-Pacific Roundtable, Kuala Lumpur, 5-8 June 1997.
2   Thomas Homer-Dixon, 'Global Dangers, Changing Dimensions of International Security', in Michael E. Brown, Sean M. Lynn-Jones & Steven E. Miller, eds., (Cambridge,Mass: MIT Press, 1996), pp. 144-179.

cities by 2025 (it is calculated Asia already possesses 13 of the world's 15 most polluted cities). The spread of deregulating policies is likewise dislocating communities and patterns of social organisation with disturbing effects on crime and disorder. China is estimated to have a floating internal migrant population of about 50 million.[3]

While East Asia's economies grew faster than the rest of the world in the last 30 years of the century, it is estimated that the region's forest cover declined by 50% and fish stocks diminished by 50%.[4] Competition for access to these resources throughout Asia-Pacific (and especially to marine resources in the Southern Hemisphere) is likely to sharpen. Unless major changes are secured in patterns of energy use in Asia, the rate of environmental degradation will profoundly worsen. The IBRD has estimated that between 1995-2004 some $US 2 trillion will be invested in power plants, water systems and other infrastructures if the rates of economic growth are to be sustained.

Economic Security

All this certainly reinforces a conclusion that the economic dimension of security and well-being for countries in East Asia is indeed real, and will likely assume an even larger dimension. The intrinsically transnational character of the challenges reinforces a disposition that exists domestically within several Asian countries (more notably in South East Asia, but also in Japan and China) to view regional security itself as not being confined to the traditional military dimension alone, but to embrace economic, environmental and other factors. Regional cooperation should, in these terms, be directed to a management order that sustains a balance of interest, as much as (or as a substitute for) a balance of power between states. The culture of conventional strategic security thinking about East Asia in Asia-Pacific more generally (in the US, Australia and elsewhere) resists the notion of comprehensive security[5] and places greatest emphasis on traditional ways, including the balance of power approach.

3   Sewell, op. cit.
4   James Clad, 'The Emergence of Ecological Issues' in David Wurfel, ed., *South-East Asia in the New World Order* (Basingstoke: Macmillan Press, 1996), pp. 52-71
5   'National Security' in Anthony Milner, ed., *Comparing Cultures: Australia in Asia Series* Melbourne: Oxford University Press, 1996), pp. 182-190.

Economic interdependence as it manifests itself in East Asia is therefore no automatic guarantor of stability. The transnational nature of the challenges reinforces the point that collective cooperative responses in the region are indispensable to resolution or successful management of the problems. That poses an added challenge to a region where formalised, institutionalised region-wide cooperation is of comparatively recent origin.

Overall Political Security Outlook

The end of the Cold War removed the global prospect of great power war. Overarching global confrontation no longer figures in strategic security calculation. The overall regional security environment within Asia-Pacific is more benign, stable and peaceful in the 1990s than at any time previously in the century.[6] There is more than one reason to explain this.

The autonomous political choices of the great majority of East Asian states to commit to economic modernisation through a range of remarkably analogous economic policies, provide the clearest and most compelling factor in the background to the present outlook. Economic dynamism may therefore be the primary explanation for, and it may also be the primary influence on, the prospects for enduring stability, at least in the medium term. There is sufficient reason to be wary about the possible adverse consequences that derive from the very economic success itself,[7] but no country regards military aggression as a means to secure its interests.

The Asia-Pacific region is, it can be reasonably suggested, managing the post-Cold War World rather better than other regions - the former Soviet Union (FSU), the Middle East, Africa or even Western Europe. The ethnic and particularist conflicts in other regions have not manifested themselves in East Asia, at least to the same degree. Of course, there is no guarantee that things will continue as they are. But this situation has developed in the absence of established mature region-wide institutions for security management. In terms of conventional threat, Northeast Asia is blessed with certain inherent

6   C. Morrison, ed., *Asia-Pacific Security Outlook 1997* (East-West Centre, Honolulu, 1997), p. 1.

7   James L. Richardson, 'The Asia-Pacific: Geopolitical Cauldron or Regional Community?' in Gary Klintworth, ed., *Asia-Pacific Security, Less Uncertainty, New Opportunities* (New York: St Martins Press, 1996), pp. 11-12.

defensive advantages (mountainous terrain, large territory that lends strategic depth, island locations that afford protection) which make offensive operations difficult. Indeed, it has been claimed that no other area of the world, where the great powers interact one with another, offers more defensive advantage than Northeast Asia.[8]

Key security arrangements are a stabilising factor. The US is committed in Asia-Pacific because it is in her vital interests to be so. The existence of US bilateral security treaties with selected partners, and most notably with Japan, affords an insurance premium that offers reassurance to governments in the East Asia region. There exists amongst those governments, nonetheless, scepticism about American will.[9]

What would be the circumstances of regional destabilisation, that would in fact prompt the US without equivocation, to act militarily on the Asian mainland? The answer to that question is far from clear. Doubts find expression, therefore, in regional thinking in Asian capitals, where eventual American withdrawal is not dismissed as a possibility. The security assurances offered by the US alliances (and the regional presence of US defence forces), constitute one explanation for the overall benign Asia-Pacific regional security environment, but they are not the full explanation. The US has, moreover, its own agenda in East Asia relating to the spread of democracy, human rights and pluralism. For several governments in the region, such policy is perceived as a very recipe for destabilisation. Reliance upon the US is, therefore, problematic.[10]

The collective efforts undertaken to create the foundations for region-wide cooperation, may also account for the persistence of a basically stable regional environment. The benign regional security outlook provides the opportunity to fashion a framework for, and the habits of, regional order management. The absence of mature formalised intergovernmental regional institutions is, however, explicable in several ways. The region is geographically and strategically disparate, and it is diverse in culture, social systems and

---

8   E. Gholz, D. Press and H. Sapolsky, 'Coming Home America: the Strategy of Restraint in the Face of Temptation', *International Security*, Vol. 21, No. 4 (Spring 1997), pp. 31-32

9   Robert Scalapino, 'The US Commitment to Asia' in Desmond Ball, ed., *Transformation of Security in the Asia-Pacific Region* (London: Frank Cass 1996), p. 68.

10   S. Sheldon, 'Alternative Visions of Security in the Asia-Pacific' *Pacific Affairs*, Vol. 69, No. 3 (Fall 1996), pp. 381-396.

politics. The creation and sustenance of any region-wide system is a formidable undertaking.[11] And, unlike Europe and elsewhere, it is not being pursued against the compelling background of the Cold War.

The brand of multilateralism taking root in East Asia during the second half of the 20th century has been predominantly sub-regional in character. This has found expression in South East Asia with the establishment of the Association of South East Nations (ASEAN). Such regionalism has been grounded in intense networking, collegiality, and ease and informality of dealings rather than legalism and a panoply of formalised intergovernmental commitments. If, however, the proof of the pudding lies in the eating, then ASEAN's contribution over the 30 years of its existence to area stability has been real, and has confounded those outside sceptics who questioned its original durability and relevance.

ASEAN now sees for itself a more ambitious role in developing the sinews of greater region-wide cooperation, throughout Asia-Pacific by way of the ASEAN Regional Forum (ARF), launched in 1994. The Forum constitutes the first attempt to create a multilateral region-wide management system for addressing issues of Asian-Pacific political security. ASEAN has been responsible as well, for energising the non-governmental strategic studies process (so called Track Two) which is considered to complement, and even influence, the regional intergovernmental process. This is a multi-layered effort not all of which owes it existence, by any means, to ASEAN. ASEAN's capacity for ongoing constructive regional leadership will be affected by the 1997 decisions over enlargement of the Association to include Myanmar, Laos and Cambodia as well as the earlier one to admit Vietnam. These countries add to the diversity and disparity of the membership. Myanmar's poor international reputation over human rights, and Cambodia's vulnerability to internal political turbulence, suggest that the cohesion and sense of purpose of ASEAN's earlier years may be harder to sustain.

A new regional security architecture can only be established gradually, through a building-block approach which could well include consolidation of sub-regional dialogues under the broad regional umbrella.[12] The basic point that 'the approach shall be evolutionary taking place in three stages, namely the promotion of confidence

11   S. Morimoto, 'A Security Framework for the Asia-Pacific Region' in Desmond Ball, ed., op. cit., pp. 202-203.

12   ibid., p. 223.

building measures (CBM), the development of preventive diplomacy and elaboration of approach to conflicts' was articulated in the Chairman's Statement at the second ARF meeting in August 1995. Behind that prescription lies an understanding that process is, or can be, as important as outcome in the particular circumstances of the contemporary Asia-Pacific; and that such new regional architecture should be grounded in inclusiveness and the principle of security 'with' others, and not security 'against' others (individually or collectively). For its founding fathers, it is important that ARF is an indigenous creation of the region, not a foreign implant or copy.[13]

Great Power View of Multilateralism

The development of ARF is evidence of the role that middle level Asia-Pacific players can pursue in the construction of a new management order for the region.[14] Amongst major regional powers, the US was a late convert to the multilateral security framework approach.Under President Bush, Washington staked its preference in the 'hub and spokes' system of bilateral security alliances, with the US as the sole hub of the network. President Clinton modified that position and endorsed ARF multilateralism, but Washington made it clear, nonetheless, that any multilateral dialogue framework is to be viewed clearly as a supplement to America's bilateral security alliance system in the region, and that the US-Japan alliance in particular would continue 'to serve as the irreplaceable core of any regional security regimes' and remained in 'the vital national security interest of both signatories, and the region as a whole....'[15]

Washington was, and is not, convinced about the contribution the dialogue framework can really make to regional security. It is sceptical that process can be as significant as outcome in the circumstances of Asia-Pacific, at least as the basis for workable order - and notably in North East Asia. But, more importantly, the US position confirmed that it resists unqualified acknowledgment of the 'inclusivist' stance to security management which informs the ASEAN-derived approach.

13   A. Acharya, 'A Regional Security Community in South-East Asia' in Desmond Ball, ed., op. cit., p. 186.
14   Yoshihide Soeya, ' The Japan-US Alliance in a Changing Asia' *Japan Review of International Affairs*, Vol. 10, No. 4 (Fall 1996), pp. 265-276.
15   S. Sato & J. Kahan, 'Japan-US Alliance and Security Regimes', in *East Asia, Workshop Report* (Institute for International Policy Studies, 1994), p. 3 and p. 22.

The American judgement is that the circumstances in Asia-Pacific where there is no consensual source of threat, are not conducive to collective security; and US leadership interests are best served by giving first priority to selected bilateral security treaties. The extent to which this influences the American approach to the further substantive evolution of ARF, and the extent to which US reservations also shape the attitudes of America's active bilateral security treaty partners (Japan and Australia) remains to be seen.

China has displayed a positive but cautious attitude to the ARF dialogue. It has participated in the exchanges on the overall regional security outlook. It has indicated willingness to agree to some multilateral confidence building measures in the region. Chinese reticence about transparency concerning its defence modernisation programme is reflected, however, in a view that CBM should not be confined to military affairs alone.[16] Chinese adherence to the view that security should be approached more comprehensively, sits readily in one sense, however, with a similar predisposition in South East Asia and Japan. Japan, in particular, is committed to military transparency.

Beijing's preparedness to participate in regional multilateral solutions also found expression in its involvement in arrangements to meet the problems of North Korean nuclear capability (KEDO). China's overall interest in the multilateral approach is proof of concern to ensure stability in its near-abroad; and evidence of Beijing's desire to play a role in organising and maintaining regional security. A Chinese policy of genuine engagement (and the proof of the pudding lies still in the eating), would mean a greater prospect of China, along with other ARF members, being held accountable for actions (for example, in the South China Sea) than if it were estranged from cooperative international relations in the region.[17]

There is no automatic monopoly on political-security dialogue in the region. The potentiality of Asia Pacific Economic Cooperation (APEC) as an additional forum for such dialogue at the highest political level, enjoys American support. Not all Asian governments share, however, an enthusiasm to lend APEC specific political-security competence. There is no difficulty with the proposition that political

16   Xu Jian, 'Economic Cooperation and Regional Harmony in the Asia-Pacific', *CCIS International Review*, No. 3 (1996), p. 71.
17   B. Garrett and B. Glaser, *Does China want the US out of Asia?*, Pacific Forum, Centre for Strategic and International Studies (CSIS), Pacnet, May 1997.

leaders, when gathered together at an annual summit, must be free to range over any subjects they care to. But this is not quite the same things as officially bestowing a mandate upon APEC. Time may indeed change attitudes. APEC as an annual summit experience is still evolving. Its potential for nourishing trust building at the highest political level should not be ignored. For those East Asian countries that favour a regional order based on a balance of interests, rather than a balance of power, APEC could indeed provide the best opportunity to pursue the development of an order in that sense.

Exclusive Regionalism

The institutions for regional cooperation in Asia-Pacific are of recent creation. The region itself, as its very geographical nomenclature implies, is an artificial construct.[18] But the countries of East Asia, buoyed by economic success, fully expect to have a determining say in the form and nature of regional cooperation for Asia-Pacific. Any effort to force models from elsewhere upon East Asian regional governments is never likely to succeed. Indeed, such attempts could prove counterproductive in the sense that they could incite instincts that exist already, amongst some countries, in favour of an exclusive brand of East Asian regionalism.

These found expression in the original proposition for an East Asian Economic caucus (EAEC) pursued by Malaysia, but robustly opposed by the US and Australia. The subsequent institutionalisation of the Asia Europe meeting (ASEM) as a biennial collective summit of Asian and European leaders is potentially significant not just for the fact that the leaders of the two regions meet regularly on a equal basis, but for the habits of exclusive East Asian interaction that ASEM will engender. Likewise the innovation of summits between ASEAN and North East Asian leaders (Japan, China and ROK) would, if regularised, nourish exclusiveness.

While the institutionalisation of regionalism is of recent vintage, a sense of 'United Asia' has gained some momentum. The common achievements of economic success as well as the shared pressure from values driven foreign policy by the US and others over democracy, and human rights, have served to inculcate greater awareness of community of interest amongst East Asian governments. While the end

18 Paul Evans,'The Prospects for Multilateral Security Cooperation in the Asia-Pacific Region' in Desmond Ball, ed., op.cit., pp. 202-203.

of the Cold War witnessed the end of a *global Western security community*, the extent to which it is replaced by a *global Western values community* committed to the systematic (and, at times, coercive) spread of those values, could well determine the extent to which 'United Asia' takes further shape in the form of exclusive regionalism. The position and attitude of Japan would be a key consideration in any such development. A modern and successful Asia in the twenty first century, with the capacity to set and carry through a global agenda, and to add an Asian 'voice' to those of Western Europe and North America in international affairs, will necessitate greater cohesion, regional identity and common purpose than presently exist given the diversity of cultural, social, and political identity within the region.

Security Perceptions and Concerns

Whilst, as we shall see, there are certain points of recurrent friction, strategic security concerns are less focused at this time on immediate or medium term prospects for direct aggression, than on the engulfing effects of potential disorder created by new large power rivalries or, more speculatively, by the possible effects of the collapse of a major state.[19] The way, therefore, in which China's emergence is managed by China itself, and assisted by the region collectively, is the critical longer term security preoccupation; a consideration of equal weight is the manner in which the US as an avowed leader in East Asia, adjusts to the reality of China's peaceful emergence (providing it is peaceful), and allows China reasonable space, while maintaining its own legitimate regional interests.

It is axiomatic that China's emergence must occur in a way that instils confidence in the region, especially but not only amongst larger powers. The role of medium and smaller powers must be as facilitators of the process of convergence. China needs to recognise that regional neighbours and partners possess a legitimate interest in Beijing's policy intentions. Traditional disdain for foreign interest will need to be tempered. Emergent China is, however, no longer a revolutionary power bent upon spreading revolution. In contrast to much of the past 150 years, China today faces no external threat. Its domestic economic prospects are not assured given the immense challenge of such vast

19   C. Morrison, ed., *Asia Pacific Security Outlook 1997* (Honolulu: East-West Centre, 1997), p. 6.

economic and social modernisation. It may be unwise to draw premature conclusions about the imminent emergence of a new major international power.[20] But existentially China will, by its very being, exercise profound impact upon the region, even if it does not assert leadership as a specific foreign policy goal.

Specialists in China emphasise the country's absolute requirement for economic and social modernisation, which will take 'several generations'[21] and necessitate, above all, an international environment of long term peace and stability. Currently, foreign trade accounts for 40% of China's GNP. Combined with a heavy dependence on external investment and technologies, it would seem China has no interest in, nor history of, belligerent expansionism. It has expended efforts to improve diplomatic relations with neighbours like Vietnam which have sufficient historical reason, though, to be prudent about the emergent China. In this context, it is apt to recall that pre-colonial South East Asian neighbours had a long tradition and experience of living and dealing with an ascendant China. At bottom, it is in the direct national interest of such neighbours to now respond positively to constructive Chinese diplomatic approaches - indeed there is little alternative. Such neighbours can perceive little interest in subscribing to a policy of containment of modern China, let alone combining in any security alliance against the Big Neighbour. The basic ASEAN position is that all great power rivalry should be eschewed in its region - and it, therefore, views China and the US through a similar prism.

China accords ASEAN a prominent position amongst its international interlocutors while at the same time maintaining territorial claims in the South China Sea that are contested by a number of South East Asia countries. With South Korea, Japan, India, Russia, and the Central Asian Republics, China has made conscious diplomatic efforts, over a reasonably short period of time, to set relations on a sounder footing. With India, China has sought to explore confidence and security building measures which suggests it is indeed becoming more receptive to the approaches that ARF seeks to fashion in Asia-Pacific.[22]

---

20   H. Harding, 'A Chinese Colossus', in Desmond Ball, ed., op. cit., p. 105.

21   Z. Shiliang, 'Prospects for Asian-Pacific Security in the Early 21st Century' *International Review*, No. 3 (July 1996), CCIS, pp. 26-27.

22   Rosemary Foot, 'Chinese-Indian Relations and the Process of Building Confidence: Implications for the Asia-Pacific', *Pacific Review*, Vol. 9, No. 1 (1996), p. 58.

Sense of Threat

Amongst some realists, there is particular concern to dispel emphatically all presumption of a threat-free Asia-Pacific. China's emergence is viewed inevitably as providing a disruption in the power equation of Northeast Asia. Whilst common sense always dictates prudence in calculating the future, some pessimistic forecasting presently comes close to suggesting that the region is in fact inherently unstable. Sharp emphasis upon intensifying economic rivalry, ideological and territorial disputes, historical animosities, and the danger of military conflict notably in Northeast Asia, are presented in combination as evidence of dangerous uncertainty in Asia-Pacific.[23]

As a guide to strategy, uncertainty per se is a notably imprecise foundation for clear thinking. Some pessimistic predictions may reflect a partiality for current issues or 'an intense short-term policy orientation closely tied to the agenda of government decision-making on defence and military issues'.[24] The suggestion by Paul Dibb[25] that 'the dominance of uncertainty will mean that planners will want to hedge their bets; deterrence against potential shocks to the regional order will mean planning a base force *larger* (emphasis added) than one designed only for one or two credible contingencies...' seems to illustrate this.

In contrast, the more consensual view of the security outlook alluded to above is that in the short to medium term it is remarkably benign. There are uncertainties, but these need not be dramatised to the point of exaggeration. Leadership changes (in Indonesia) or uncertain political settlements (in Cambodia) may provide the occasions for turbulence and internal instabilities, but not of a kind that would compel substantial outside interference. There would be a shared regional interest to contain any such internal disorder so that it did not threaten wider achievements. No East Asian regional power in the next ten years has either the intention or capability to assert regional

23   P. Dibb, 'Emerging Geopolitics of the Asia-Pacific Region', Strategic and Defence Studies Centre, Working Paper 296, 1996, pp. 2-9.
24   B. Buzan, *Introduction to Strategic Studies, Military Technology and International Relations* (Macmillan, 1987), cited by R. Leaver, 'Australia and Japan in the Post-Cold War World', in G. Klintworth, ed., *Asia-Pacific Security* (New York: St Martins Press, 1996), p. 52.
25   P. Dibb, 'Emerging Geopolitics of the Asia-Pacific Region', Strategic and Defence Studies Centre, Working Paper 296, 1996, pp. 2-9.

dominance; and in the case of China, the capability for so doing will not be secured for several decades.

Arms Modernisation

Nevertheless, there is considerable speculation about the real significance of current arms modernisation in East Asia, where virtually all countries are engaged in acquisition programmes including development of force projection. These programmes are not threat-driven, but rather contingency-related, and a reflection of successful economic advance by many countries, where there are more funds for defence. The defence share of national GDP in the region is actually declining.[26] Many weapons inventories in the region include armaments of pre-1960 design.

The modernisation programmes start, therefore, from a low base but they do reveal some symmetry in the capabilities being acquired[27]: maritime reconnaissance and multi-role fighter aircraft, missiles, surface vessels including chiefly destroyers and frigates as well as submarines and a very limited number of carriers, moderate numbers of artillery and radar and electronic systems. Such acquisition programmes are a case principally of keeping up with the neighbours; and amongst other things, of increasing resource protection capacity. The business of establishing and expanding defence relationships within and across the region is influenced by the extent to which would-be partners are viewed to possess up-to-date equipment. The acquisition programmes do not seem to be motivated by an intention to secure and maintain technological edge over neighbours. There are exceptions. Australia has traditionally sought to maintain just such an edge, while fostering bilateral defence relations in its neighbourhood (Malaysia, Singapore, Indonesia). There is an implicit contradiction here. It is likely that Australia will look to sustain that advantage through its 1996 revitalised security alliance within the US,[28] although the growing availability of technologies and capabilities throughout the region will make it harder to do so.

26   C. Morrison, op. cit., p. 5.
27   P. Wattanayagorn and D. Ball, 'A Regional Arms Race?' in Desmond Ball, ed., op. cit., p. 161.
28   See 'Rethinking Australia's Defence, Strategic Comments', *IISS*, No. 4 (1997).

Amongst larger powers, Japan remains the biggest spender by a considerable margin.[29] Under its modernisation programme, the down-sizing of the Self-Defence Force (SDF) and cuts in armour and surface naval vessel numbers may provide a measure of reassurance to neighbours. There is widespread scepticism that China's published defence expenditure figures represent a true indication of actual disbursement. Official figures of around $7 billion annually need to be inflated, according to informed analysts, by a factor of two to four at least.[30] Even so, Japan's expenditure would still be superior, and Chinese capabilities lag significantly behind other regional powers in state-of-the art equipment. Japanese analysts themselves are not fazed, it seems, by China's defence modernisation which in 1996 they laconically concluded is 'expected to gradually proceed at a moderate pace'.[31] Even by the period 2025-2050, China's force projection capability will continue to be limited, particularly in comparison with the US.[32] China poses no threat to the physical security of the US itself. Its airforce has been assessed as roughly comparable to that of Malaysia. Its capabilities are inferior to those of Taiwan. To some neighbours, its large, albeit antiquated forces, cannot however be ignored.

Points of Friction

Disputed land and sea boundaries comprise the essential core of current regional friction points. Some of them are longstanding, variously involving China and India, Japan and China, Japan and Russia, China and Vietnam, China and Malaysia, and other South East Asian states, as well as dividing the South East Asian states themselves. To these should be added activities like piracy, smuggling, illegal refugees, drugs and poaching of marine resources. As serious as some of these abrasive problems undoubtedly are, notably the disputed islands in the South China Sea (the Spratlys),

29   G. Cheeseman and R. Leaver, 'Trends in Arms Spending and Conventional Arms Trade', in G. Klintworth, ed., *Asia-Pacific Security* (New York: St Martins Press, 1996), p. 199.
30   David Shambaugh, 'China's Challenge to Asian Security', *Survival*, Vol. 36, No. 2, p. 54.
31   'Defence of Japan White Paper 1996', Japanese Defence Agency, Tokyo, p. 45.
32   P. Kriesberg, 'Threat Environment for a United Korea: 2010', *Journal of Korean Defence Analysis*, Vol. VIII, No. 1 (1996), pp. 90-91.

with their possible implications for freedom of maritime passage, none threaten the security or actual existence of the claimants. National survival is not at stake anywhere.[33]

Periodic clashes between claimants, of greater or lesser severity, can however be anticipated. The prospect that such disputes could become the calculated cause of war with major regional consequences, does not seem probable. By its decision in 1995 to accept, through ARF, multilateral discussion with other claimants to the Spratly Islands (based on the UN Law of the Sea), China would seem to have made a choice to follow a pathway of preventive diplomacy. China's apparent preference is that the issue of sovereignty be quarantined, whilst agreements on joint development between claimants are pursued.

The points of friction are potentially more acute in Northeast Asia, at least in terms of likely repercussions from any miscalculation. The fact that interests of all the major regional powers intersect in this area indicates the stakes are higher. The US assesses tensions on the Korean Peninsular to be the principal threat to East Asian stability.[34] Nonetheless, all great powers evidently share an interest that peace and stability be preserved there. Korean reunification is an important but subordinate objective which both North and South seem, for differing reasons, disposed to defer.[35] The likelihood of total economic and social collapse in the North cannot be discounted, although all forecasts of imminent disaster have thus far proven misplaced. China, whose actions can obviously play a key part in influencing the shape of events in the Peninsular, has successfully cultivated relations with South Korea, maintaining at the same time stable ties with the North, whilst removing some of the preferential aspects of the earlier relationship. China was an active participant behind-the-scenes in negotiations to secure the nuclear agreement (KEDO) with the North. The sort of relationship that China might evolve with a reunified Korea, and, in particular, the future of the US military presence on the Peninsular once reunification occurs, are questions that will shape the strategic environment in Northeast Asia. It seems a reasonable bet that

---

33   'National Security Strategy, for a New Century', US White House National Security Council., May 1997.

34   S. Sheldon, op. cit., p. 390.

35   P. Kriesberg, 'Threat Environment for a United Korea: 2010', *Journal of Korean Defence Analysis*, Vol. VIII, No. 1 (1996), pp. 90-91.

if and when reunification eventuates, China would press for the removal of the US defence presence.

The nuclear ambitions of North Korea (DPRK) engaged the US directly in the Peninsular given the global security dimension of nuclear non-proliferation. The impressive tempo of the US effort, with carrot-and-stick diplomacy, laid the basis, for the first time, of cooperative engagement with the DPRK. While past experience points to the inherent unpredictability of the DPRK regime, there is no reason to anticipate a major irrational act that would compromise the position Pyongyang has secured through direct dealings with the US. Devastating floods, failed crops and poor harvests have severely debilitated the economy; and manifold shortages of fuel and material must have undermined the DPRK's military capacity to fight and win over the forces of South Korea (ROK).

The area of friction most likely to provoke great power involvement concerns Taiwan. Its eventual reunification with China in terms of the 'one China' policy recognised in the 1972 Shanghai Communique between the US and the PRC is, for Beijing, the irreducible cornerstone of Northeast Asian regional order. While stressing attachment to peaceful reunification and formally committed to 'one country, two systems' as the basis for reunification, China has watched the emergence of a majority in Taiwan that is now opposed to reunification,[36] even as commercial, economic and people-to-people links between the two continue to multiply significantly. In Taiwan reunification also remains the official goal, but this is now overshadowed by pursuit of policies that point rather to *de facto* independence and which have severely disconcerted Beijing. They led in 1996 to admonitory displays of Chinese military prowess in the Taiwan Straits, and a robust American response.

In the circumstances, the July 1997 resumption of Chinese sovereignty over Hong Kong contains implications of considerable significance not just for the outside view of China itself, but for Taiwan-China relations too. Continuing toleration by Beijing of Hong Kong's autonomous status in respect to the rule of law and basic freedoms will materially strengthen China's stance regarding Taiwan.[37] It will also improve China's international reputation,

36   J-P Cabestan, 'Taiwan's Mainland Policy, Normalisation Yes, Reunification Later', *China Quarterly*, No 148 (December 1996), pp. 1260-1283.
37   Michael Yahuda, *Hong Kong: China's Challenge* (London: Routledge, 1996), pp. 2-20.

strengthen its economic prospects and reduce anxieties in both North East and South East Asia. There can be little question China's leaders seek a successful transition of sovereignty. There are grounds to be optimistic. But dark predictions from several quarters persist. Such views will condition outside attitudes and judgements about China's ongoing treatment of Hong Kong after July 1997. It remains vital to distinguish between criticisms designed to justify the direst predictions, and the actual reality. This is not just because of the relevance to Hong Kong itself, but also to Taiwan and the future of Northeast Asian regional order.

The Big Power Relations

In the broader strategic context, the triangle of relationships encompassing China-US, China-Japan and Japan-US is the core of Northeast Asian stability, and indeed of the wider region. It has been claimed that the health or condition of each of these three relationships individually will affect the health or condition of the remaining two. If one goes sour, they all go sour.

United States

There is no question that, since the end of the Cold War, the United States has experienced difficulty in establishing international priorities through which to calculate and manage divergent interests with and in Asia-Pacific. The articulation of policy has betrayed contradictions, sometimes inconsistency. There are several explanations for this state of affairs which are beyond the scope of this contribution, but which relate back to domestic challenges inside America and its society, as well as a view of America's place in the world.[38] There is a multitude of voices raised inside Washington with predictions and advice for the administration about the future for the US in the region, and, in particular, with regard to China.[39] That phenomenon is always a problem for outsiders in determining the precise course of US policy action on many foreign issues. Such opinion has, of course, ready

---

38   Robert. Scalapino 'The US Commitment to Asia' in Desmond Ball, ed., op. cit., p70.

39   The publication of Samuel Huntington's book, *The Clash of Civilisations and the Remaking of World Order* (Simon and Schuster, 1996), with its prediction of inevitable conflict between the Western (US) and Confucian (Chinese) worlds, fuelled the public commentary and debate in Washington.

access to the media whose impact upon foreign policy-making is considerable.

Two features affecting immediate US regional policy-making are evident. First, since the advent of the second-term Clinton Presidency in January 1997, the traditional Euro-centricity of the US foreign policy establishment has been more prominent. The concentration upon European policy, in particular, the expansion of NATO, has been notable for the energy and purpose brought to bear, from the White House downwards. One question is how far such Euro-centricity will remain, throughout the Clinton second term, an obstruction, as it has been before in other Presidencies, to clear American thinking about the Asia-Pacific region.[40] In Asia-Pacific, moreover, and in marked contrast to Europe, key US official and diplomatic positions have stood vacant both in Washington and in important regional capitals for long periods. Substantial budgetary cuts in the State Department and related agencies during recent years must also have had an adverse impact on US policy towards Asia-Pacific at the very time when clear and consistent policy articulation is needed.

Second, as a consequence of this, it seems increasingly the lead role in Asia-Pacific policy has come to reside in the hands of the Pentagon. The only major non-economic US policy document on East Asia in five years, the 1995 Nye report, is a Pentagon policy paper. The revitalisation of key military alliances with Japan, and with Australia in 1996, and the subsequent publication of draft guidelines for Japanese and US military cooperation, point as well to the influence of the Pentagon. Any preponderance of defence policy in statecraft always runs the risk that threat analysis comes to occupy the key place in external policy thinking, even where the strategic environment may be essentially benign. The risk is that governmental responses are formulated then outside the ambit of foreign policy and international relations more generally. Such preponderance is sometimes also evident in Australia where the Defence and the Foreign Affairs Departments compete for primacy in external policy making, with Defence able to count upon the seemingly omnipresent sense of

40 R. Trood, ed., *Security in the Asia-Pacific Region* (Selochan: Australian Defence Studies Centre, 1993), p. 10.

threat inside the Australian community at large, in a bid to maintain pre-eminence.[41]

The revitalisation of bilateral military alliances in times of peace, in the absence of a declared or prospective enemy, is historically unusual. There is an obvious danger in Asia-Pacific that such actions may be self-fulfilling prophecies, as countries excluded from the alliance question whether they are not the putative enemy. The Chinese reactions to the revitalisation of the US alliances in 1996 were uniformly negative. Beijing saw in such actions confirmation of its belief that the US and its allies were bent upon containment of China.[42] The US denied such intent, pursued a programme of high level contacts (suspended after Tiananmen Square in 1989) and attempted to assuage Chinese concerns with bilateral defence/military contacts. But the principal significance of the alliance revitalisation was its timing. At the very moment when China was gingerly committing itself to the new multilateral security dialogue framework of ARF, the US was moving to reinvigorate certain key bilateral alliances, underlining a message thereby that its attachment to the inclusiveness principle behind the ARF vision of regional security management is, at best, qualified.

The security treaties illustrate US commitment to bilateralism as the way to underpin its leadership in East Asia and the region more widely. Bilateralism is the means by which, in Asia-Pacific, the US keeps its hands free to act as it sees fit when it must. American commitment to multilateralism, at the global and the regional level, remains ambivalent. This is not surprising for an historically unique superpower that has yet to define its role in the contemporary world. With the passage of time, with the decline of American's relative power, especially in the international economic arena, with the deepening acceptance that a range of key transnational problems embracing the environment, pollution, migration, crime, drugs, terrorism, and weapons proliferation can only be approached multilaterally, plus the desire or need to share the burden of sustaining peace and prosperity, such ambivalence about multilateralism may modify - but it will not happen quickly.

41   R. Leaver, 'Australia and Japan in the Post-Cold War World', in Gary Klintworth, ed., *Asia-Pacific Security* (New York: St Martins Press, 1996), p. 52.
42   Wan Guang, 'Questions in US Readjustment of External Strategy', *International Review*, CCIS, Beijing, No. 3 (July 1996), p. 133.

At the regional and global level, it is possible that one will witness greater American predisposition to build coalitions of like-minded to deal with specific issues, and to place more weight on regional organisations and decision-making mechanisms. The United States will serve, and seek to serve, as a catalyst in all such endeavours, but it may do so as *a* leader, not *the* leader.[43] That may not necessarily be easy for the US. Such an approach will require the sharing of decision-making, as well as the sharing of burdens. Moreover, in a globalising interdependent world with no fixed international order, different countries will align with different partners on different issues at different times. In this multifarious environment, contradictions and tensions in international relations may well grow more evident, including Asia-Pacific. It will be as much a diplomatic challenge for the strong and powerful as for the small and insubstantial.

For the US, in East Asia, the need to harmonise its deep ideological commitment to democracy and human rights with the imperatives of international relations and of its national interests, is likely to continue to pose a key challenge.

China

China's attitude to the US is conditioned basically by the need for access to American investment, ideas and technology to consolidate its successful modernisation programme. Beijing professes a desire for a good and rewarding relationship with the US, and it does not believe a military confrontation is likely.[44] At the same time, it is aware that strategic realists in the US assert that to preserve a leadership role, America must maintain mechanisms and policies to deter potential competitors from assuming larger regional or global roles. Beijing, which has its own share of realists, criticises what it perceives to be the US refusal to accept, and adjust to, the emergence of a multi-polar world. Washington is determined, in Beijing's eyes, to preserve East Asian regional order on a uni-polar basis, with US leadership paramount.

American pressures over human rights and democracy are interpreted in Beijing as attempts to destabilise the Chinese

43   R. Scalapino, op. cit., p 81.
44   There are, however, conflicting public voices in Beijing that include the threat to China from a hegemonic US. See Richard Bernstein & Ross H. Munro, *The Coming Conflict with China* (New York: A. A. Knoopf, 1997), p. 25.

Government, whose legitimacy is thereby questioned.[45] American opposition to Beijing as the site for the Olympic Games, the long and complex dealings within the US over Chinese admission to the World Trade Organisation (WTO), the annual Washington debates over MFN treatment for China and a host of lesser events, have been interpreted as a failure to respect the dignity and place of China in the international arena. In this context, the shame and humiliation of China's colonial experiences are asserted often in ways calculated to stir Chinese nationalist instincts.[46]

In China's relations with Japan, the primacy of economics has been paramount since World War II. It is claimed that the scale of economic interdependence between the two countries is unprecedented, and constitutes one of the most solid links in international affairs.[47] In political-security terms, through its 1972 normalisation of relations with Japan (hard on the heels of normalisation with the US), China, in effect, joined Japan in the new power system in Asia, and recognised the utility of the Japan-US security relationship; and became a *de facto* Cold War strategic partner. The 1972 communiques issued at the time of normalisation of both relationships contained identical language and said: 'Neither power should seek hegemony in the Asia Pacific region, and each is opposed to the efforts by any other country or group of countries to seek such hegemony'. Here lies the bedrock for the triangle of North East Asian relationships.

Japan

Like China, Japan also seems to anticipate a changing place in the management of the Asia Pacific order. Japan's political-security policies towards East Asia have, in large measure in the past, been simply a reflection of, or a support for, American political-security policies in the region. While countries in the region have been tenaciously pushing for a more autonomously structured regional order, Japan has been inhibited because of the Japan-US Security Treaty whose redefinition in 1996 does, on the face of it, envisage a

45 A. Choate, 'Confidence Building in the US-China Relationship', Paper prepared for ASEAN ISIS, 1997.
46 Kazuo Ogura, 'Japan's Asia Policy, Past and Future', *Japan Review of International Affairs*, Vol. 10, No. 1 (1996), pp. 9-15.
47 Akira Iriye, *China and Japan in the Global Setting* (Cambridge, Mass: Harvard University Press, 1994), p. 91.

more active Japanese security role. This redefinition, however, has to reconcile the constraints of the war-renouncing Japanese Constitution with participation in the overall framework of US strategy towards East Asia. Japan's strategy towards East Asia remains in essence to cooperate with the US strategy towards East Asia; and effectively precludes a substantively independent Japanese approach.[48]

Two factors, among others, would seem to point to an emerging Japanese policy that is more independent, and reflects therefore more directly Japan's major global economic status. First, the emergence of China. Japan confronts the prospect of being overtaken, in the 21st century, as the economic engine of East Asia. As a regional player itself, Japan has to make adjustments in ways that it deems will safeguard the country's prosperity and security. The possibility that Washington and Tokyo may differ over appropriate responses to an emerging China seems to be more likely than not. Already differences exist about Russia, and what part it might play in the future, with Japan taking a more restrained view - because of the unresolved Kurile Islands territorial dispute - than the US, which is more sanguine over Russia's intentions. Under the redefined US-Japan Security Treaty, greater consultation between the two governments about many issues, but especially about China, will be indispensable.[49] In the past American views have been paramount. Japan will expect, presumably, that its perceptions and judgements should now receive equal weight.

Second, in the context of Asia in the 21st century, Japan clearly envisages a leadership role.[50] Whilst the US-Japan Treaty provides essential security reassurance to the region, Japanese policies, which derive uniquely from it, will not necessarily strengthen Tokyo's credentials for the leadership it might seek, and for which it might need to compete with China. The choice Japan may confront is whether to be more 'Asian' or remain the principal 'Western' representative in East Asia.

In addition, further change in the US-Japan security relationship is likely. A gradual but significant reduction of the US military presence in Okinawa and elsewhere in Japan is forecast by Japanese specialists, because such reduction now commands wide public

---

48 Michael Yahuda, *Hong Kong, China's Challenge* (London: Routledge, 1996), p. 9.
49 Michael Mochizuki, 'US Foreign Policy Challenges: Japan', *Brookings Review*, Vol. 15, No. 2 (Spring 1997), p. 13.
50 Kazuo Ogura, op. cit., pp. 9-15.

support in Japan.[51] The US will be obliged to make changes so that those assets that are judged absolutely critical to US East Asia policy can remain hosted by Japan. At the same time, any attempt to restructure elements of the alliance must be sensitive to the impact on East Asia generally, where some neighbours remain wary of resurgent Japanese militarism without the constraint that the US alliance is seen to provide. The ability of Tokyo to assuage such anxieties may necessitate of itself an autonomous Japanese policy in East Asia.

As the century draws to a close, more insistent worries are voiced outside Japan about that country's plutonium economy, and her intentions concerning nuclear weapon acquisition. This is clearly an issue closely linked to the US commitment in East Asia, and the availability of the American nuclear deterrent. Nuclear proliferation, and the strengthening of China's nuclear capability, are related factors in this equation for Japan. The problems on the Korean Peninsular graphically underline the interconnectedness between the global and regional dimension of the nuclear factor, and explain the purpose and resolve of the US.

What is true of the Korean Peninsular, it may reasonably be argued, is even more true of North East Asia as a whole. Nowhere else, in the post-Cold War world, are three nuclear weapon states, and one nuclear capable state (Japan), interacting so closely within such a relatively confined geographical area. The potentially destabilising dimension of nuclear proliferation points heavily in the direction of the real contribution that genuine nuclear disarmament could make to North East Asian stability and security. For this, US leadership would be indispensable. China, for its part, has indicated in the UN a willingness, in principle, to begin negotiations about an eventual Convention for nuclear disarmament. But without American support, serious collective nuclear disarmament, with its considerable potential to reduce the possibilities for destabilisation in North East Asia, would hardly be feasible. In a direct sense, such an initiative should command equal priority with the prospective next (third) round of Strategic Arms Reduction Talks (START) between Russia and the US.

Conclusion

The pace and extent of economic advance in East Asia, in less than thirty years, is equivalent to modernisation in North America and in

---

51   Michael Mochizuki, op. cit., p. 13.

Western Europe that took closer to one hundred years. Speculation abounds as to whether the rate of East Asian advance is sustainable. The manner in which profound but unforeseen change altered the basis of order in the world over the last decade of the century suggests, too, that prediction about East Asian stability should be prudent.

Notwithstanding some pessimistic analysis to the contrary, there is nothing which would lend substantive credence, however, to the view that East Asia is inherently unstable. The commitment to economic modernisation by a wide number of East Asian countries remains the pre-eminent influence upon regional order; which is not the same thing as asserting that concentration upon economic development is a guarantee that conflict will not eventuate. As this chapter has endeavoured to show, the consequences of economic transformation itself - for instance, ecological damage, resource depletion - could provide seeds for conflict. But there is no evidence that any regional country calculates that its economic or political interests would be served by planning for aggression. Misunderstandings, especially between the larger powers, could still, nonetheless, produce miscalculation which, in turn, could destabilise the security environment; that is why the task of fashioning an effective regional infrastructure for inclusive dialogue and inclusive interaction remains the key task for large and small regional countries alike. Trust building, in a region that lacks a tradition of regionalism, will always require perseverance. APEC with its summit-level annual meetings offers a pre-eminent opportunity to create and nurture the building of trust . For that opportunity the region is obliged to US statecraft. The ARF provides the potential to foster security dialogue, preventive diplomacy and conflict prevention at a more practical operational level. Here perseverance and patience will be at a premium, especially amongst those (larger) powers who seek to shape regional order. Whether there is, or is not, a distinctively 'Asian way' of approaching the management of regional stability, the models and the approach must clearly be tailored to the circumstances that prevail, or are in prospect.

Chapter 15

Reflections on Security

Bryce Harland

This volume brings together a series of well-informed, thoughtful and stimulating essays which were based on papers delivered at the 32nd Otago Foreign Policy School. The contributors have dealt in depth with various aspects of what is a broad subject-Security in a post-Cold War World. What I can usefully do is to try to pull together some of the threads and attempt to give an overall view of the subject.

The first question that arises in my mind is, what is security? Each contributor seemed to have his or her own definition of the word, some of which overlapped more than others. To me, security means essentially what President Roosevelt called 'freedom from fear'. The idea was easy to grasp when it first became popular during the Second World War. When the United Nations was set up in 1945, its first objective was 'To save succeeding generations from the scourge of war', and the principal means was to be the Security Council. Security was understood to be the antithesis of war. Not long after 1945, the meaning began to be widened, and the word sometimes took on sinister connotations. Security even became a means of waging the Cold War. Of late, the meaning has been stretched in other ways, until it seems to encompass almost the whole field of international affairs. That may be helpful at times, but to me security still describes the condition in which people do not live under constant threat, but can pursue their own avocations safe and undisturbed, and build confidently for the future. It is legitimate to ask, 'Whose security?' but it is difficult to formulate the question in general terms.

The 'post -Cold War World' presumably began in 1991, with the collapse of the Soviet Union. The main feature of the period since then has been a change in the nature of threats to international security. The threat of nuclear war has receded, though it has by no means disappeared. It has been succeeded by a spate of civil wars - not mere threats but actual conflicts within states, often waged in the most ruthless manner. Far from reducing the quantum of human suffering, as was widely hoped, the end of the Cold War has increased it many times over. In some substantial parts of the world, civil order has almost totally collapsed, and left behind a condition not unlike the State of Nature, as seen by Thomas Hobbes - a war of all against all. And even in those cases like Afghanistan or Lebanon, where outside powers have brought about the collapse, they have great difficulty in putting things together again. In a wider range of areas, lawlessness and crime have grown to the point where personal security can no longer be taken for granted. And in others, not so remote from New Zealand, hostility between great powers has risen to a height comparable with that reached during the Cold War. No wonder security has become such a widespread concern.

One problem left over from the Cold War is how to prevent nuclear war. Nuclear deterrence worked during the Cold War, but its relevance has been reduced by the collapse of the Soviet Union. Conventional arms are the ones that actually do the damage - noone has been killed by a nuclear weapon since 1945. But while large numbers of nuclear weapons still exist, in various parts of the world, the possibility of their being used, in one way or another, cannot be entirely excluded. So the fear they aroused at an earlier stage still persists. Efforts continue to be made through the United Nations and through other channels, to reduce the danger - notably by banning nuclear weapons testing and by stopping the spread of nuclear weapons. Progress has been made in these areas, and hopefully will continue to be made. The larger goal of total elimination remains elusive - not least because Saddam Hussein has demonstrated repeatedly the possibilities for cheating on even the most carefully drafted international documents.

But the difficulty of preventing nuclear war pales beside the problem of civil war. The causes vary. In Rwanda, over-population played a significant part. In the case of Bosnia, the ending of the Cold War was itself a major factor in the outbreak of internal conflict. As soon as the external threat from the Soviet Union went, peoples who had been living together in peace and relative prosperity began to indulge again their old animosities, with horrendous consequences. Not until external pressure was applied, with great force, did the fighting stop, and then with little prospect of lasting peace. The United Nations and other international organisations have worked long and hard to promote reconciliation, and have at least saved many lives, but the fighting went on until the arrival of international forces that were too powerful to defy. Without the deployment of such forces, on a scale the governments concerned are seldom willing to contemplate when they don't feel threatened themselves, the international community cannot usually achieve much more than to relieve suffering to bind up the wounds.

The challenge the world faces, again and again, is how to give antagonistic groups in the same society scope to work out their own destinies without, in the process, destroying the framework of the state they live in, and causing great suffering. The idea that the right of self-determination can be realised within an existing state, without secession from it, is attractive to bystanders like us, but it does not always satisfy the aspirations of the peoples in question. That being the case, it is hard to see how civil wars can be prevented by international action. The best that can realistically be expected is that such wars can be limited in scope and effect, and the way kept open for their ultimate settlement by negotiation.

One thing the organised international community could do to help avert civil wars is to consider more carefully in advance the likely effect of any action taken to encourage and support disaffected groups in other countries. However good the motives, such actions can lead to internal conflict, the break-up of states, and great suffering. If limiting human suffering is a goal shared by people all over the world - as we would all like to believe - then the pressing problem is to discourage divergent groups within a single society from pursuing their individual aspirations to the point of conflict. This must surely be an element - if a negative one - in any programme of Preventive Diplomacy.

Within the Asia-Pacific region, the most serious problem at present is the growing tension between the United States and Asian countries, including China. Since the end of the Cold War, the Americans have found less need for Asian allies and have felt free to pursue their own interests more vigorously. The two they focus on are trade and human rights. Even when the two are not directly linked, threats are made to limit Asian access to the American market - threats which could encourage Asians to close ranks against the US. At the same time, the spectacular growth of the Chinese economy has made that country increasingly attractive to American business. It is regarded as a market no firm can afford to abandon to its rivals. So far, business pressures have balanced those from other groups and restrained the Clinton administration from carrying out the threats. But the repeated crises of the last few years have affected public attitudes on both sides, and generated growing mutual hostility.

The Taiwan Straits crisis of 1996 brought this to the surface. It reminded all involved how fragile the security of the region is, and its prosperity as well. Yet voices continue to be heard in the United States calling for 'containment' of China, as if that were as feasible now as it was at the height of the Cold War. And voices in China reply, in tones of rising nationalism, accusing America of seeking to frustrate China's emergence on the world stage. Taiwan is the issue that could most easily set off a conflict - partly because it has such strong support in the US Congress. The main constraint is economic. Taiwan now has close ties with the Mainland, and depends heavily on them. If economic rationality prevails, it should preclude a conflict from which both sides would suffer much, and gain little. But rationality has not always prevailed, especially when pitted against the emotional power of nationalism, and the 'missionary spirit'.

For New Zealand, as for Australia, the situation is fraught with risk. Both of us now depend on trade with Asian countries, including China, from which we have benefited greatly. Any conflict between America and China would affect both of us severely. But some Australians are coming to see China as a 'threat', and even to echo the American call for 'containment', while the New Zealanders I meet are more inclined to see China as an 'opportunity'. They are receptive to the point I keep making, that if New Zealand ever has to choose between America and China, it could only lose. The New Zealand Foreign Minister, Mr McKinnon, says in his contribution here that the government sees the reemergence of China, and the change that has to be made in the structure of regional relations to accommodate the new balance not as a threat but as a unique opportunity for New Zealand and for the wider region. Mr McKinnon goes on to point out that, in the field of defence, New Zealand is at present not carrying out its declared policy and maintaining the capabilities of our forces. 'Our partners are letting us know', he notes, that 'our credibility is in question'. New Zealand benefits greatly from our relations with other countries in Asia and the Pacific. We can hardly expect to go on doing so to the full if we do not pull our weight in helping to maintain the security of the region.

To return to the global picture, since the end of the Cold War the world has been no more secure than it was in the course of that prolonged struggle. The area of acute insecurity has in fact widened, because the United States is no longer prepared to police regions where it has no direct interest. It has such interests in Asia and the Pacific, and maintains powerful military forces there. But the growing tension in its relations with China could lead to conflict, which would affect every country in the region and many outside it as well.

At the risk of introducing morals into politics, I would suggest that the root cause of these problems, both global and regional, is to be found in Manichaeism - in the black-and-white outlook that says always I am right and you are wrong. I am a patriot, you are a nationalist. What I stand for is Good, and what you stand for is Evil. It is strange how hard these crude old beliefs die - even when they have caused so much trouble. Ideals, and ideologies, may change, with changing circumstances, but idealism, like hope, 'springs eternal in the human breast'. As the great Oxford philosopher, Isaiah Berlin, put it in one of his essays:

> Faith in universal, objective truth ... in the possibility of a perfect and harmonious society, wholly free from conflict or injustice or oppression ... [is] an ideal for which more human beings have, in our time, sacrificed themselves and others than, perhaps, for any other cause in human history.

If there is any answer to the problems we have been discussing, problems in which arrogance and self-righteousness play large parts, it probably lies in that old-fashioned virtue, 'tolerance'. (There is a fine irony in the fact that last year, 1996, was declared beforehand 'The United Nations Year of Tolerance'.) The point was made over 300 years ago by Oliver Cromwell, in a letter he wrote to the General Assembly of the Church of Scotland in 1650 - 'I beseech you, in the bowels of Christ, think it possible you may be mistaken'.

Index